Managing For Dummies, 2nd Edition

P9-DBK-138

Daily Affirmations for Managers

- ✔ The energy of your area and the people in it starts with you. Be an energizing manager.
- ✔ Managing is a people job. Put people first.
- ✔ Managing is what you do with people, not to people.
- ✔ Walk your talk; back up your words with actions. People believe what they see more than what they hear.
- ✔ "If it's to be, it begins with me."
- ✔ You gain power when you share power with your employees.
- ✔ The best business is common sense.
- ✔ Always ask: What do your customers value, and how do you know that they value it?
- ✔ The best performance starts with clear goals.
- ✔ You get what you reward.
- ✔ The more mistakes you make, the closer you are to the right answer.
- ✔ If you can't measure performance, you can't manage it.
- ✔ Remember: It's not personal, it's business.
- ✔ If you don't like the way things are today, be patient. Everything will change tomorrow.
- ✔ Make work fun. Doing so is good for you and for the bottom line.
- ✔ Don't sweat the small stuff (it's all small stuff).
- ✔ The simple approach is often the best approach.

For Dummies: Bestselling Book Series for Beginners

Managing For Dummies,® 2nd Edition

Cheat Sheet

Ten Ways to Motivate Employees

Employees may not need a pay raise as much as they do personal thanks from their manager for a job well-done. Following is the top ten list of motivators for today's employees:

- ✔ Personally thank employees for doing a good job — one on one, in writing, or both. Do it promptly, often, and sincerely.

- ✔ Be willing to take time to meet with and listen to employees — as much time as they need or want.

- ✔ Provide specific feedback about performance of the employee, the department, and the organization.

- ✔ Strive to create a work environment that is open, trusting, and fun. Encourage new ideas and initiative.

- ✔ Provide information about upcoming products and strategies, how the company makes and loses money, and how each employee fits into the overall plan.

- ✔ Involve employees in decisions, especially those decisions that affect them.

- ✔ Encourage employees to have a sense of ownership in their work and their work environment.

- ✔ Create a partnership with each employee. Give people a chance to grow and learn new skills. Show them how you can help them meet their goals within the context of meeting the organization's goals.

- ✔ Celebrate successes of the company, the department, and the individuals in it. Take time for team- and morale-building meetings and activities.

- ✔ Use performance as the basis for recognizing, rewarding, and promoting people. Deal with low and marginal performers so that they improve their performance or leave the organization.

Copyright © 2003 Wiley Publishing, Inc.
All rights reserved.
Item 1771-6.
For more information about Wiley Publishing, call 1-800-762-2974.

For Dummies: Bestselling Book Series for Beginners

Praise for Managing For Dummies, 2nd Edition

"Bob Nelson and Peter Economy have demonstrated a rare talent for distilling the most complex and essential elements of good management into an easily digestible, understandable, and practical text. Although intended primarily for new managers, the wise tenets they have selected and carefully explained are as valuable to CEOs of large corporations as they are to novice professionals just beginning their management careers."

> — Ron Vukas, Former Executive Vice President, The Institute of Real Estate Management

"Everywhere I opened this book, I found concepts I could immediately apply in my job and in the job of managing others to get their best performance."

> — Bill Taylor, Lark In The Morning, Inc.

"Bob Nelson's *Managing For Dummies,* 2nd Edition contains sound, practical management advice developed with a pleasing touch of humor. The book avoids traditional management theory in favor of useful, applications-oriented management information and techniques that can be used immediately on the job.

> — Michael Cicero, Coordinator, General Business Program, Highline Community College

"This is *the* one handbook that I keep close by as a reference for daily work problems. It serves as both a guide and refresher for a myriad of situations that arise at work."

> — Sam Steinhardt, Executive Director, Stanford Center for Innovations in Learning

"*Managing For Dummies,* 2nd Edition is dynamite! Whether you are a rookie or management pro, it will help blast you to stellar managerial performance. *Managing For Dummies,* 2nd Edition has the latest information on the best ways to manage yourself, your subordinates, and your organization to outstanding performance. This extraordinary book is the next best thing to an MBA!"

> — Dr. W. Bradley Zehner II, Associate Professor of Strategic Management, Pepperdine University

"Every manager will benefit from the sound advice found in *Managing For Dummies,* 2nd Edition; especially the belief that management can and must be fun."

> — Felix Mussenden, President and Chief Operating Officer, Universal Studios

"While it seems that most management fads are here today and gone tomorrow, there are precious few sources that present the essential basics of managing a business in a way that is at once understandable, useful, *and* fun to read. *Managing For Dummies,* 2nd Edition has a real knack for accomplishing all of these goals."

> — William K. VanCanagan, J.D., L.L.M., Partner, Datsopoulos, MacDonald, & Lind

"This book recognizes that it is a new world of management out there. But it takes the best of proven, older principles to apply to the new workplace."

> — Rick Crandall, PhD, Speaker and Author, *Marketing Your Services: For People Who Hate to Sell*

"This is a valuable book for any manager, or any aspiring manager. It provides a useful, easy-to-read description of the tools that an effective manager must draw from. I like its breadth and diversity of topics, from interviewing to budgeting, from technology to teambuilding, from coaching to compensation. They're put together in a practical package that'll make sense to anyone in the world of business."

> — Oren Harari, PhD, Professor of Mangement, Graduate School of Business, University of San Francisco

"Nelson and Economy have crafted the ABC's of MBA! Novice managers will be relieved; experienced managers will be renewed. An excellent and powerful resource for everyone charged with helping others perform effectively."

> — Chip R. Bell, Senior Partner, Performance Research Associates, Inc.

Managing
FOR
DUMMIES®
2ND EDITION

by Bob Nelson and Peter Economy

Foreword by Ken Blanchard

Wiley Publishing, Inc.

Managing For Dummies®, 2nd Edition

Published by
Wiley Publishing, Inc.
909 Third Avenue
New York, NY 10022
www.wiley.com

WILEY

Wiley Publishing, Inc. is a trademark of Wiley Publishing, Inc.

About the Authors

Bob Nelson, PhD, (San Diego, California) is founder and president of Nelson Motivation, Inc., a management training and products firm headquartered in San Diego, California. As a practicing manager, researcher, and best-selling author, Bob is an internationally recognized expert in the areas of employee motivation, recognition and rewards, productivity and performance improvement, and leadership.

Bob has published 20 books and sold more than 2.5 million books on management, which have been translated in some 20 languages. He has been featured extensively in the media on television: CNN, PBS, and CNBC; on radio: NPR, Business News Network, and USA Radio Network; and in print: *The New York Times*, *The Wall Street Journal*, *USA Today,* and *Fortune* magazine among others. He writes a weekly column for *American City Business Journals*, a monthly column for *Corporate Meeting & Incentives* magazine, and a quarterly column for *SAM's Club Source* magazine, which has a circulation of 5 million business owners. He earned his BA in communications from Macalester College, his MBA in organizational behavior from UC Berkeley, and his PhD in management from the Peter F. Drucker Graduate Management Center of the Claremont Graduate University.

To schedule Dr. Bob Nelson or one of his associates to present to your organization, association, or conference, call Nelson Motivation Inc. in San Diego at 800-575-5521 or 858-487-1046. For more information about available products or services offered by Nelson Motivation Inc., including registration for Bob's free Tip of the Week, visit his website at www.nelson-motivation.com or contact Bob directly at BobRewards@aol.com.

Peter Economy (La Jolla, California) is associate editor of *Leader to Leader*, the award-winning magazine of the Peter F. Drucker Foundation for Nonprofit Leadership, and author of numerous books, including *Leadership Ensemble: Lessons in Collaborative Management from the World's Only Conductorless Orchestra* (with Harvey Seifter), *Why Aren't You Your Own Boss?* (with Paul and Sarah Edwards), *At the Helm: Business Lessons for Navigating Rough Waters* (with Peter Isler), *Enterprising Nonprofits: A Toolkit for Social Entrepreneurs* (with Greg Dees and Jed Emerson), *Home-Based Business For Dummies* (with Paul and Sarah Edwards), and many others. Peter combines his writing expertise with more than 15 years of management experience to provide his readers with solid, hands-on information and advice. He received his bachelor's degree (with majors in economics and human biology) from Stanford University and is currently pursuing his MBA at the Edinburgh Business School. Visit Peter at his Web site: www.petereconomy.com.

Dedication

To any manager who has struggled to do the job and every employee who has had to live with the consequences.

Authors' Acknowledgments

Throughout our careers, we have been fortunate to have had experienced mentors to model the right kinds of management skills and techniques that we advocate in *Managing For Dummies,* 2nd Edition.

Bob recalls three influential mentors in particular. Jim Reller, a delegator par excellence in Bob's first corporate position at Control Data Corporation, who often gave out assignments with a disclaimer such as, "I could probably do this task faster than you, but I believe you'll learn a lot from the process"; Dr. Ken Blanchard, also known as *The One Minute Manager,* who Bob worked with for more than ten years, demonstrated how to get the best efforts from people by using the softer side of management and never directly telling them what to do; and Dr. Peter F. Drucker who Bob worked with in his PhD studies at Claremont Graduate University.

In Peter's case, Richard Vaaler, contracting officer for the Department of Defense, taught the benefits of upholding high ethical standards and making things happen. At Horizons Technology, Inc., CFO Debbie Fritsch demonstrated the importance of hiring and developing superior employees and challenging authority. Pat Boyce, president, taught Peter to look beyond the obvious to ferret out the truth and also showed him the value of becoming one with your customers. Jim Palmer, chairman, embodied the value of painting the big picture — a vision for all employees to strive for.

These people taught more than just the technical skills of assigning work, conducting a performance appraisal, or disciplining an employee. They also emphasized the people side of management: how to motivate employees by example, reward them when they exceed your expectations, and make each customer feel like he or she is your only customer — even if you have thousands of others.

Bob and Peter are also especially appreciative of all the folks at Wiley Publishing, Inc. — including Pam Mourouzis, who has been with us since the very beginning, Allyson Grove, who helped keep everything on track, and copyeditor extraordinaire Chad Sievers — for their infinite wisdom, guidance, and support on this project.

On the personal side, Bob would like to acknowledge the ongoing love and support of his father Edward, his wife Jennifer, and his children, Daniel and Michelle. Peter acknowledges his mother Betty Economy Gritis, his wife Jan, and his children, Peter J, Skylar Park, and Jackson Warren, for their everlasting love and for putting up with his crazy life. May the circle be unbroken.

Publisher's Acknowledgments

We're proud of this book; please send us your comments through our Dummies online registration form located at www.dummies.com/register/.

Some of the people who helped bring this book to market include the following:

Acquisitions, Editorial, and Media Development

Project Editor: Allyson Grove

(Previous Edition: Pam Mourouzis)

Acquisitions Editor: Pam Mourouzis

Copy Editor: Chad R. Sievers

(Previous Edition: Leah Cameron)

Technical Editor: William Taylor

Editorial Manager: Jennifer Ehrlich

Editorial Assistants: Melissa Bennett, Elizabeth Rea

Cartoons: Rich Tennant, www.the5thwave.com

Production

Project Coordinator: Nancee Reeves

Layout and Graphics: Amanda Carter, Joyce Haughey, Michael Kruzil, Jacque Schneider, Julie Trippetti, Jeremey Unger

Proofreaders: Laura Albert, Dave Faust, Andy Hollandbeck, Charles Spencer, TECHBOOKS Production Services

Indexer: TECHBOOKS Production Services

Publishing and Editorial for Consumer Dummies

Diane Graves Steele, Vice President and Publisher, Consumer Dummies

Joyce Pepple, Acquisitions Director, Consumer Dummies

Kristin A. Cocks, Product Development Director, Consumer Dummies

Michael Spring, Vice President and Publisher, Travel

Brice Gosnell, Publishing Director, Travel

Suzanne Jannetta, Editorial Director, Travel

Publishing for Technology Dummies

Andy Cummings, Vice President and Publisher, Dummies Technology/General User

Composition Services

Gerry Fahey, Vice President of Production Services

Debbie Stailey, Director of Composition Services

Contents at a Glance

Table of Contents

Foreword

*W*hen I first heard about *Managing For Dummies,* 2nd Edition, I have to admit that I was a bit apprehensive. After all, most of the managers I know are far from dummies. In fact, they tend to be highly educated, hardworking, and intelligent — not dumb by any stretch of the imagination.

Then I got a chance to see what was in the book, and my apprehension quickly shifted to enthusiasm. Here was the practice of management simplified to its essential ingredients, presented in a lively, fun, and practical format! This was one-stop shopping at its finest: a step-by-step guide for what you need, when you need it. I said to myself, "Finally a book on managing that doesn't make you feel like an idiot!"

I suppose I shouldn't have been surprised. After all, I have worked closely with Bob Nelson for more than ten years and have seen firsthand his ability to build a team and get results. His knack for writing about managing in a clear and practical manner has always been evident — from his best-selling trade book on employee recognition, *1001 Ways to Reward Employees,* to his work as one of my coauthors on our recent textbook, *Exploring the World of Business.* Bob has a rare blend for a writer: He is both an astute observer of management and a skilled practitioner. You'll find the fruits of his labor with Peter Economy both insightful and highly practical. They have digested management practices, activities, and skills into a what-you-need-to-know, when-you-need-to-know-it format that both works and is fun in the process.

If clarity is a virtue, Bob and Peter should be the patron saints. They have demonstrated this fact and in the process taken the mystery out of managing. And not a minute too soon, given the complexity of the global business environment and the rapid change that is all around us today.

Thank you for this gift to managers everywhere! This is one book I will be delighted to give to those managers I most want to succeed.

— Ken Blanchard, coauthor
The One Minute Manager

Introduction

Congratulations! As a result of your astute choice of material, you're about to read a completely fresh approach to the topic of management. If you've already read other books about management, you have surely noticed that most of them fall into one of two categories: (1) deadly boring snooze-o-rama that makes a great paperweight, or (2) recycled platitudes glazed with a thin sugar-coating of pop psychobabble, which sounds great on paper but fails abysmally in the real world.

Managing For Dummies, 2nd Edition is different. First, this book is fun. Our approach reflects our strong belief and experience that management can be fun, too. You can get the job done and have fun in the process. We even help you to maintain a sense of humor in the face of the seemingly insurmountable challenges that all managers have to deal with from time to time. On some days, you'll face challenges — perhaps to your limit or beyond. However, on many more days, the joys of managing (teaching a new skill to an employee, helping land a new customer, accomplishing an important assignment, and so on) can bring you a sense of fulfillment that you never imagined possible.

Second, popular business books seem to be here today and gone tomorrow. Like it or not, many managers (and the companies they work for) seem to be ruled by the business fad of the month. In *Managing For Dummies,* 2nd Edition, we buck the trend by concentrating on tried-and-true solutions to the most common situations that real supervisors and managers face: solutions that stand up over time and can be used in turbulent times. You won't find any mumbo-jumbo here — just practical solutions to everyday problems.

Managing For Dummies, 2nd Edition breaks the rules. It provides a comprehensive overview of the fundamentals of effective management presented in a fun and interesting format. It neither puts you to sleep nor is so sugarcoated that it rots your teeth. We know from personal experience that managing can be an intimidating job. New managers — especially ones promoted into the position for their technical expertise — are often at a loss as to what they need to do. Don't worry. Relax. Help is at your fingertips.

About This Book

Managing For Dummies, 2nd Edition is perfect for all levels of managers. New managers and managers-to-be can find everything you need to know to be successful. Experienced managers are challenged to shift your perspectives and to take a fresh look at your management philosophies and techniques. Despite the popular saying about teaching old dogs new tricks, you can always make changes that ease your job — and the jobs of your employees — and make them more fun and a lot more effective.

But, even the most experienced manager can feel overwhelmed from time to time — new tricks or not.

For Bob, it was when he was giving an important business presentation before a group of international executives — only to be told by one of the executives that his pants zipper was unzipped. Although Bob did score bonus points for getting his audience's attention with this novel fashion statement, he could've done so in a more conventional way.

For Peter, it was when he reprimanded an employee for arriving late to work and later learned that the employee was late because she had stopped at a bakery on the way to work to buy Peter a cake in celebration of Boss's Day. Needless to say, the event wasn't quite as festive as it could've been!

Face it: Whether you're new to the job or are faced with a new task in an old job, all managers feel overwhelmed sometimes. The secret to dealing with such feelings is to discover what you can do better (or differently) to obtain the results you want. When you do make a mistake, pick yourself up, laugh it off, and learn from it. We wrote this book to make learning easier so that you won't have to learn the hard way.

How to Use This Book

Despite the obvious resemblance of this book to one of the yellow bricks on Dorothy's road to Oz, the proper way to use this book is not as a doorstop or a makeshift paperweight. You can use this book in one of two ways:

- ✔ If you want to find out about a specific topic, such as delegating tasks or hiring employees, you can flip to that section and get your answers quickly. Faster than you can say, "Where's that report I asked for last week?" you'll have your answer.

- ✔ If you want a crash course in management, read this book from cover to cover. Forget going back to school to get your MBA — you can save your money and take a trip to the Bahamas instead.

This book is unique because you can read each chapter without having to read what comes before. Or you can read each chapter without reading what comes after. Or you can read the book backwards or forwards. Or you can just carry it around with you to impress your friends.

Conventions Used in This Book

As you'll soon see, new terms are in italics for easy reference, and Web sites appear in monofont. Neat, huh?

Foolish Assumptions

As we wrote this book, we made a few assumptions about you, our readers. For example, we assumed that you're either a manager — or a manager-to-be — and that you're truly motivated to discover some new approaches to managing organizations and to leading people. We also assumed that you're ready, willing, and able to commit yourself to becoming a better manager.

How This Book Is Organized

Managing For Dummies, 2nd Edition is organized into seven parts. Each part covers a major area of management practice. The chapters within each part cover specific topics in detail. Following is a summary of what you'll find in each part.

Part 1: So, You Want to Be a Manager?

Successful managers master several basic skills. This part begins with a discussion of what managers are and what they do, and then looks at the most basic management skills: organization, delegation, and leadership.

Part II: Managing: The People Part

The heart of management boils down to getting tasks done through others. This process starts with hiring talented workers and extends to motivating and coaching them to go above and beyond expectations.

Part III: Making Things Happen

Making things happen is another important aspect of managing that starts with knowing where you're going and how to tell when you've arrived. In this part, we consider goal setting, measuring and monitoring employee performance, and conducting performance appraisals.

Part IV: Working with (Other) People

Successful managers have discovered that building bridges to other workers and managers — both inside and outside the organization — is important. This part covers communicating, making presentations, building high-performance teams, and dealing with office politics.

Part V: Tough Times for Tough Managers

As any manager can testify, management is not all fun and games. In fact, managing can be downright difficult at times. In this part, we consider some of the toughest tasks of managing: managing change, disciplining and firing employees, and managing "me."

Part VI: Tools and Techniques for Managing

Being a manager requires that you learn and apply certain technical tools and skills. This part discusses guidelines for accounting and budgeting and working with today's technologies.

The most successful managers know that standing still in business is the same as falling behind. Good managers always look to the future and make plans accordingly. Developing and training employees and creating a learning workplace are also covered in this part.

Part VII: The Part of Tens

Finally, we include the Part of Tens: a quick-and-dirty collection of chapters, each of which gives you ten (or so) pieces of information that every manager needs to know. Look to these chapters when you need a quick refresher on managing strategies and techniques.

Icons Used in This Book

To guide you along the way and point out the information you really need to know, this book uses icons along its left margins. You'll see the following icons in this book:

This icon points to tips and tricks that make managing easier.

If you don't heed the advice next to these icons, the situation may blow up in your face. Watch out!

Remember these important points of information, and you'll be a much better manager.

This icon points out wise sayings and other kernels of wisdom that you can take with you on your journey to becoming a better manager.

These anecdotes from Bob and Peter and other real-life managers show you the right — and sometimes wrong — way to be a manager.

Where Do I Go from Here?

If you're a new or aspiring manager, you may want to start at the beginning (isn't that a novel concept?) and work your way through to the end. Simply turn the page and take your first step into the world of management.

If you're already a manager and are short of time (and what manager isn't short of time?), you may want to turn to a particular topic to address a specific need or question. The Table of Contents gives a chapter-by-chapter description of the topics in this book. You can also find specific topics in the index.

Enjoy your journey!

Part I
So, You Want to Be a Manager?

The 5th Wave   By Rich Tennant

Remember Robin— lead, follow, or get out of the forest.

In this part . . .

*B*efore you can become an effective manager, you need to master some basic skills. In this part, we find out what management is, and we cover some of the most important managing skills, including delegating tasks to employees and becoming a leader.

Chapter 1

You're a Manager — Now What?

Congratulations! Because you're reading this book, you're probably

  ✔ A manager

  ✔ A manager-to-be

  ✔ An individual who is uncontrollably attracted to books with bright yellow and black covers (not that there's anything wrong with that!)

Of course, if you're simply curious and want to discover the intimate details about the kinds of management techniques that can help you get the best from your employees every day of the week, then welcome!

Managing is truly a calling — one that, as managers, the authors are proud to have answered. *We're the few. The proud. The managers.* In the world of business, no other place allows you to have such a direct, dramatic, and positive impact on the lives of others and on the ultimate success of your enterprise. (Except, perhaps, for the guy who is in charge of fixing the Xerox machine.)

Identifying the Different Styles of Management

One definition describes management as *getting things done through others.* Another definition more specifically defines management as *making something planned happen within a specific area through the use of available resources.* Seems simple enough. But why do so many bright, industrious people have trouble managing well? And why do so many companies today seem to offer a flavor-of-the-month training program? How often have you been introduced to some hot new management concept — guaranteed to turn your organization around in no time flat — only to watch it fade away within a few months, if not sooner? Of course, as soon as one management fad disappears, another is waiting in the wings to replace it.

> "What? You didn't catch onto that concept of Six Sigma? That's okay — we decided that it doesn't really work anyway. Now, we want you to pay close attention to this video on Armadillo Management (hard on the outside, soft on the inside!) — it's the latest thing. The big guy read an article about it in *The Wall Street Journal* and wants us to implement it throughout our North American operations right away!"

Unfortunately, good management is a scarce commodity — at once precious and fleeting. Despite years of management theory's evolution and the comings and goings of countless management fads, many workers — and managers, for that matter — have developed a distorted view of management and its practice, with managers often not knowing the right approach to take, or exactly what to do. And, as the saying goes, "If it's foggy in the pulpit, it'll be cloudy in the pew."

Do you ever hear any of the following statements at your office or place of business?

✔ We don't have the authority to make that decision.

✔ She's in charge of the department — fixing the problem is her responsibility, not ours.

✔ Why do they keep asking us what we think when they never use anything we say?

✔ I'm sorry, but that's our policy. We're not allowed to make exceptions.

✔ If my manager doesn't care, I don't either.

✔ It doesn't matter how hard you work; no one's going to notice anyway.

✔ You can't trust those employees — they just want to goof off.

When you hear statements like these at work, red lights should be flashing before your eyes, and alarm bells should be ringing in your ears. Statements like these indicate that managers and employees aren't communicating effectively — that managers don't trust their employees, and that employees lack confidence in their managers. If you're lucky, you can find out about these kinds of problems while you still have a chance to do something about them. If you're not so lucky and you miss the clues, you may be stuck making the same mistakes again and again.

The expectations and commitments that employees carry with them on the job are in large part a product of the way that their managers treat them. Following are the most commonly adopted styles of management. Do you recognize your management style?

Tough guy (or gal) management

Okay. Here's the $64,000 question: What is the best way to make something planned happen? Everyone seems to have a different answer to this question. Some people see management as something you do to people — not with them. Does this type of manager sound familiar? "We're going to do it my way. Understand?" Or perhaps the ever-popular threat: "It had better be on my desk by the end of the day — or else!" If worse comes to worst, a manager can unveil the ultimate weapon, "Mess up one more time, and you're out of here!"

This type of management is often known as *Theory X management,* which assumes that people are inherently lazy and need to be driven to perform. Managing by fear and intimidation is always guaranteed to get a response. The question is: Do you get the kind of response that you really want? When you closely monitor your employees' work, you usually end up with only short-term compliance. In other words, you never get the best from others by building a fire under them — you have to find a way to build a fire within them.

Sometimes managers have to take command of the situation. If a proposal has to be shipped out in an hour and your customer just sent you some important changes, take charge of the situation to ensure that the right people are on the task — that is, if you're serious about keeping your customer. When you have to act quickly with perhaps not as much discussion as you would like, however, it's important to apologize in advance and let people know why you're doing things the way you are.

Nice guy (or gal) management

At the other end of the spectrum, some people see management as a nice-guy or nice-gal kind of idea. *Theory Y management* assumes that people basically want to do a good job. In the extreme interpretation of this theory, managers are supposed to be sensitive to their employees' feelings and be careful not to do anything that may disturb their employees' tranquility and sense of self-worth.

> "Uh, there's this little problem with your report; none of the numbers are correct. Now, don't take this personally, but we need to consider our alternatives for taking a more careful look at these figures in the future."

Again, managers may get a response with this approach (or they may choose to do the work themselves!), but are they likely to get the best possible response? No, the employees are likely to take advantage of the managers.

The ideal compromise

Good managers realize that they don't have to be tough all the time — and that nice guys and gals often finish first. If your employees are diligently performing their assigned tasks and no business emergency requires your immediate intervention, you can step back and let them do their jobs. Not only do your employees learn to be responsible, but you also can concentrate your efforts on what is most important to the bottom-line success of your organization.

A manager's real job is to inspire employees to do their best and establish a working environment that allows them to reach their goals. The best managers make every possible effort to remove the organizational obstacles that prevent employees from doing their jobs and to obtain the resources and training that employees need to do their jobs effectively. All other goals — no matter how lofty or pressing — must take a back seat.

Bad systems, bad policies, bad procedures, and poor treatment of others are organizational weaknesses that managers must be talented at identifying and repairing or replacing. Build a strong organizational foundation for your employees. Support your people, and they will support you. Time and time again, when given the opportunity to achieve, workers in all kinds of businesses, from factories to venture capital firms, have proven this rule to be true. If you haven't seen it at your place of business, you may be mistaking your employees for problems. Quit squeezing them and start squeezing your organization. The result is employees who want to succeed and a business that flourishes right along with them. Who knows, your employees may even stop hiding when they see you coming their way!

Squeezing employees may be easier than fighting the convoluted systems and cutting through the bureaucratic barnacles that have grown on your organization. You may be tempted to yell, "It's your fault that our department didn't achieve its goals!" Yes, blaming your employees for the organization's problems may be tempting, but doing so isn't going to solve the problems. Sure, you may get a quick, short-lived response when you push your people, but ultimately, you're failing to deal with the organization's real problems.

We all want to "win." The challenge of management is to define winning in such a way that it feels like winning for everyone in the organization. This, of course, is extremely difficult. People are often competing with co-workers for a "piece of the pie" rather than trying to make the pie bigger. It's your job to help make a bigger pie.

Quick Fixes Don't Stick

Despite what many people want you to believe, management is not prone to simple solutions or quick fixes. Being a manager is not simple. Yes, the best management solutions tend to be common sense; however, turning common sense into common practice is sometimes difficult.

Management is an attitude — a way of life. Management is a very real desire to work with people and help them succeed, as well as a desire to help your organization succeed. Management is a life-long learning process that doesn't end when you walk out of a one-hour seminar or finish viewing a 25-minute video. Management is like the old story about the happy homeowner who was shocked to receive a bill for $100 to fix a leaky faucet. When asked to explain the basis for this seemingly high charge, the plumber said, "Tightening the nut cost you $5. Knowing which nut to tighten cost you $95!"

Management is a people job. If you're not up to the task of working with people — helping them, listening to them, encouraging them, and guiding them — then you shouldn't be a manager.

Because management is such a challenge, an entire management training industry has sprung up, ready to help managers find out how to solve their problems. Unfortunately, trainers often focus on creating instant gratification among course attendees, many of whom have spent hundreds and even thousands of dollars to be there. "Let's give them so much stuff to use that it will be their fault if they never use any of it!"

Once, Peter went to one of those touchy-feely offsite management meetings meant to build teamwork and communication among the members of the group. Picture this: Just after lunch, a big tray of leftover veggies, bagels, fruit, and such was sitting on a table at the side of the room. The facilitator rose from his chair, faced the group, and said, "Your next task is to split yourselves into four groups and construct a model of the perfect manager by using only the items on that tray of leftovers." A collective groan filled the room. "I don't want to hear any complaints," the trainer said. "I just want to see happy people doing happy things for the next half-hour."

The teams feverishly went about their task of building the perfect manager. With some managers barely throttling the temptation to engage each other in a massive food fight, the little figures began to take shape. A banana here, a carrot stick there . . . and voilà! After a brief competition for dominance, the winners were crowned. The result? We thought you'd never ask. Check out Figure 1-1.

We have to admit that the result was kind of cute (and kind of tasty, too), but did it really make a difference in the way in which these managers managed their employees when they returned to the office the next day? We don't think so. Was the seminar a nice break from the day-to-day office routine? Yes. Was it a meaningful teaching tool with lasting impact? No.

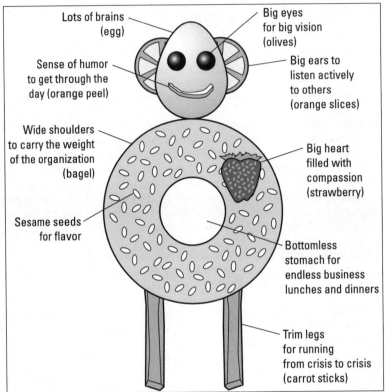

Big eyes
for big vision
(olives)

Lots of brains
(egg)

Big ears to
listen actively
to others
(orange slices)

Sense of humor
to get through the
day (orange peel)

Wide shoulders
to carry the weight
of the organization
(bagel)

Big heart
filled with
compassion
(strawberry)

Sesame seeds
for flavor

Bottomless
stomach for
endless business
lunches and dinners

Trim legs
for running
from crisis to crisis
(carrot sticks)

Figure 1-1:
The Veggie
Manager.

Meeting the Management Challenge

When you're assigned a task in a nonmanagement position, completing it by yourself is fairly simple and straightforward. Your immediate results are in direct response to your effort. To accomplish your task, you first review the task, you decide how best to accomplish it, and then you set schedules and milestones for its successful completion. Assuming that you have access to the tools and resources necessary to accomplish your task, you can probably do it yourself quickly and easily. You're an expert doer — a bright, get-things-done type of person.

However, if you hold a management position, you were probably selected because you proved yourself to be very skilled in the areas that you're now responsible for managing. For example, Peter's friend, John, was a member of a team of software programmers developing a complex application for portable computers. When he was a team member, everything was fine. He came to work in a T-shirt and jeans — just like the rest of his teammates — and often spent time with his programmer friends after hours. The bond that the team shared changed, however, when John was selected to manage the team.

In his new role of manager, John first changed offices. Instead of sharing an open bay with the other programmers, he moved into his very own office — one with four walls and a window looking out over the parking lot. A secretary was assigned to guard his door. Of course, the jeans and T-shirt had to go — they were replaced with a business suit and tie. Instead of having fun programming, John was now concerned about more serious topics such as cost overruns, schedule delays, and returns on investments. As John's role changed, so did John. And as John changed, so did his relationship with his coworkers. He was no longer a coworker; he was the Boss. To achieve his goals, John quickly had to make the transition from a doer to a manager of doers.

When you want to get a task done through someone else, you employ a different set of skills than when you do the task yourself. All of a sudden, because of this simple decision to pass the responsibility for completion of a task on to someone else, you introduce an interpersonal element into your equation. "Oh, no! You mean I have to actually work with people?" Being good technically at your job is not enough — no matter how good your technical skills are. Now you must have good planning, organization, leadership, and follow-up skills.

In other words, in addition to being a good doer, you have to be a good manager of doers.

The old rules don't work anymore

If this challenge isn't already enough, managers today face yet another challenge — one that has shaken the foundations of modern business. The new reality is the partnership of managers and workers in the workplace.

Originally, management was about dividing the company's work into discrete tasks, assigning the work to individual workers, and then closely monitoring the workers' performance and steering them toward accomplishing their tasks on time and within budget. The old reality of management often relied on fear, intimidation, and power over people to accomplish goals. If things weren't going according to management's plan, then management commanded its way out of the problem: "I don't care what you have to do to get it done — just get it done. Now!" The line between managers and workers was drawn clearly and drawn often.

The new business environment

In the new business environment, what's going on inside the organization is a reflection of what's going on outside the organization. The following factors are creating rapid and constant change in today's new business environment:

- ✔ A surge of global competition
- ✔ New technology and innovation
- ✔ The flattening of organizational hierarchies
- ✔ Widespread downsizing, reengineering, and layoffs
- ✔ The rise of small business
- ✔ The changing values of today's workers
- ✔ The increasing demands for better customer service

Sure, managers still have to divide and assign work, but workers are taking on more of that responsibility. Most importantly, managers are finding out that they can't command their employees' best work — they have to create an environment that fosters their employees' desire to do their best work. In short, the new reality is the partnership of managers and workers in the workplace.

The landscape of business worldwide has changed dramatically during the past couple of decades. If you don't change with it, you're going to be left far behind your competitors. You may think that you can get away with treating your employees like "human assets" or children, but you can't. You can't because your competitors are discovering how to unleash the hidden power of their employees. They're no longer just talking about it; they're doing it!

It's a new army

A few years ago, Bob made a presentation to a group of high-tech managers. As he was wrapping up his presentation, he opened the floor to questions. A hand shot up. "With all the downsizing and layoffs that we've endured, people are lucky to get a paycheck, much less anything else. Why do we have to bother to empower and reward employees?" Before Bob had a chance to respond, another manager in the audience shot back, "Because it's a new army."

Watch out! Technology explosion ahead!

In the new world of information technology, the old ways of doing business are being turned on their sides. With the presence of computer networks, e-mail, and voice mail, the walls that divide individuals, departments, and organizational units have come crashing down. In the words of Frederick Kovac, vice president of planning for the Goodyear Tire and Rubber Company, "It used to be, if you wanted information, you had to go up, over, and down through the organization. Now you just tap in. Everybody can know as much about the company as the chairman of the board."

This response really sums it all up. In business, times are changing. Now that employees have tasted the sweet nectar of empowerment, you can't turn back. Companies that stick with the old way of doing business — the hierarchical, highly centralized model — will lose employees and customers to those companies that use the new ways of doing business and make them a part of their corporate culture. The best employees will leave the old-model companies in droves, seeking employers who treat them with respect and who are willing to grant them greater autonomy and responsibility.

That leaves you with the employees who don't want to take risks or rock the boat. You get the yes-men and yes-women. No one will challenge your ideas because they're afraid to. No one will suggest better or more efficient ways to do business because they know that you won't listen or care anyway. Your employees won't bother to go out of their way to help a customer because you don't trust them to make the most basic decisions — the ones that can make the biggest difference to the satisfaction, or the lack thereof, of your precious customers.

Imagine the difference between an employee who tells your key customer, "Sorry, my hands are tied. I am not allowed to make any exceptions to our policies," and the employee who tells that customer, "Sure, I'll do everything in my power to get you your order by your deadline." With whom do you think your customers prefer to do business? With whom would you prefer to do business? (***Hint:*** Don't even think about the first alternative!)

Managers used to rent behavior. Some workers used to be called "hired hands." Today, hiring your hands is not good enough. You must find a way to engage their souls and bring their best efforts to the workplace each and every day.

Trust is not a four-letter word

Companies that provide exceptional customer service unleash their employees from the constraints of an overly controlling hierarchy and allow front-line workers to serve their customers directly and efficiently. For example, while many companies devote forests of paper to employee manuals, Nordstrom, Inc., devotes exactly one page to its manual.

Figure 1-2 shows you what is on that page.

You may think that a *small* company with five or ten employees can get away with a policy like that, but certainly not a big company like yours. However, Nordstrom is not a small business by any stretch of the imagination — unless you consider a company with 50,000 or so employees and more than $5 billion in annual sales small.

The ultimate employee letter

In his book *Please Don't Just Do What I Tell You! Do What Needs to Be Done* (Hyperion, 2002), Bob talks about the "Ultimate Expectation" of every employer — for employees to do what needs to be done. In the letter that follows from manager to employee, Bob clearly outlines this expectation.

Dear Employee:

You've been hired to handle some pressing needs we have. If we could have gotten by in not hiring you, we would have. But we've determined that we needed someone with your skills and experience and that you were the best person to help us with our needs. We have offered you the position and you've accepted. Thanks!

During the course of your employment, you will be asked to do many things: general responsibilities, specific assignments, group and individual projects. You will have many chances to excel and to confirm that we made a good choice in hiring you.

However, there is one foremost responsibility that may never be specifically requested of you but that you need to always keep in mind through the duration of your employment. This is the Ultimate Expectation, and it is as follows:

ALWAYS DO WHAT MOST NEEDS TO BE DONE WITHOUT WAITING TO BE ASKED.

We've hired you to do a job, yes, but more important, we've hired you to think, to use your judgment and to act in the best interest of the organization at all times.

If we never say this again, don't take it as an indication that it's no longer important or that we've changed our priorities. We are likely to get caught up in the daily press of business, the never-ending changes of the operation, and the ongoing rush of activities. Our day-to-day practices make it look like this principle no longer applies. Don't be deceived by this.

Please don't ever forget The Ultimate Expectation. Strive to have it always be a guiding principle in your employment with us, a philosophy that is always with you, one that is constantly driving your thoughts and actions.

As long as you are employed with us, you have our permission to act in our mutual best interests.

If at any time you do not feel we are doing the right thing — the thing you most believe would help us all — please say so. You have our permission to speak up when necessary to state what is unstated, to make a suggestion, or to question an action or decision.

This doesn't mean we will always agree with you, nor that we will necessarily change what we are doing; but we always want to hear what you most believe would help us better achieve our goals and purpose and to create a mutually successful experience in the process.

You will need to seek to understand how (and why) things are done the way they are done before you seek to change existing work processes. Try to work with the systems that are in place first, but tell us if you think those systems need to be changed.

Discuss what is presented here with me and others in the organization so that we might all become better at applying The Ultimate Expectation.

Sincerely,

Your Manager

How does management at a large business like Nordstrom get away with such a policy? They do it through trust.

We're glad to have you with our Company. Our number one goal is to provide outstanding customer service.

Set both your personal and professional goals high.

Nordstrom Rules:

Rule #1: Use your good judgement in all situations.

There will be no additional rules. Please feel free to ask your department manager, store manager, or division general manager any question at any time.

(Source: *Business and Society Review*, Spring 1993, n85)

First, Nordstrom hires good people. Secondly, the company gives them the training and tools to do their jobs well. Then management gets out of the way and lets the employees do their work. Nordstrom knows that it can trust its employees to make the right decisions because the company knows that it has hired the right people for the job and has trained them well.

We're not saying that Nordstrom doesn't have problems — every company does. But Nordstrom has taken a proactive stance in creating the environment that employees most need and want.

Can you say the same for your organization?

When you trust your employees, they respond by being trustworthy. When you recognize them for being independent and responsive to their customers, they continue to be independent and responsive to their customers. And when you give them the freedom to make their own decisions, they make their own decisions. With a little training and a lot of support, these decisions are in the best interest of the company because the right people at the right level of the organization make them.

Explaining the New Functions of Management

Remember the four "classic" functions of management — plan, organize, lead, and control — that you learned in school? (Yeah. We were asleep in that class, too.) These management functions form the foundation from which every manager works. Although these basic functions are fine for taking care of most of your day-to-day management duties, they fail to reflect the new reality of the workplace and the new partnership of managers and workers. What is needed is a new set of management functions that builds upon the four classic functions of management. You're in luck. The sections that follow describe the functions of the new manager in the 21st-century workplace.

Energize

Today's managers are masters of making things happen — starting with themselves. "If it's to be, it's to begin with me." Think of the best managers you know. What one quality sets them apart from the rest? Is it their organizational skills, their fairness, or their technical ability? Perhaps their ability to delegate or the long hours that they keep sets them apart.

Although all these traits may be important to a manager's success, we haven't yet named the unique quality that makes a good manager great. The most important management function is to get people excited and inspired, that is, to *energize* them.

You can be the best analyst in the world, the most highly organized executive on the planet, or fair beyond reproach, but if the level of excitement that you generate can be likened more to that of a dish rag than to that of a spark plug, then you're handicapped in your efforts to create a truly great organization. ("Everyone follow me!" she said as her staff went back to sleep.)

Great managers create far more energy than they consume. The best managers are organizational catalysts. Instead of taking energy from an organization, they channel and amplify it to the organization. In every interaction, effective managers take the natural energy of their employees, add to it, and leave the employees in a higher energy state than when they started the interaction. Management becomes a process of transmitting the excitement that you feel about your organization and its goals to your employees in terms that they can understand and appreciate. Before you know it, your employees are as excited about the organization as you are, and you can simply allow their energy to carry you forward.

A picture is worth a thousand words. This statement is as true for the pictures that you paint in the minds of others as for the pictures that people paint on canvas or print on the pages of magazines and books. Imagine taking a vacation with your family or friends. As the big day draws near, you keep the goal exciting and fresh in the minds of your family or friends by creating a vision of the journey that awaits you. Vivid descriptions of white sand beaches, towering redwoods, glittering skylines, secluded lakes, hot food, and indoor plumbing paint pictures in the minds of each of your fellow travelers. With this vision in mind, everyone works toward a common goal of having a successful vacation.

What managers really do

With tongue planted firmly in cheek, we universally agree that all managers perform five functions in an organization. These five functions are as follows:

✔ **Eat:** Management clearly has its rewards, one of which is an expense account and all the company-paid lunches and dinners you can get away with. And if those yo-yos in accounting dare to question the business purpose of your meals, you can always threaten to leave them off your list of invitees.

✔ **Meet:** Meetings are truly a perk of management. The higher you rise in an organization, the more time you spend in meetings. Instead of doing productive work, you now spend more time than ever listening to presentations that have no relevance to your department, drinking three-day-old coffee, and keeping close tabs on your watch as your meeting drags on and on — well past its scheduled ending time.

✔ **Punish:** With so many wayward employees, the best managers learn to punish early and punish often. What better way to show your employees that you care? Punishment also sends a welcome signal to upper management that you don't put up with any nonsense from your underlings.

✔ **Obstruct:** When you ask managers what single achievement makes them proudest, they are likely to bring out policies as thick as the Yellow Pages that were carefully drafted over many years. A close look at the policy may reveal a package of deftly written red tape that does more to prevent good customer service than it does to support it.

✔ **Obscure:** Managers are masters at the art of miscommunication. No one knows better than a manager that information is power, that an individual who has it has the power, and that an individual who doesn't is lost. With potential enemies all around, why give anyone else a chance to get an advantage over you? "Hey! That information is on a need-to-know basis only!" And for heaven's sake, why let your employees in on the inner workings of the organization? They wouldn't appreciate or understand it anyway, right?

Actually, this *isn't* the list of the functions of management. Although the list may ring true in many cases, we were just pulling your leg.

Successful managers create compelling visions — pictures of a future organization that inspire and compel employees to bring out their best performance.

Empower

Have you ever worked for someone who didn't let you do your job without questioning your every decision? Maybe you spent all weekend working on a special project only to have it casually discarded by your boss. "What were you thinking when you did this, Elizabeth? Our customers will never buy into that approach!" Or maybe you went out of your way to help a customer, accepting a return shipment of an item against company policy. "Why do you think we have policies — because we enjoy killing trees? No! If we made exceptions for everyone, we'd go out of business!" How did it feel to have your sincere efforts at doing a great job disparaged? What was your reaction? Chances are, you didn't bother making the extra effort again.

Despite rumors to the contrary, when you empower your employees, you do not stop managing. What changes is the way you manage. Managers still provide vision, establish organizational goals, and determine shared values. However, managers must establish a corporate infrastructure — skills training, teams, and so on — that supports empowerment. And although all your employees may not want to be empowered, you still have to provide an environment that supports those employees who are eager for a taste of the freedom to apply their personal creativity and expertise to your organization.

Great managers allow their employees to do great work. This role is a vital function of management, for even the greatest managers in the world can't succeed all by themselves. To achieve the organizations' goals, managers depend on their employees' skills. Effective management is the leveraging of the efforts of every member of a work unit toward a common purpose. If you're constantly doing your employees' work for them, not only have you lost the advantage of the leverage that your employees can provide you, but you're also putting yourself on the path to stress, ulcers, and worse.

However, far worse than the personal loss that you suffer when you don't empower employees is that everyone in your organization loses. Your employees lose because you aren't allowing them to stretch themselves or to show creativity or initiative. Your organization loses the insights that its creative workforce brings with it. Finally, your customers lose because your employees are afraid to provide them with exceptional service. Why should they if they're constantly worried that you will punish them for taking initiative or for pushing the limits of the organization to better serve your customers?

As William McKnight, former CEO of manufacturing giant 3M put it, "The mistakes people make are of much less importance than the mistakes management makes if it tells people exactly what to do."

Support

A manager's job is no longer that of a watchdog, police officer, or executioner. Increasingly, managers must be coaches, colleagues, and cheerleaders for the employees they support. The main concern of today's managers needs to be shaping a more supportive work environment that enables each employee to feel valued and be more productive.

When the going gets tough, managers support their employees. Now, this doesn't mean that you do everything for your employees or make their decisions for them. It does mean that you give your employees the training, resources, and authority to do their jobs, and then you get out of the way. You're always there for your employees to help pick up the pieces if they fall, but fall they must if they're going to learn. The idea is the same as learning to skate: If you're not falling, you're not learning.

The key to creating a supportive environment is establishing trust or *openness* throughout an organization. In an open environment, employees can bring up questions and concerns. In fact, they're encouraged to do so. When the environment is truly open, an individual can express concerns without fear of retribution. Hidden agendas do not exist, and people feel free to say the same things in business meetings that they'd say after work. When employees see that their managers are receptive to new ideas, they're more likely to feel invested in the organization, and to think of more and better ways to improve systems, to solve problems, to save money, and to better serve customers.

Managers also support each other. Personal fiefdoms, fighting between departments, and withholding information have no place in the modern organization; companies cannot afford to support these dysfunctional behaviors. All members of the organization — from the top to the bottom — must realize that they play on the same team. To win, team members support each other and keep their coworkers apprised of the latest information. Which team are you on?

Communicate

Without a doubt, communication is the lifeblood of any organization, and managers are the common element that connects different levels of employees with one another. We have seen firsthand the positive effects on a business and its employees of managers who communicate, and the negative effects on a business and its employees of managers who don't.

Managers who don't communicate effectively are missing out on a vital role of management.

Communication is a key function for managers today. Information is power, and as the speed of business accelerates, information must be communicated to employees faster than ever. Constant change and increasing turbulence in the business environment necessitate more communication, not less. Who's going to be around in five years? The manager who has mastered this function or the one who has not?

With the proliferation of e-mail, voice mail, and the other new means of communication in modern business, managers simply have no excuse not to communicate with their employees. You can even use the telephone or try a little old-fashioned face-to-face talk with your employees and coworkers.

To meet the expectations that you set for them, your employees have to be aware of your expectations. A goal is great on paper, but if you don't communicate it to employees and don't keep them up-to-date on their progress toward achieving that goal, how can you expect them to reach it? Simply, you can't. It would be like training for the Olympics but never being given feedback on how you're doing versus the competition.

Employees often appreciate the little things — an invitation to an upcoming meeting, praise for a job well done, or an insight into the organization's finances. Not only does sharing this kind of information make a business run better, but it also creates tremendous goodwill and cements the trust that bonds your employees to the organization and to the successful completion of the organization's goals.

Taking the First Steps toward Becoming a Manager

Believe it or not, many managers are never formally trained to be managers. For many of you, management is just something that's added to your job description. One day, you may be a computer programmer working on a hot new Web browser, and the next day you may be in charge of the new development team. Before, you were expected only to show up to work and create a product. Now you're expected to lead and motivate a group of workers toward a common goal. Sure, you may get paid more to do the job, but the only training you may get for the task is in the school of hard knocks.

Managers (or managers-to-be) can easily discover how to become good managers by following the recommendations in the sections that follow. No one way is absolutely right or absolutely wrong; each has its pluses and minuses.

I meet, you meet, we all meet

According to the experts, managers are attending more meetings than ever. Although meetings take up more than 25 percent of an average businessperson's time, the figure rises to 40 percent for middle managers and up to a staggering 80 percent for executives. What's even more shocking is that about half of every hour spent in meetings is wasted due to the inefficiency and ineffectiveness of the participants.

A world-class teacher

By many measures, Jack Welch is considered to be one of the United States' top business leaders. Welch, who until recently was chairman of General Electric, radically transformed his company's culture while dramatically improving its performance — and in the process created some $57 billion in value.

Although Welch did many different things to make the transformation a reality, one of the most telling was his takeover of GE's training facility in Ossining, New York. As Welch realized, designing a new culture is one thing, but getting the word out to employees and making it stick is another thing altogether. By directing the class curricula for all levels of workers, and by personally dropping into the training center every two weeks or so to meet with students, Welch was able not only to determine what message would be communicated to GE employees, but also to ensure that the message was received loudly and clearly. If the employees were confused, they had ample opportunity to ask Welch for clarification.

In a gesture that was at once symbolic and real, Welch directed the ceremonial burning of the old-school General Electric "Blue Books." The Blue Books were a series of management training manuals that prescribed how GE managers were to get tasks done in the organization. Despite the fact that the use of these books for training had been mothballed for some 15 years, they still exerted tremendous influence over the actions of GE managers. Citing the need for managers to write their own answers to day-to-day management challenges, Welch swept away the old order by removing the Blue Books from the organization's culture once and for all. Now, GE managers are taught to find their own solutions rather than to look them up in a dusty old book.

Look and listen

If you're fortunate enough to have had a skilled teacher or mentor during the course of your career, you're treated to an education in management that's equal to or better than any MBA program. You learn firsthand the right and wrong ways to manage people. You learn what it takes to get things done in your organization, and you learn that customer satisfaction involves more than simply giving your customers lip service.

Unfortunately, any organization with good management also has living, breathing examples of the wrong way to manage employees. You know whom we're talking about: the manager who refuses to make decisions, leaving employees and customers hanging. Or the boss who refuses to delegate even the simplest decision to employees. Or the supervisor who insists on managing every single aspect of a department — no matter how small or inconsequential: "No, no, no! The stamp goes on the envelope first, and then the address label, not the other way around!" Examples of the right way to manage employees are, regrettably, still few and far between.

Top five management Web sites

Wondering where to find the best information on the Web about the topics addressed in this chapter? You've come to the right place! Here are our top five favorites:

✔ Harvard Business School Working Knowledge: www.hbsworkingknowledge.hbs.edu

✔ Fast Company magazine: www.fastcompany.com

✔ ManagementFirst: www.managementfirst.com

✔ The McKinsey Quarterly: www.mckinseyquarterly.com

✔ ManagementLearning.com Ltd.: www.managementlearning.com

You can benefit from the behaviors that poor managers model. When you find a manager who refuses to make decisions, for example, carefully note the impact that the management style has on workers, other managers, and customers. You feel your own frustration. Make a mental note: "I'll never, ever demotivate another person like that." Indecision at the top inevitably leads to indecision within all ranks of an organization — especially when employees are punished for filling the vacuum left by indecisive managers. Employees become confused, and customers become concerned as the organization drifts aimlessly.

Observe the manager who depends on fear and intimidation to get results. What are the real results of this style of management? Do employees look forward to coming to the office every day? Are they all pulling for a common vision and goal? Are they extending themselves to bring innovation to work processes and procedures? Or are they more concerned with just getting through the day without being yelled at? Think about what you would do differently to get the results that you want.

You can always learn something from other managers — whether they're good managers or bad ones.

Do and learn

Perhaps you're familiar with this old saying (attributed to Lao Tze):

> *Give a man a fish, and he eats for a day,*
>
> *Teach a man to fish, and he eats for a lifetime.*

Such is the nature of managing employees. If you make all the decisions, do the work that your employees are able to do given the chance, and try to carry the entire organization on your own shoulders, you're harming your employees and your organization far more than you can imagine. Your employees never find out how to succeed on their own, and after a while, they quit trying. In your sincere efforts to bring success to your organization, you stunt the growth of your employees and make your organization less effective and vital.

Simply reading a book (even this one) or watching someone else manage — or fail to manage — isn't enough. To take advantage of the lessons that you learn, you have to put them into practice. Keep these key steps in mind.

1. **Take the time to assess your organization's problems.** Which parts of your organization work, and which don't? Why or why not? You can't focus on all your problems at one time. Concentrate on a few problems that are the most important, and solve them before you move on to the rest.

2. **Take a close look at yourself.** What do you do to help or hinder your employees when they try to do their jobs? Do you give them the authority to make decisions? Just as important, do you support them when they go out on a limb for the organization? Study your personal interactions throughout your business day. Do they result in positive or negative outcomes?

3. **Try out the techniques that you learn from your reading or from observing other managers at work.** Go ahead! Nothing changes if you don't change first. "If it's to be, it's to begin with me."

4. **Step back and watch what happens.** We promise that you can see a difference in the way you get tasks done and in the way your customers and employees respond to your organization's needs and goals.

Chapter 2

Delegation: Getting Things Done without Getting Done In

. . . .

In This Chapter
▶ Managing through delegation
▶ Debunking the myths about delegation
▶ Putting delegation to work
▶ Choosing which tasks to delegate
▶ Checking up on your employees

. . . .

The power of effective management comes not from your efforts alone (sorry to burst your bubble) but from the sum of all the efforts of your work group. If you're responsible for only a few employees, with extraordinary effort, you perhaps can do the work of your entire group if you so desired (if you want to be a complete stranger to your friends and family).

However, when you're responsible for a much larger organization, you simply can't be an effective manager by trying to do all your group's work. In the best case, the group probably views you as a *micromanager* — a manager who gets too involved in the petty details of running an organization — with more time for other people's work than for your own. In the worst case, your employees may take less responsibility for their work because you're always there to do it (or check it) for them. Why should they bother trying to do their best job if you're just going to take the assignment back anyway?

Managers assign the responsibility for completing tasks through *delegation*. But as we explain in this chapter, simply assigning tasks and then walking away is not enough. For delegation to be effective, managers must also give authority to their employees and ensure that employees have the resources necessary to complete tasks effectively. Finally, managers who delegate like experts can monitor the progress of their employees toward meeting their assigned goals.

Delegating: The Manager's No. 1 Tool

Now that you're a manager, you're required to develop skills in many different areas. Not only do you need good technical, analytical, and organizational skills, but most important, you also must have good people skills. Of all the people skills, the one skill that can make the greatest difference in your effectiveness is the ability to delegate well. Delegating is a manager's No. 1 management tool, and the inability to delegate well is the leading cause of management failure.

So why do managers have such a hard time delegating? A variety of reasons exist:

✔ You're too busy and just don't have enough time.

✔ You don't trust your employees to complete their assignments correctly or on time.

✔ You don't know how to delegate effectively.

Or perhaps you're still not convinced that managers need to delegate at all. If you're a member of this large group of reluctant managers *(Hey! You there in the back! Yeah, you know who you are!)*, then the following list is why you must let go of your preconceptions and inhibitions and start delegating today:

✔ **Your success as a manager depends on it!** Managers who can successfully manage team members — each of whom has specific responsibilities for a different aspect of the team's performance — prove that they're ready for bigger and better challenges. Bigger and better challenges are often accompanied by bigger and better titles, paychecks, and the other niceties of business life, such as offices with windows and computers that actually work on occasion.

✔ **You can't do it all.** No matter how great a manager you are, carrying the entire burden of achieving your organization's goals by yourself isn't in your interest unless you want to work yourself into an early grave. Besides, wouldn't it be nice to see what life is like outside the four walls of your office?

✔ **Your job is to concentrate your efforts on the things that you can do and your staff can't.** They pay you the big bucks to be a manager — not a super programmer, accounting clerk, or customer service representative. Do your job, and let your employees do theirs.

✔ **Delegation gets workers in the organization more involved.** When you give responsibility and authority to employees to carry out tasks — whether individually or in teams — they respond by becoming more

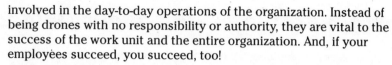
involved in the day-to-day operations of the organization. Instead of being drones with no responsibility or authority, they are vital to the success of the work unit and the entire organization. And, if your employees succeed, you succeed, too!

✔ **Delegation gives you the chance to develop your employees.** If you make all the decisions and come up with all the ideas, your employees never learn how to take initiative and be responsible for seeing tasks through to successful completion. And if they don't learn, guess who's going to get stuck doing everything forever? (*Hint:* Take a look in the mirror.) In addition, keep in mind that learning and development opportunities are increasingly reported as one of the top motivators by today's employees.

As a manager, you're ultimately responsible for all your department's responsibilities. However, for most managers, personally executing all the tasks necessary for your department to fulfill its responsibilities and for you to achieve your organizational goals is neither practical nor desirable.

Say, for example, that you're the manager of the accounting department for a software development firm. When the firm had only five employees and sales of $500,000 a year, it was no problem for you to personally bill all your customers, cut checks to vendors, run payroll, and take care of the company's taxes every April. However, now that employment has grown to 150 employees and sales are at $50 million a year, you can't even pretend to do it all — you don't have enough hours in the day. (The last time we checked, each day still had only 24 hours — they're not making any more.) Now you have specialized employees who take care of accounts payable, accounts receivable, and payroll, and you have farmed out the completion of income tax work to a CPA.

Each employee that you've assigned to a specific work function has specialized knowledge and skills in his or her area of expertise. Sure, you could personally generate payroll if you had to, but, if you've hired someone to do that job, why would you want to? And, by the way, your payroll clerk is probably a lot better and quicker at it than you are.

On the other hand, you're uniquely qualified to perform numerous responsibilities in your organization. These responsibilities may include developing and monitoring your operations budget, conducting performance appraisals, helping to plan the overall direction of your company's acquisitions, and selecting the flavor of the coffee that your department stocks. Later in this chapter — in the section, "Reviewing the Good and Bad of Delegation" — we tell you which tasks to delegate to your employees and which ones to retain. First, however, consider some of the popular misconceptions about delegation.

Explaining the Myths about Delegation

Admit it: You may have many different reasons to rationalize to yourself why you can't delegate work to your employees. Unfortunately, these reasons are guaranteed to get in the way of your ability to be an effective manager. Do any of the following myths sound familiar to you? Now tell the truth!

Myth No. 1: You can't trust your employees to be responsible

If you can't trust your employees, whom can you trust? Assume that you're responsible for hiring at least a portion of your staff. Now, forgetting for the moment the ones that you didn't personally hire, you likely went through quite an involved process to recruit your employees. Remember the mountain of resumes that you had to sift through and then divide into winners, potential winners, and losers? After hours of sorting and then hours of interviews, you selected the best candidates — the ones with the best skills, qualifications, and experience for the job.

You selected your employees because you thought that they were talented people deserving of your trust. Now your job is to give them your trust without strings attached.

You usually reap what you sow. Your staff members are ready, willing, and able to be responsible employees; you just have to give them a chance. Sure, not every employee is going to be able to handle every task that you assign. If that's the case, find out why. Does he or she need more training? More time? More practice? Maybe you need to find a task that is better suited to his or her experience or disposition. Or perhaps you simply hired the wrong person for the job. If that's the case, face up to the fact and fire or reassign the employee before you lose even more time and money. To get responsible employees, you have to give responsibility.

Myth No. 2: When you delegate, you lose control of a task and its outcome

If you delegate correctly, you don't lose control of the task or its outcome. What you lose control of is the way that the outcome is reached. Picture a map of the world. How many different ways can a person get from San Francisco to Paris? One? One million? Some ways are quicker than others. Some are more scenic, and others require a substantial resource commitment. Do the differences in these ways make any of them inherently wrong? No.

In business, you have countless ways to get a task done. Even for tasks that are spelled out in highly defined steps, — "we've always done it that way" — you can always leave room for new ways to make a process better. Why should your way be the only way to get the task done? "Because I'm the boss!" Sorry, wrong answer. Your job is to describe to your employees the outcomes that you want and then to let them decide how to accomplish the tasks. Of course, you need to be available to coach and counsel them so that they can learn from your past experience if they want, but you need to let go of controlling the how and instead focus on the what and the when.

Myth No.3: You're the only one who has all the answers

You're joking, right? If you think that you alone have all the answers, have we got a thing or two to tell you! As talented as you may be, unless you're the company's only employee, you can't possibly have the only answer to every question in your organization.

On the other hand, a certain group of people deals with an amazing array of situations every day. The group talks to your customers, your suppliers, and each other — day in and day out. Many members of the group have been working for the company far longer than you, and many of them will be there long after you're gone. Who are these people? They are your employees.

Your employees are a wealth of experience and knowledge about your business contacts and the intimate, day-to-day workings of the organization. They are often closer to the customers and problems of the company than you are. To ignore their suggestions and advice is not only disrespectful but also shortsighted and foolish. Don't ignore this resource. You're already paying for it — whether you use it or not!

Myth No.4: You can do the work faster by yourself

You may think that you're completing tasks faster when you do them than when you assign them to others, but this belief is merely an illusion. Yes, discussing and assigning a task to one of your employees may require slightly more time when you first delegate that task, but if you delegate well, the second through nth times take substantially less time. Not only does doing the task yourself actually cost you more time, but also you're robbing your employees of a golden opportunity to develop their work skills.

And, what happens when you do it yourself instead of delegating it? When you do the task, you're forever doomed to doing the task — again and again and again. When you teach someone else to do the task and then assign him or her responsibility for completing it, you may never have to do it again. Not only that, but your employee may come to do it faster than you can. Who knows, he or she may even improve the way that you've always done it.

Myth No.5: Delegation dilutes your authority

Actually, delegation does exactly the opposite — it extends your authority. You're only one person, and you can do only so much. Imagine all 10, 20, or 100 members of your team working toward your common goals. You still set the goals and the timetables for reaching them, but each employee chooses his or her own way of getting there.

Do you have less authority because you delegate a task and transfer authority to an employee to carry out the task? Clearly, the answer is no. What do you lose in this transaction? Nothing. Your authority is extended, not diminished. The more authority you give to employees, the more authority your entire work unit has, and the better able your employees are to do the jobs you hired them to do.

As you grant others authority, you gain an efficient and effective workforce — employees who are truly empowered, excited by their jobs, and working as team players — and the ability to concentrate on the issues that deserve your undivided attention.

Myth No.6: The company recognizes your employees for doing a good job and not you

Letting go of this belief is one of the biggest difficulties in the transition from being a doer to being a manager of doers. When you're a doer, you're rewarded for writing a great report, developing an incredible market analysis, or programming an amazing piece of computer code. When you're a manager, the focus of your job shifts from your performance in completing individual tasks to your performance in reaching an overall organizational or project goal through the efforts of others. Although you may have been the best darn marketing assistant in the world, suddenly, that talent doesn't matter anymore. Now you're expected to develop and lead a team of the best darn marketing analysts in the world. The skills required are quite different, and your success is a result of the indirect efforts of others and your behind-the-scenes support.

Wise managers know that when their employees shine, they shine, too. The more you delegate, the more opportunities you give your employees to shine. Give your workers the opportunity to do important work and to do it well. And when they do well, make sure that you tell everyone about it. Give your employees credit for their successes publicly and often, and they will be more likely to want to do a good job for you on future assignments. Don't forget: When you're a manager, you're being primarily measured on your team's performance — not so much what you're personally able to accomplish. Chapter 5 covers everything you ever wanted to know about employee motivation and rewards — and even a few things you maybe didn't want to know!

Myth No. 7: Delegation decreases your flexibility

When you do everything yourself, you have complete control over the progress and completion of tasks, right? Wrong! How can you when you're balancing multiple priorities at the same time and dealing with the inevitable crisis of the day? Being flexible is pretty tough when you're doing everything yourself. Concentrating on more than one task at a time is impossible. While you're concentrating on that one task, you put all your other tasks on hold. Flexibility? Not!

The more people you delegate to, the more flexible you can be. As your employees take care of the day-to-day tasks necessary to keep your business running, you're free to deal with those surprise problems and opportunities that always seem to pop up at the last minute.

Myth No. 8: Your employees are too busy

If that belief isn't a cop out, we don't know what is! What exactly are your employees doing that they don't have the time to learn something new — something that can make your job easier and boost the performance of your work unit, all at the same time?

Think about yourself for a moment. What about your job makes you want to return day after day? No, we're not talking about your paycheck or the lunch truck. We're willing to bet that the satisfaction you feel when you take on a new challenge, meet it, and succeed is reason enough.

Now consider your employees — their job satisfaction is no different from yours. They want to test themselves against new challenges and succeed, too. But how can they if you don't delegate new tasks to them? Too many managers have lost good employees because they failed to meet employees' needs to stretch and to grow in their jobs. And too many employees have become mindless drones because their managers refuse to encourage their creativity and natural yearning to learn. Don't learn this lesson the hard way!

Myth No. 9: Your workers don't see the big picture

Well, actually, this myth may be true, but only because you make it so. How can your employees see the big picture if you don't share it with them? Your employees are often specialists in their jobs or fields of expertise. They naturally develop severe cases of tunnel vision as they pursue the answers to their assignments or process their routine transactions. As we discuss in Chapter 1, your job is to provide your employees with a vision of where you want to go and the priorities of what needs to be achieved, and then allow them to find the best way to attain those goals.

Unfortunately, many managers withhold vital information from their employees — information that can make them much more effective in their jobs — in hopes that by doing so, they can maintain a close rein on their behavior and stay "in control." By keeping their employees in the dark, these managers don't create the better outcomes that they hope for. Instead, they cripple their organization and their employees' ability to learn, grow, and become a real part of the organization.

You have to trust your employees

These myths aside, delegation can be scary, at least at first. But like anything else, the more you do it, the less scary it gets. When you delegate, you're putting your trust in another individual. If that individual fails, then you're ultimately responsible — regardless of who you give the task to. A line like this probably won't go very far with your boss: "Yeah, I know that we were supposed to get that proposal to the customer today, but Joe dropped the ball." When you delegate tasks, you don't automatically abdicate your responsibility for their successful completion.

Beginning to delegate tasks to your employees is sort of like bungee jumping for the first time: You jump off that little platform hundreds of feet above the ground and hope that the cord doesn't break. And don't forget that your employees may be a little nervous, too. The thought of taking on a new task may cause some hesitance on their part. This hesitance requires more support from you as your employees discover how to become comfortable with their new roles.

As a part of this process, you also need to understand each of your employees' strengths and weaknesses. You probably aren't, for example, going to delegate a huge task to someone who has been on the job for only a few months.

Taking the Six Steps to Delegate

Delegation doesn't just happen. Just like any other task that you perform as a manager, you have to work at it. The six steps to effective delegation are the following:

1. **Communicate the task.** Describe exactly what you want done, when you want it done, and what end results you expect. Ask for any questions.

2. **Furnish context for the task.** Explain why the task needs to be done, its importance in the overall scheme of things, and possible complications that may arise during its performance.

3. **Determine standards.** Agree on the standards that you plan to use to measure the success of a task's completion. Make these standards realistic and attainable.

4. **Grant authority.** You must grant employees the authority necessary to complete the task without constant roadblocks or standoffs with other employees.

5. **Provide support.** Determine the resources necessary for your employee to complete the task and then provide them. Successfully completing a task may require money, training, or the ability to check with you about progress or obstacles as they arise.

6. **Get commitment.** Make sure that your employee has accepted the assignment. Confirm your expectations and your employee's understanding of and commitment to completing the task.

Clearly, delegation benefits both workers and managers alike when you do it correctly. So why aren't you delegating more work to your employees? It's not too late to start!

Reviewing the Good and Bad of Delegation

Theoretically, you can delegate anything to your employees. Of course, if you delegate all your duties, then why is your company bothering to pay you? Clearly, you have tasks that you make an effort to delegate to your employees and tasks that you retain for yourself. Remember, you're the manager and your employees aren't.

When you delegate, begin with simple tasks that don't substantially impact the firm if they aren't completed on time or within budget. As your employees gain confidence and experience, delegate higher-level tasks. Carefully assess the level of your employees' expertise, and assign tasks that meet or slightly exceed that level. Set schedules for completion and then monitor your employees' performance against them. This is a good opportunity to see if an employee isn't being challenged or is bored. After you get the hang of it, you find that you really have nothing to be afraid of when you delegate.

Always delegate these things

Certain tasks naturally lend themselves to being delegated. As a manager, you can take every possible opportunity to delegate the following kinds of work to your employees.

Detail work

Truly, the devil is in the details. As a manager, you have no greater time-waster than getting caught up in details — you know, tasks such as double-checking pages, spending days troubleshooting a block of computer code, or personally auditing your employees' timesheets. The old saying says that 20 percent of the results come from 80 percent of the work, which illustrates why the company selected you to be a manager. You can no doubt run circles around almost anyone on those detailed technical tasks that you used to do all the time.

But now that you're a manager, you're being paid to orchestrate the workings of an entire team of workers toward a common goal — not just to perform an individual task. Leave the detail to your employees, but hold them accountable for the results. Concentrate your efforts on tasks that have the greatest payoff and that allow you to most effectively leverage the work of all your employees.

Information gathering

Browsing the Web for information about your competitors, spending hours poring over issues of *Fortune* magazine, or moving into your local library's reference stacks for weeks on end is not an effective use of your time. Despite the fact, most managers get sucked into the trap. Not only is reading through newspapers, reports, books, magazines, and the like fun, but it also provides managers with an easy way to postpone the more difficult tasks of management. You're being paid to look at the big picture — to gather a variety of inputs and make sense of them. You can work so much more efficiently when someone else gathers needed information, which frees you to take the time you need to analyze the inputs and to devise solutions to your problems.

Repetitive assignments

What a great way to get routine tasks done: assign them to your employees. "Here you go — this should keep you busy for the next few years." Many of the jobs in your organization occur again and again; drafting your weekly production report, reviewing your biweekly report of expenditures versus budget, and approving your monthly phone bill are just a few examples. Your time is much too important to waste on routine tasks that you mastered years ago.

If you find yourself involved in repetitive assignments, first take a close look at their particulars. How often do the assignments recur? Can you anticipate the assignments in sufficient time to allow an employee to be successful in completing it? What do you have to do to train your employees in completing the tasks? After you figure all this out, develop a schedule and make assignments to your employees.

Surrogate roles

Do you feel that you have to be everywhere all the time? Not only can't you be everywhere all the time, but also you shouldn't be everywhere all the time. Every day, your employees have numerous opportunities to fill in for you. Presentations, conference calls, client visits, and meetings are just a few examples. In some cases, such as in budget presentations to top management, you may be required to attend. However, in many other cases, whether you attend personally or send someone to take your place really doesn't matter.

The next time someone calls a meeting and requests your attendance, send one of your employees to attend in your place. This simple act benefits you in several different ways. Not only do you have an extra hour or two in your schedule, but also your employee can present you with only the important outcomes of the meeting. In any case, your employee has the opportunity to take on some new responsibilities, and you have the opportunity to spend the time you need on your most important tasks. Not only that, but your employee may discover something new in the process.

Future duties

As a manager, you can always be on the lookout for opportunities to train your staff in their future job responsibilities. For example, one of your key duties may be to develop your department's annual budget. By allowing one or more of your employees to assist you — perhaps in gathering basic market or research data — you can give your employees a taste of what goes into putting together a budget.

And don't fall into the trap of believing that the only way to train your employees is to sign them up for an expensive class taught by someone with a slick, color brochure who knows nothing about your business. Opportunities to train your employees abound within your own business. An estimated 90 percent of all development occurs on the job. Not only is this training free, but also by assigning your employees to progressively more important tasks, you build their self-confidence and help to pave their way to progress in the organization.

When delegation goes wrong

Sometimes delegation goes wrong — way wrong. How can you identify the danger signs before it's too late, and what can you do to save the day? You can monitor the performance of your workers in several ways:

✔ **Personal follow-up:** Supplement your formal tracking system with an informal system of visiting your workers and checking their progress on a regular basis.

✔ **Sampling:** Take periodic samples of your employees' work and check to make sure that the work meets the standards you agreed to.

✔ **Progress reports:** Regular progress reporting from employees to you can give you advance notice of problems and successes.

✔ **A formalized tracking system:** Use a formal system to track assignments and due dates. The system can be manual (think: big chart pinned to your wall) or computerized.

If you discover that your employees are in trouble, you have several options for getting everything back on track:

✔ **Increased monitoring:** Spend more time monitoring employees who are in trouble, keeping closer track of their performance.

✔ **Counseling:** Discuss the problems with your employees and agree on a plan to correct them.

✔ **Rescinding authority:** If problems continue despite your efforts to resolve them through counseling, you can rescind your employees' authority to complete the tasks independently. (They still work on the task, but under your close guidance and authority.)

✔ **Reassigning activities:** The ultimate solution when delegation goes wrong. If your employees can't do their assigned tasks, give the tasks to workers who are better suited to perform them successfully.

Avoid delegating these things

Some tasks are part and parcel of the job of being a manager. By delegating the following work, you fail to perform your basic management duties.

Long-term vision and goals

As a manager, you're in a unique position. Your position at the top provides you with a unique perspective on the organization's needs — the higher up you are in an organization, the broader your perspective. As we discuss in Chapter 1, one of the key functions of management is vision. Although employees at any level of a company can help provide you with input and make suggestions that help to shape your perspectives, developing an organization's long-term vision and goals is up to you. Simply, every employee can't decide what direction the organization should move. An organization is much more effective when everyone moves together in the same direction.

Positive performance feedback

Rewarding and recognizing employees when they do good work is an important job for every manager. If this task is delegated to lower-level employees, however, the workers who receive it won't value the recognition as much as if it came from their manager. The impact of the recognition is therefore significantly lessened (assuming it gets done at all!).

Performance appraisals, discipline, and counseling

In the modern workplace, a strong relationship between manager and employee is often hard to come by. Most managers are probably lucky to get off a quick "good morning" or "good night" between the hustle and bustle of a typical workday. Given everyone's hectic schedules, you may have times when you don't talk to one or more of your employees for days at a time. "Oh, hello. Haven't we met each other before? You seem so familiar."

However, sometimes you absolutely have to set time aside for your employees. When you discipline and counsel your employees, you're giving them the kind of input that only you can provide. You set the goals for your employees, and you set the standards by which you measure their progress. Inevitably, you decide whether your employees have reached the marks you've set or whether they have fallen short. You can't delegate away this task effectively — everyone loses as a result.

Politically sensitive situations

Some situations are just too politically sensitive to assign to your employees. Say, for example, that you're in charge of auditing the travel expenses for your organization. The results of your review show that a member of the corporation's executive team has made several personal trips on company funds. Do you assign the responsibility for reporting this explosive situation to a worker? "Gee, Susan, I was hoping that you could present this information to the Board — I don't think I want to be around when the news hits!" No!

Not only do such situations demand your utmost attention and expertise, but also placing your employee in the middle of the line of fire in this potentially explosive situation is also unfair. Being a manager may be tough sometimes, but you're paid to make the difficult decisions and to take the political heat that your work generates.

Personal assignments

Occasionally, your boss assigns a specific task to you with the intention that you can personally perform it. He or she may have very good reasons for doing so: You may have a unique perspective that no one else in your organization has, or you may have a unique skill that needs to be brought to bear to complete the assignment quickly and accurately. Whatever the situation, if a task is assigned to you with the expectation that you, and only you, carry it out, then you can't delegate it to your staff. You may decide to involve your staff in gathering input, but you must retain the ultimate responsibility for the final execution of the task.

Confidential or sensitive circumstances

As a manager, you're likely privy to information, such as wage and salary figures, proprietary data, and personnel assessments that your staff isn't. Release of this information to the wrong individuals can be damaging to an organization. Salary information should be kept confidential, for example. Similarly, if your competitors get their hands on some secret process that your company has spent countless hours and money to develop, the impact on your organization and employees can be devastating. Unless your staff has a compelling need to know, then you should retain assignments involving these types of information yourself.

Checking Up Instead of Checking Out

Now delegation gets tough. Assume that you've already worked through the initial hurdles of delegation — you assigned a task to your employee, and you're anxiously waiting to see how she performs. You defined the scope of the task and gave your employee the adequate training and resources to get it done. Not only that, but also you told her what results you expect and exactly when you expect to see them. What do you do next?

Here's one option: An hour or two after you make the assignment, you check on its progress. In a couple more hours, you check again. As the deadline rapidly approaches, you increase the frequency of your checking until finally, your employee spends more time answering your questions about the progress she has made than she spends actually completing the task. Not only that, but every time you press her for details about her progress, she gets a little more distracted from her task and a little more frustrated with your seeming lack of confidence in her abilities. When the appointed hour arrives, she submits the result on time, but the report is inaccurate and incomplete.

Here's another option: After you make the assignment to your employee, you do nothing. Yes, you heard right. You do nothing. Instead of checking on your employee's progress and offering your support, you assign the task and move on to other concerns. When the appointed hour arrives, you're surprised to discover that the task is not completed. When you ask your employee why she didn't meet the goal that you had mutually agreed upon, she tells you that she had trouble obtaining some information and, rather than bother you with this problem, she decided to try to construct it for herself. Unfortunately, this slight diversion required an additional two days of research before she found the correct set of numbers.

Clearly, both extremes aren't productive ways to monitor the delegation process. However, in between lies the answer to how to approach this delicate but essential task. Depending on the situation, this may mean daily or weekly progress updates from your employee.

Each employee is unique. One style of monitoring may work with one employee but not work with another. New or inexperienced employees naturally require more attention and hand-holding than employees who are seasoned at their jobs — whether they realize it or not. Veteran employees don't need the kind of day-to-day attention that less experienced employees need. In fact, they may resent your attempts to closely manage the way in which they carry out their duties.

Effective monitoring of delegation requires the following:

- ✔ **Tailor your approach to the employee.** If your employee performs his or her job with minimal supervision on your part, then establish a system of monitoring with only a few, critical checkpoints along the way. If your employee needs more attention, create a system (formal, in writing, or informal) that incorporates several checkpoints along the way to goal completion.

- ✔ **Diligently use a written or computer-based system for tracking the tasks that you assign to your employees.** Use a daily planner, personal digital assistant, or project management software program to keep track of the what, who, and when of task assignments. Making a commitment to get organized is important. Do it!

✔ **Keep the lines of communication open.** Make sure that your employees know that you want them to let you know if they can't surmount a problem. This, of course, means making time for your employees when they come by to ask you for help. Find out whether they need more training or better resources. Finding out too early — when you can still do something about it — is better than finding out too late.

✔ **Follow through on the agreements that you make with your employees.** If a report is late, then hold your employees accountable. Despite the temptation to let these failures slip ("Gee, he's had a rough time at home lately"), ignoring them does both you and your employees a disservice. Make sure that your employees understand the importance of taking personal responsibility for their work and that the ability of your group to achieve its goals depends on their meeting commitments. Be compassionate if your employee has indeed gone through a tough personal challenge (mother died, spouse diagnosed with cancer, and so on) — you may need to assign someone else to cover his or her duties for a short period of time. If, however, an employee consistently misses goals and shows no hope of improvement, then perhaps he or she is in the wrong job.

✔ **Reward performance that meets or exceeds your expectations, and counsel performance that falls below your expectations.** If you don't let your employees know when they fail to meet your expectations, then they may continue to fail to meet your expectations. Do your employees, your organization, and yourself a big favor and bring attention to both the good things and the bad things that your employees do. Remember the old saying (which happens to be an accurate one), praise in public and criticize privately. You can find many more details about counseling employees in Chapters 6 and 9.

Top five delegation Web sites

Wondering where to find the best information on the Web about the topics addressed in this chapter? Well, you've come to the right place! Here are our top five favorites:

✔ Wise Women Network: www.wisewomen. org.nz/words/fiona/delegate.htm

✔ Center for Service and Leadership: www.gmu.edu/student/csl/ delegation.html

✔ ITtoolkit.com: www.ittoolkit.com/ articles/projects/ease_ delegation.htm

✔ Networking Times: www.networking times.com/journal/0204/ leadership.phtml

✔ IAHCSMM: www.iahcsmm.com/ leadership_0700.htm

Chapter 3

Lead, Follow, or Get Out of the Way

*W*hat makes a leader? Experts have written countless books, produced endless videos, and taught interminable seminars on the topic of leadership. Still, leadership is a quality that eludes many who seek it.

Studies show that the primary traits that all effective leaders have in common are (1) a positive outlook and (2) forward thinking. They have a positive outlook and are sure of themselves and their ability to influence others and impact the future. Although similar, leadership and management are different; leadership goes above and beyond management. A manager can be organized and efficient at getting tasks done without being a leader — someone who inspires others to achieve their best. In short, managers manage processes; they lead people. According to management visionary Peter Drucker, leadership is the most basic and scarcest resource in any business enterprise. We concur wholeheartedly.

Everyone in an organization wants to work for great leaders. Employees want the men and women they work for to exhibit leadership. "I wish that my boss would just make a decision — I'm just spinning my wheels until she does. I guess I'll just wait here until she lets me know what she wants me to do." And wait they do — until the boss finally notices that the project is two months behind. Top executives want the men and women who work for them to exhibit leadership. "You need to take responsibility for your department and pull the numbers into the black before the end of the fiscal year!" And employees want their peers to show leadership. "If he's not going to straighten out that billing process, then I'll just have to work around it myself!"

A leader is many things to many people. In this chapter, we discuss the key skills and attributes that make good managers into great leaders. As this chapter explains, leadership requires the application of a wide variety of skills. No single trait, when mastered, suddenly makes you an effective leader. "You mean that I can't become a great leader just from watching this video?" However, you may notice that some leadership skills that follow are also key functions of management — ones that we review in Chapter 1. This similarity is no coincidence. By the way, for an in-depth look at leadership, you should check out *Leadership For Dummies* (Wiley) by Marshall Loeb.

Understanding the Differences between Management and Leadership

Being a good manager is quite an accomplishment. Management is by no means an easy task, and mastering the wide range of varied skills that is required can take many years. The best managers get their jobs done efficiently and effectively — with a minimum of muss and fuss. Like the person behind the scenes of a great performance in sports or the theater, the best managers are often those employees whom you notice the least.

Great managers are experts at taking their current organizations and optimizing them to accomplish their goals and get their jobs done. By necessity, they focus on the here and now — not on the tremendous potential of what the future can bring. Managers are expected to make things happen now — not at some indefinite, fuzzy point in the future. "Don't tell me what you're going to do for me next year or the year after that! I want results, and I want them now!" Having good managers in an organization, however, isn't enough.

Great organizations need great management. However, great management doesn't necessarily make a great organization. For an organization to be great, it must also have great leadership.

Leaders have vision. They look beyond the here and now to see the vast potential of their organizations. And although great leaders are also effective at getting things done in their organizations, they accomplish their goals in a way different from managers.

How so? Managers use values, policies, procedures, schedules, milestones, incentives, discipline, and other mechanisms to push their employees to achieve the goals of the organization.

Leaders, on the other hand, challenge their employees to achieve the organization's goals by creating a compelling vision of the future and then unlocking their employees' potential. Think about some great leaders. President John F. Kennedy challenged the American people to land a man on the moon. We did. Lee Iacocca challenged the management and workers of the Chrysler Corporation to bring their company out of the clutches of financial disaster and to build a new corporation that would lead the way in product innovation and profitability. They did. Jack Welch of General Electric challenged his workers to help the company attain first or second place in every business that it owned. They did.

All these leaders share a common trait. They all painted compelling visions that grabbed the imagination of their followers and then challenged them to achieve these visions. Without the vision that leaders provide and without the contributions of their followers' hard work, energy, and innovation, the United States would never have landed a man on the moon, the name Chrysler would have slipped quietly into history, and General Electric wouldn't be the hugely successful firm that it is today.

Figuring Out What Leaders Do

The skills required to be a leader are no secret; some managers have figured out how to use the skills and others haven't. And although some people seem to be born leaders, anyone can discover what leaders do and how to apply these skills themselves.

Inspire action

Despite what some managers believe, most workers want to feel pride for their organization and, when given the chance, would give their all to a cause they believe in. A tremendous well of creativity and energy is just waiting to be tapped in every organization. Leaders use this knowledge to inspire their employees to take action and to achieve great things.

Leaders know the value of employees and their critical importance in achieving the company's goals. Do the managers in your company know the importance of their employees? Check out what these managers had to say in Bob Nelson's *1001 Ways to Reward Employees:*

✔ Former chairman and CEO of the Ford Motor Company Harold A. Poling said, "One of the stepping stones to a world-class operation is to tap into the creative and intellectual power of each and every employee."

✔ According to Paul M. Cook, founder and CEO of Raychem Corporation, "Most people, whether they're engineers, business managers, or machine operators, want to be creative. They want to identify with the success of their profession and their organization. They want to contribute to giving society more comfort, better health, [and] more excitement."

✔ Hewlett-Packard cofounder Bill Hewlett said, "Men and women want to do a good job, a creative job, and if they are provided the proper environment, they will do so."

Unfortunately, few managers reward their employees for being creative or for going beyond the boundaries set by their job descriptions. Too many managers search for workers who do exactly what they are told — and little else. This practice is a tremendous waste of worker creativity, ideas, and motivation.

Use your influence as a manager to help your employees create energy in their jobs instead of draining it from them with bureaucracy, red tape, policies, and an emphasis on avoiding mistakes.

Leaders are different. Instead of draining energy from their employees, leaders unleash the natural energy within all employees. They do so by clearing the roadblocks to creativity and pride from the paths of their workers and by creating a compelling vision for their employees to strive for. Leaders help employees to tap into energy and initiative that the employees didn't know they had.

Create a compelling vision for your employees and then clear away the roadblocks to creativity and pride. Your vision must be a stretch to achieve, but not so much of a stretch that the vision is impossible to achieve.

Communicate

Leaders make a commitment to communicate with their employees and to keep them informed about the organization. Employees want to be an integral part of their organizations and want their opinions and suggestions to be heard. Great leaders earn the commitment of their workers by building communication links throughout the organization — from the top to the bottom, from the bottom to the top, and from side to side.

So how do you build communication links in your organization? Consider the experiences of the following business leaders as listed in Bob's *1001 Ways to Reward Employees:*

- According to Donald Petersen, former president and CEO of Ford Motor Company, "When I started visiting the plants and meeting with employees, what was reassuring was the tremendous, positive energy in our conversations. One man said he'd been with Ford for 25 years and hated every minute of it — until he was asked for his opinion. He said that question transformed his job."

- Andrea Nieman, administrative assistant with the Rolm Corporation, summarized her company's commitment to communication like this: "Rolm recognizes that people are the greatest asset. There is no 'us' and 'them' attitude here; everyone is important. Upper management is visible and accessible. There is always time to talk, to find solutions, and to implement changes."

- Said Robert Hauptfuhrer, former chairman and CEO of Oryx Energy, "Give people a chance not just to do a job but to have some impact, and they'll really respond, get on their roller skates, and race around to make sure it happens."

When Bob became a department manager at Blanchard Training and Development, he made a commitment to his team of employees to communicate with them. To make his commitment real, Bob added specifics: He promised that he would report the results of every executive team meeting within 24 hours. Bob's department valued his team briefings because, through this communication, he treated all individuals as colleagues — not as underlings.

Great leaders know that leadership isn't a one-way street. Leadership today is a two-way interchange of ideas where leaders create a vision and workers throughout an organization develop and communicate ideas of how best to reach the vision. The old one-way, command-and-control model of management doesn't work anymore. Commanding workers may have worked all right in the traditional U.S. Army, but as a daily means of managing a company, it doesn't work well at all. Most employees aren't willing to simply take orders and be directed all day long. If you think your employees want to be ordered around, you're only fooling yourself.

Support and facilitate

Great leaders create environments in which employees are safe to speak up, to tell the truth, and to take risks. The numbers of managers who punish their employees for pointing out problems that they encounter, for disagreeing with the conventional wisdom of management, or for merely saying what is on their minds is incredible. Even more incredible, many managers punish their employees for taking risks and losing, instead of helping their employees win the next time around.

Great leaders support their employees and facilitate their ability to reach their goals. The head of an organization where Peter once worked did just the opposite. Instead of leading his employees with vision and inspiration, he pushed them with the twin cattle prods (120 volts DC!) of fear and intimidation. The management team members lived in constant fear of his temper, which could explode without warning and seemingly without reason. More than a few managers wore the psychological bruises and scars of his often-public outbursts. Instead of contributing to the good of the organization, some managers simply withdrew into their shells and said as little as possible in this leader's presence. Consider these managers' statements in *1001 Ways to Reward Employees:*

✔ Catherine Meek, president of compensation consulting firm Meek and Associates, says, "In the 20 years I have been doing this and the thousands of employees I have interviewed in hundreds of companies, if I had to pick one thing that comes through loud and clear it is that organizations do a lousy job of recognizing people's contributions. That is the number one thing employees say to us. 'We don't even care about the money; if my boss would just acknowledge that I exist. The only time I ever hear anything is when I screw up. I never hear when I do a good job.'"

✔ According to Lonnie Blittle, an assembly line worker for Nissan Motor Manufacturing Corporation U.S.A., "There was none of the hush-hush atmosphere with management behind closed doors and everybody else waiting until they drop the boom on us. They are right down pitching in, not standing around with their hands on their hips."

✔ James Berdahl, vice president of marketing for Business Incentives, says, "People want to feel empowered to find better ways to do things and to take responsibility for their own environment. Allowing them to do this has had a big impact on how they do their jobs, as well as on their satisfaction with the company."

Instead of abandoning their employees to the sharks, great leaders throw their followers life preservers when the going gets particularly rough. Although leaders allow their employees free rein in how they achieve their organizations' goals, leaders are always there in the background — ready to assist and support workers whenever necessary. With the added security of this safety net, employees are more willing to stretch themselves and to take chances that can create enormous payoffs for their organizations.

Surveying Leading Leadership Traits

Today's new business environment is unrelenting change. About the only constant you can be sure of anymore is that everything will change. And after it changes, it will change again and again.

Key business trends to watch out for

According to Stanley Bing, the incredibly insightful columnist for Fortune magazine, many trends are sweeping the business landscape. One major trend is the necessity for managers to talk the talk and walk the walk. While talking the talk means to sound like you know what you're doing, walking the walk takes this idea a step farther and requires that you also look like you know what you're doing — whether you do or not.

As the related graph shows, the percentage of executives who can talk the talk and those executives who can walk the walk has been increasing since 1970. However, the ability of managers to talk the talk and walk the walk at the same time has steadily declined from its peak some 20 years ago. Here is some advice from Bing regarding these critical leadership skills:

✔ "First, always talk the talk, even when others don't seem to understand what you're saying. It's all about consistency and perception — so keep it up!

✔ Second, if you're not in a position to talk the talk, either because someone superior is doing so or because you've got your mouth full, default to walking the walk exclusively, thereby projecting the necessary executive qualities in dignity and silence.

✔ Third, don't try doing both together until you're very good at it. There's nothing more pathetic than somebody attempting to walk/talk concurrently and getting his ankles all bollixed up while irreverent employees stand around chortling. So practice!"

(Source: Fortune)

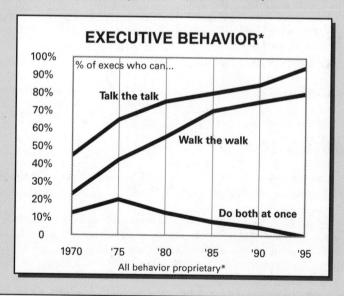

EXECUTIVE BEHAVIOR*

% of execs who can...

Talk the talk

Walk the walk

Do both at once

1970   '75   '80   '85   '90   '95

All behavior proprietary*

Get used to it now, because business will continue to transform in the foreseeable future. Although so much in business is shifting, great leadership remains steadfast — like a sturdy rock standing up to the storms of change.

Numerous traits of great leaders have remained the same over the years and are still highly valued today. The following sections discuss the leading leadership traits.

Optimism

Great leaders always see the future as a wonderful place. Although they may find much adversity and hard work on the way to achieving their goals, leaders always look forward to the future with great promise and optimism. This optimism becomes a glow that radiates from all great leaders and touches all those employees who come into contact with them.

People want to feel good about themselves and their futures, and they want to work for winners. Workers are therefore naturally attracted to people who are optimistic rather than pessimistic. Who wants to work for someone who enjoys nothing more than spouting doom and gloom about the future of a business? Negative managers only demotivate their employees and coworkers and lead workers to spend more time polishing their resumes than they do concentrating on improving their organizations.

Optimism is infectious. Before long, a great leader can turn an organization full of naysayers into one that's overflowing with positive excitement for the future. This excitement results in greater worker productivity and an improved organizational environment. Morale increases, and so does the organization's bottom line.

Be an optimist. Let your excitement rub off on those people around you.

Confidence

Great leaders have no doubt — at least not in public — that they can accomplish any task that they set their minds to.

"What? A 10,000 foot-high mountain is in the way? No problem — we'll climb it. You say that a vast ocean is separating us from our goal? No sweat — we'll swim it. Hmmm . . . a bottomless crevasse is blocking our path? Fine — we'll leap it. Whatever the challenge may be, we'll find a way to surmount it."

Confident leaders make for confident followers, which is why organizations led by confident leaders are unstoppable. An organization's employees mirror the behavior of their leaders. When leaders are tentative and unsure of themselves, so are workers (and the bottom-line results of the organization). When leaders display self-confidence, workers follow suit, and the results can be astounding.

Be a confident leader. You inspire the best performance of your employees at the same time as you help them to become more confident in their abilities.

Integrity

One trait that sets great leaders apart from the rest of the pack is integrity: ethical behavior, values, and a sense of fair play. Honest people want to follow honest leaders. In a recent survey, integrity was the most desired trait that employees wanted from their leaders. When an organization's leaders conduct themselves with integrity, the organization can make a very real and positive difference in the lives of its employees, its customers, and others who come in contact with it. This, in turn, results in positive feelings from employees about the organization.

Most working Americans devote a third (or more) of their waking hours to their jobs. Whether the organization makes light fixtures, disposes radioactive waste, develops virtual reality software, or delivers pizzas, people want to be part of an organization that makes a positive difference in people's lives. Sure, money is important — people have to make car payments and buy baby shoes — but few would not count this *external* reward a secondary consideration to the *internal* rewards that they derive from their work.

Decisiveness

The best leaders are decisive. If employees make the same complaint again and again, they say that their bosses won't make decisions. Despite the fact that making decisions is one of the key reasons that people are hired to be managers, too few are willing to risk the possibility of making a wrong decision. Instead of making wrong decisions — and having to face the consequences — many so-called leaders prefer to indefinitely postpone making a decision, instead continually seeking more information, alternatives, and opinions from others. They hope that, eventually, events may overtake the need to make the decision, or perhaps that someone else may step up to the plate and make the decision for them.

Great leaders make decisions. Now, this statement doesn't mean that great leaders make decisions in a shoot-from-the-hip, cavalier, gotta-do-it-right-now fashion. No, great leaders take whatever time is necessary to gather whatever information, people, or resources they need to make an informed decision within a reasonable time frame. If the data is immediately available, so be it. If not, then a leader carefully weighs the available data versus the relative need of the decision and acts accordingly.

Be decisive. Don't wait for the course of events to make decisions for you. Sometimes making a decision — even if you make the wrong decision — is better than making no decision at all.

Fostering Collaborative Leadership

A new kind of leadership is gaining traction in an increasing number of organizations: *collaborative leadership*. When leaders lead collaboratively, they share leadership with others in the organization. And, not just with other managers and supervisors, but with employees at all levels — from the shop floor to the front line and everywhere else.

So, what exactly does collaborative leadership look like in the workplace? Here are a few examples:

- To encourage collaborative leadership, banking powerhouse J.P. Morgan Chase maintains a flat organization with only four levels of employees worldwide: managing director, vice president, associate, and analyst. With fewer lines of reporting, every employee has the opportunity — and the responsibility — to play a much greater role in leading and in making decisions.

- W.L. Gore and Associates — manufacturer of a variety of products including Gore-Tex — is famous for its unique lattice organizational structure that encourages collaborative leadership. W.L. Gore and Associates has no formal hierarchy — ranks, titles, and layers of management don't exist. The company only has *sponsors* and *associates*. Sponsors must attract and engage a sufficient number of associates to get their projects off the ground.

- To achieve its ultimate goal of "the genuine care of and comfort of our guests," management of the Ritz-Carlton Hotel Company promotes lateral service — a philosophy that encourages every employee to handle whatever problem comes his or her way, without consulting higher-ups regardless of their place on the organizational chart.

- Aside from president Carol Sturman, employees of Woodland Park, Colorado-based Sturman Industries don't have titles, the organization is flat, and all employees are encouraged to play an active role in decision making. Even high-level corporate policies, such as the company's drug-free workplace policy and the company's at-will employment policy are subject to vigorous discussion, debate, and input by all employees before they're adopted.

In his book *Leadership Ensemble: Lessons in Collaborative Management from the World's Only Conductorless Orchestra*, Peter takes a very close look at the unique brand of collaborative leadership practiced by New York City's Orpheus Chamber Orchestra. Orpheus is one of the world's truly great orchestras, and it is one of very few to perform without a conductor. The vast majority of orchestras are noted not because of the musicians who play the music — but because of their conductors, who are often visionary, charismatic (and autocratic) leaders. The conductor calls all the shots when it comes to the notes that an orchestra's musicians play, and how and when they play them.

By forgoing the traditional model of a conducted orchestra — with one leader and many followers — Orpheus fosters a culture of collaboration where every musician can be a leader, and is expected to play an active role in the shaping of the group's final product: its music. Does this system work? Yes. Orpheus's performances have been acclaimed throughout the world, and the group has numerous Grammy-winning albums and other awards to its credit.

At the heart of the Orpheus Process — the system of collaborative leadership that has brought the group great success over its three-decade history — are eight principles. These principles include:

- **Put power in the hands of the people doing the work.** Those employees closest to the customers are in the best position to know the customers' needs, and they're in the best position to make decisions that directly impact their customers.

- **Encourage individual responsibility for product and quality.** The flip side of putting power in the hands of the people doing the work is requiring employees to take responsibility for the quality of their work. When employees are trusted to play an active role in their organization's leadership, they'll naturally respond by taking a personal interest in the quality of their work.

- **Create clarity of roles.** Before employees can be comfortable and effectively share leadership duties with others, they first have to have clearly defined roles so that they know exactly what they are responsible for, as well as what others are responsible for.

- **Foster horizontal teamwork.** Because no one person has all the answers to every question, effective organizations rely on horizontal teams — both formal and informal — that reach across department and other organizational boundaries. These teams obtain input, solve problems, act on opportunities, and make decisions.

- **Share and rotate leadership.** By moving people in and out of positions of leadership — depending on the particular talents and interests of the individuals — organizations can tap the leadership potential that resides within every employee, even those employees who aren't a part of the formal leadership hierarchy.

✔ **Discover how to listen, discover how to talk.** Effective leaders don't just listen; effective leaders talk — and they know the right times (and the wrong times) to make their views known. Effective organizations encourage employees to speak their minds and to contribute their ideas and opinions — whether or not others agree with what they have to say.

✔ **Seek consensus (and build creative systems that favor consensus).** One of the best ways to involve others in the leadership process is to invite them to play a real and important role in the discussions and debates that lead to making important organizational decisions. Seeking consensus requires a high level of participation and trust, and it results in more democratic organizations.

✔ **Dedicate passionately to your mission.** When people feel passion for the organizations in which they work, they care more about them and about their performance. This caring is expressed in the form of increased employee participation and leadership.

Collaborative leadership is growing in popularity in all kinds of organizations in all kinds of places. Why? Collaborative leadership is growing because organizations today can't afford to limit leadership to just a few individuals at the top. To survive and prosper, today's organizations need to get the most out of every employee. Every employee needs to take a leadership role in his or her organization, to make decisions, to serve customers, to support colleagues, and to improve systems and procedures. Employees — and leaders — who can't meet this challenge may soon find that they will be left behind by others who can.

Top five leadership Web sites

Wondering where to find the best information on the Web about the topics addressed in this chapter? Well, you've come to the right place! Here are our top five favorites:

✔ Leader to Leader magazine: `www.pfdf.org/leaderbooks/l2l/index.html`

✔ Fast Company magazine: `www.fastcompany.com`

✔ Leadervalues: `www.leader-values.com`

✔ Center for Leadership and Change Management: `http://leadership.wharton.upenn.edu`

✔ The Leadership Network: `http://leadership.gc.ca`

Part II
Managing: The People Part

The 5th Wave — By Rich Tennant

©RICHTENNANT

"Frankly, I liked it better when we ran around barking like heck and scaring them into the pen."

In this part . . .

If nothing else, managing is a people job. The best managers work well with all people. In this part, we show you how to hire great employees, inspire employees to achieve their best performance, and to coach employees.

Chapter 4

Hiring: The Million-Dollar Decision

- -

- -

Good employees are hard to find. If you've had the recent privilege of advertising for a job opening, you know good employees aren't easy to come by. Here's the scenario: You place the advertisement and then wait for the resumes of the best and brightest candidates to find their way into your mailbox. In just a couple days, you're pleased beyond your wildest dreams as you see the stack of resumes awaiting your review. How many are there — 100? 200? Wow! What a response!

Your glee quickly turns to disappointment, however, as you begin your review. "Why did this guy apply? He doesn't have half the required number of years of experience!" "What? She's never even done this kind of work before." "Is this guy joking? He must have responded to the wrong advertisement!"

Finding and hiring the best candidates for a job has never been easy. Unfortunately, with all the streamlining, downsizing, and rightsizing going on in business nowadays, a lot of people are looking for work — and, chances are, very few of them have the exact qualifications that you're looking for. Your challenge is to figure out how to pluck the best candidates out of the sea strewn with the wreckage of corporate castoffs. The lifetime earnings of the average American worker are calculated at approximately $1 million. Hiring really is a million-dollar decision!

Your mission, should you decide to accept it, is to locate the most highly quali-fied candidates for your job opening. You will have a wide range of tools at your disposal, but your budget is limited. You will have to use cunning and you will have to be resourceful but, above all, you will have to keep your wits about you at all times. When you've located your candidates, your task is to narrow your selection down to one person and to ensure that the recruitment is executed with his or her successful entry into the firm. You must succeed in your mission — we cannot afford the alternative. Good luck. This tape will self-destruct in five seconds.

Defining the Characteristics of Your New Employees

Employers look for many qualities in candidates. What do you look for when you interview? The following list gives you an idea of the qualities that employers consider most important when hiring new employees. Other char-acteristics may be particularly important to you.

- ✔ **Hard working:** Hard work can often overcome a lack of experience or training. You want to hire people who are willing to do whatever it takes to get the job done. Conversely, no amount of skill can make up for a lack of initiative or work ethic. Although you won't know for sure until you make your hire, careful questioning of candidates can give you some idea of their work ethic (or, at least, what they want you to believe about their work ethic).

- ✔ **Good attitude:** Although what constitutes a "good" attitude is different for different people, a positive, friendly, willing-to-help perspective makes life at the office much more enjoyable and makes everyone's job easier. When you interview candidates, consider what they'll be like to work with for the next five or ten years. Skills are important, but attitude is even more important. This is the "mantra" for the success of Southwest Airlines: "Hire for attitude, train for success." And consider what the new CEO of General Electric says: With every hire the company makes, they look for *givers,* not *takers.*

- ✔ **Experienced:** When Peter graduated from Stanford University, he naively thought that he'd be hired immediately based on the weight of his institution's diploma. However, Peter lacked a critical element — experience — that's so important in the hiring process. An interview gives you the opportunity to ask very pointed questions that require your candidates to demonstrate to you that they can do the job. Initially, Peter didn't see why this would be necessary.

✔ **Go-Getter:** The ability to take initiative to get work done. In a recent Internet survey that Bob conducted for his book *1001 Ways to Take Initiative at Work,* initiative was ranked as the top reason that employees were able to get ahead where they work.

✔ **Team player:** Teamwork is critical to the success of today's organizations that must do far more with far fewer resources than their predecessors. The ability to work with others effectively is a definite must for employees today.

✔ **Smart:** Smart people can often find better and quicker solutions to the problems that confront them. In the world of business, work smarts are more important than book smarts. Unless, of course, you work for a publisher (just kidding!).

✔ **Responsible:** You want to hire people who are willing to take on the responsibilities of their positions. Questions about the kinds of projects that your candidates have been responsible for, and the exact roles they played in their success, can help you determine this important quality. Little things, like showing up for the interview and remembering the name of the company they're interviewing for, can also be key indicators of your candidates' sense of responsibility.

✔ **Stable:** You don't want to hire someone today and then find out that he or she is already looking for the next position tomorrow. You can get some indication of a person's potential stability (or lack thereof) by asking how long he or she worked with his or her previous employer and why he or she left. Not only that, but also you can enjoy listening to your candidates explain, in intimate detail, how they've finished sowing their wild oats and are now ready to settle down.

Hiring the right people is one of the most important tasks that managers face. You can't have a great organization without great people. Unfortunately, managers traditionally give short shrift to this task — devoting as little time as possible to preparation and to the actual interview process. As in much of the rest of your life, the results that you get from the hiring process are usually in direct proportion to the amount of time that you devote to it. If you devote yourself to finding the best candidates for a position, you're much more likely to find them. If you rely on chance to bring them to you, you may be disappointed by what and whom you find.

Defining the Job Before You Start

Is the position new, or are you filling an existing one? In either case, before you start the recruiting process, you need to know exactly what standards you're going to use to measure your candidates. The clearer you are about what you need, the easier and less arbitrary your selection process becomes.

If the job is new, now is your opportunity to design your ideal candidate. Draft a job description that fully describes all the tasks and responsibilities of the position and the minimum necessary qualifications and experience. If the job requires expertise in addition and subtraction, for example, then say so. Don't be shy! You're not going to fill the position with the right hire if you don't make it a key part of the job description. The more work you put into the job description now, the less work you have to do after you make your hire.

If you're filling an existing position, review the current job description closely and make changes where necessary. Again, make the job description reflect exactly the tasks and requirements of the position. When you hire someone new to fill an existing position, you start with a clean slate. For example, you may have had a difficult time getting a former employee to accept certain new tasks — say, taking minutes at staff meetings or filing travel vouchers. By adding these new duties to the job description before you open recruitment, you make the expectations clear, and you won't have to struggle with your new hire to do the job.

Finally, before you start recruiting, use the latest and greatest job description to outline the most important qualities that you're seeking in your new hire. Consult and compare notes with other managers on your team to get input on your descriptions, and ask employees for their feedback as well. Use this outline to guide you in the interview process. Keep in mind, however, that job descriptions may give you the skills you want, but they do not automatically give you the kind of employee you want — that's much more difficult to accomplish (and the reason that you spend so much time recruiting in the first place).

Making an interview outline carries an additional benefit: You can easily document why you didn't hire the candidates who didn't qualify for your positions. Pay close attention here. If a disgruntled job candidate ever sues you for not hiring him, and such lawsuits are more common than you may suspect, you'll be eternally thankful that you did your homework in this area of the hiring process.

Finding Good People

People are the heart of every business. The better the people running your business, the better the business you have. Some people are just meant to be in their jobs. You may know such individuals — someone who thrives as a receptionist or someone who lives to sell. Think about how great your organization would be if you staffed every position with people who lived for their jobs.

Likewise, bad hires can make working for an organization an incredibly miserable experience. The negative impacts of hiring the wrong candidate can reverberate throughout an organization for years. If you, as a manager, ignore the problem, you put yourself in danger of losing your good employees. We can't overemphasize the importance of hiring the right people. Do you want to spend a few extra hours up front to find the best candidates, or do you later want to devote countless hours trying to straighten out a problem employee?

Of course, as important as the interview process is to selecting the best candidates for your jobs, you won't have anyone to interview if you don't have a good system for finding good candidates. So where can you find the best candidates for your jobs?

The simple answer is everywhere. Sure, some places are better than others — you probably won't find someone to run your lab's fusion reactor project by advertising on the backs of matchbooks — but you never know where you can find your next star programmer or award-winning advertising copywriter. Who knows, he or she may be working for your competitors right now!

Bob recalls that his best experience with hiring has always come when he took a long-term view of the hire: a broad search and long hiring cycle, involving other employees in the process. The short-term, "we gotta have somebody right away" approach often results in selecting an applicant who is the lesser of a number of evils — and whose weaknesses soon become problems to the organization.

The following list presents some of the best ways to find candidates for your positions. Your job is to develop a recruitment campaign that can find the kinds of people that you want to hire. And don't rely solely on your human resources department to develop this campaign for you; you probably have a better understanding of where to find the people you need than they do (no offense to human resources departments!). Finally, make sure that your input is heeded.

✔ **Taking a close look within:** In most organizations, the first place to look for candidates is within the organization. If you do your job in training and developing employees, then you probably have plenty of candidates to consider for your job openings. Only after you exhaust your internal candidates should you look outside your organization. Not only is hiring people this way less expensive and easier, but you also get happier employees, improved morale, and have new hires who are already familiar with your organization to boot.

✔ **Personal referrals:** Whether from coworkers, professional colleagues, friends, relatives, or neighbors, you can find great candidates by referrals. Who better to present a candidate than someone whose opinion you already value and trust? You get far more insight about the candidates' strengths and weaknesses from the people who refer them than you ever get from resumes alone. Not only that, but research shows that people hired through current employees tend to work out better, stay with the company longer, and are happier. When you're getting ready to fill a position, make sure that you let people know about it.

✔ **Temporary agencies:** Hiring *temps,* or temporary employees, has become routine for many companies. When you simply have to fill a critical position for a short period of time, temporary agencies are the way to go — no muss, no fuss. And the best part is that when you hire temps, you get the opportunity to try out employees before you buy them. If you don't like the temps you get, no problem. Simply call the agency, and they send replacements before you know it. But if you like your temps, most agencies allow you to hire them at a nominal fee or after a minimum time commitment. Either way, you win.

✔ **Professional associations:** Most professions have their accompanying associations that look out for their interests. Whether you're a doctor (and belong to the American Medical Association), or a truck driver (and belong to the Teamster's Union), you can likely find an affiliated association for whatever you do for a living. Associations even have their own associations. Association newsletters, journals, and magazines are great places to advertise your openings when you're looking for specific expertise, because your audience is already prescreened for you.

✔ **Employment agencies:** If you're filling a particularly specialized position, are recruiting in a small market, or simply prefer to have someone else take care of recruiting and screening your applicants, employment agencies are a good, albeit pricey (with a cost of up to one-third of the employee's first-year salary, or more), alternative. Although employment agencies can usually locate qualified candidates in lower-level or administrative positions, you may need help from an executive search firm or *headhunter* (someone who specializes in recruiting key employees away from one firm to place in a client's firm) for your higher-level positions.

✔ **The Internet:** Every day, more and more companies discover the benefits of using the Internet as a hiring tool. Although academics and scientists have long used Internet newsgroups to advertise and seek positions within their fields, corporations are now following suit. The proliferation of corporate Web pages and online employment agencies and job banks has brought about an entirely new dimension in recruiting. Web pages let you present almost unlimited amounts and kinds of information about your firm and about your job openings — in text, audio, graphic, and video formats. Your pages work for you 24 hours a day, 7 days a week.

For an example of a particularly effective recruiting Web site, point your browser to www.qualcomm.com and click on the Careers button.

✔ **Want ads:** Want ads can be relatively expensive, but they're an easy way to get your message out to a large cross-section of potential candidates. You can choose to advertise in your local paper or in nationally distributed publications such as the *Wall Street Journal*. On the downside, you may find yourself sorting through hundreds or even thousands of unqualified candidates to find a few great ones. But that's what your human resources department is for, right?

A *great* test in hiring is do you proceed if you don't find the right candidate? It's a real testament to your values and pre-work to stick with your plan and either extend the candidate recruiting period to allow for additional candidates, or delay the recruitment for another time.

You Can Be the Greatest Interviewer in the World

After you narrow the field down to the top three or five applicants, you need to start interviewing. What kind of interviewer are you? Do you spend several hours preparing for interviews — reviewing resumes, looking over job descriptions, writing and rewriting questions until each one is as finely honed as a razor blade? Or are you the kind of interviewer who, busy as you already are, starts preparing for the interview when you get the call from your receptionist that your candidate has arrived?

The secret to becoming the Greatest Interviewer in the World is to spend some serious time preparing for your interviews. Remember how much time you spent preparing to be interviewed for your current job? You didn't just walk in the door, sit down, and get offered the job, did you? You probably spent hours researching the company, their products and services, their financials, their market, and other business information. You probably brushed up on your interviewing skills and may have even done some role-playing with a friend or in front of a mirror. Don't you think that you should spend at least as much time getting ready for the interview as the people whom you're going to interview?

Asking the right questions

More than anything else, the heart of the interview process is the questions that you ask and the answers that you receive in response. You get the best answers when you ask the best questions. Lousy questions often result in lousy answers — answers that don't really tell you whether the candidate is going to be right for the job.

A great interviewer asks great questions. "How do I ask great questions?" you ask. According to Richard Nelson Bolles, author of the perennially popular job-hunting guide *What Color Is Your Parachute?,* you can categorize all interview questions under one of the following four headings:

- ✔ **Why are you here?** Really. Why is the person sitting across from you going to the trouble of interviewing with you today? You have just one way to find out — ask. You may assume that the answer is because he or she wants a job with your firm, but you may be surprised at what you find.

  Consider the story of the interviewee who forgot that he was interviewing for a job with Hewlett-Packard. During the entire interview, the applicant referred to Hewlett-Packard by the name of one of its competitors.

- ✔ **What can you do for us?** Always an important consideration! Of course, your candidates are all going to dazzle you with their incredible personalities, experience, work ethic, and love of teamwork — that almost goes without saying. However, despite what many job seekers seem to believe, the question is not, "What can your firm do for me?" — at least not from your perspective. The question that you want an answer to is, "What can you do for us?"

  One recruiter shares a story about the job applicant who slammed his hand on her desk and demanded a signing bonus. And this was before the interview had even started! We're not surprised that this particular candidate landed neither the job nor the bonus!

- ✔ **What kind of person are you?** Few of your candidates will be absolute angels or demons, but don't forget that you'll spend a lot of time with the person that you hire. You want to hire someone whom you enjoy being with during the many work hours, weeks, and years that stretch before you — and the holiday parties, company picnics, and countless other events that you're expected to attend. (Okay, at least someone you can tolerate being with for a few hours every once in a while.) You also want to confirm a few other issues: Are your candidates honest and ethical? Do they share your views in regards to work hours, responsibility, and so forth? Are they responsible and dependable employees? Of course, all your candidates will answer in the affirmative to mom-and-apple-pie questions like these. So, how do you find the real answers?

  When Bob used to recruit, he would try to "project" the applicant in a typical, real-life scenario and then see how they would think it through. This way, there is no "right" answer and they're forced to expose their thinking process, for example, the questions they would ask, strategies they would consider, people they would involve, and so forth. Ask open-ended questions and let your candidates do most of the talking!

✔ **Can we afford you?** It does you no good if you find the perfect candidate but, at the end of the interview, you bring up the topic of pay and find out that you're so far apart that you're actually in a different state. Keep in mind that the actual wage you pay to workers is only part of an overall compensation package. Although you may not be able to pull together more money for wages for particularly good candidates, you may be able to offer them better benefits, a nicer office, a more impressive title, or a key to the executive sauna.

Interviewing do's

So what can you do to prepare for your interviews? The following handy-dandy checklist gives you ideas on where to start:

✔ **Review the resumes of each interviewee the morning before interviews start.** Not only is it extremely poor form to wait to read your interviewees' resumes during the interview, but also you miss out on the opportunity to tailor your questions to those little surprises that you invariably discover in the resumes.

✔ **Become intimately familiar with the job description.** Are you familiar with all the duties and requirements of the job? Really? Telling interviewees that the position requires duties that it really doesn't is poor form. Surprising new hires with duties that you didn't tell them about — especially when they are major duties — is definitely poor form.

✔ **Draft your questions before the interview.** Make a checklist of the key experience, skills, and qualities that you seek in your candidates and use it to guide your questions. Of course, one of your questions may trigger other questions that you didn't anticipate. Go ahead with such questions as long as they provide you with additional insights regarding your candidate and help to illuminate the information that you've outlined on your checklist.

✔ **Select a comfortable environment for both of you.** Your interviewee will likely be uncomfortable regardless of what you do. You don't need to be uncomfortable, too. Make sure that the interview environment is well ventilated, private, and protected from interruptions. You definitely don't want your phone ringing off the hook or employees barging in during your interviews. You get the best performance from your interviewees when they aren't thrown off track by distractions.

✔ **Avoid playing power trips during the course of the interview.** Forget the old games of asking trick questions, turning up the heat, or cutting the legs off their chairs (yes, some managers still do this game playing!) to gain an artificial advantage over your candidates. Get real — it's the 21st century, for heaven's sake!

✔ **Take lots of notes.** Don't rely on your memory when it comes to interviewing candidates for your job. If you interview more than a couple of people, you can easily forget who said exactly what and what your impressions were of their performances. Not only are your written notes a great way to remember who's who, but also they're an important tool to have when you're evaluating your candidates. Plus, they look impressive when you route them to your boss.

As you have no doubt gathered by now, interview questions are one of your best tools for determining whether a candidate is right for your company. Although some amount of small talk is appropriate to help relax your candidates (as sweat poured down the candidate's face, the interviewer asked the opening question with razor-like sharpness: "Hot enough for you?"), the heart of your interviews should focus on answering the questions just listed. Above all, don't give up! Keep asking questions until you're satisfied that you have all the information you need to make your decision.

And don't forget to take lots of notes as you interview your candidates. Try to avoid the temptation to draw pictures of little smiley faces or that new car you've been lusting after. Write the key points of your candidates' responses and their reactions to your questions. For example, if you ask why your candidate left her previous job, and she starts getting really nervous, make a note about this reaction. Finally, note your own impressions of the candidates:

✔ "Top-notch performer — the star of her class."

✔ "Fantastic experience with developing applications in a client-server environment. The best candidate yet."

✔ "Geez, did this one just fall off the turnip truck?"

Interviewing don'ts

The topic of interviewing don'ts is probably worth a chapter of its own. If you've been a manager for any time at all, you know that you can run into tricky situations during an interview and that certain questions can land you in major hot water if you make the mistake of asking them.

Five steps to better interviewing

Every interview consists of five key steps. They are

1. **Welcome the applicant.** Greet your candidates warmly and chat with them informally to help loosen them up. Questions about the weather, the difficulty of finding your offices, or how they found out about your position are old standbys.

2. **Summarize the position.** Briefly describe the job, the kind of person you're looking for, and the interview process that you use.

3. **Ask your questions (and then listen!).** Questions should be relevant to the position and should cover the applicant's work experience, education, and other related topics. Limit the amount of talking you do as an interviewer. Many interviewers end up trying to sell the job to an applicant instead of probing whether or not he or she is a good fit.

4. **Probe experience and find out the candidate's strengths and weaknesses.** The best predictor of future behavior is past behavior, which is why exploring an applicant's past experience can be so helpful to see what they did and how they did it! And, although asking your candidates to name their strengths and weaknesses may seem clichéd, the answers can be very revealing. Go ahead, ask them. We dare you.

5. **Conclude the interview.** Allow your candidates the opportunity to offer any further information that they feel is necessary for you to make a decision, and to ask questions about your firm or about the job. Thank them for their interest and let them know when they can expect your firm to contact them.

Some interviewing don'ts are merely good business practice. For example, accepting an applicant's invitation for a date is probably not a good idea. After a particularly drawn-out interview at a well-known high-tech manufacturer, a male candidate asked out a female interviewer. The interviewer considered her options and declined the date; she also declined to make Prince Charming a job offer.

Then you have the blunders of the major legal type — the kind that can land you and your firm in court. Interviewing is one area of particular concern in the hiring process as it pertains to the possibility of discrimination. For example, although you can ask applicants whether they are able to fulfill job functions, in the United States, you can't ask them whether they are disabled. Because of the critical nature of the interview process, you must know the questions that you absolutely should never ask a job candidate. Here is a brief summary of the kinds of topics that may, depending on the exact circumstances, get you and your firm into trouble:

- ✔ Applicant's race or skin color
- ✔ Applicant's national origin
- ✔ Applicant's sex
- ✔ Applicant's sexual orientation
- ✔ Applicant's marital status
- ✔ Applicant's religion (or lack thereof)
- ✔ Applicant's arrest and conviction record
- ✔ Applicant's height and weight
- ✔ Applicant's debts
- ✔ Applicant's disability

Legal or illegal, the point is that none of the preceding topics are necessary to determine the applicants' ability to perform their jobs. Therefore, ask questions that directly relate to the candidates' ability to perform the tasks required. To do otherwise can put you at definite legal risk. In other words, what *does* count is job-related criteria, that is, information that's directly pertinent to the candidate's ability to do the job (you clearly need to decide this *prior* to interviewing!).

Evaluating Your Candidates

Now comes the really fun part of the hiring process — evaluating your candidates. If you have done your homework, then you already have an amazing selection of candidates to choose from, you've narrowed your search down to the ones showing the best potential to excel in your position, and you've interviewed them to see whether they can live up to the promises that they made in their resumes. Before you make your final decision, you need a little bit more information.

Checking references

Wow! What a resume! What an interview! What a candidate! Would you be surprised to find out that this shining employee-to-be didn't really go to Yale? Or that he really wasn't the account manager on that nationwide marketing campaign? Or that his last supervisor was not particularly impressed with his analytical skills?

A resume and interview are great tools, but a reference check is probably the only chance you have to find out whether your candidates are who they say they are before you make a hiring decision. Depending on your organization, you may be expected to do reference checks. Or maybe your human resources department takes care of that task. Whichever the case, don't hire new employees without first doing an exhaustive check of their backgrounds.

The twin goals of checking references are to verify the information that your candidates have provided and to gain some candid insight into who your candidates really are and how they really behave in the workplace. When you contact a candidate's references, limit your questions to those that are related to the work to be done. As in the interview process, asking questions that can be considered discriminatory to your candidates is not appropriate.

Here are some of the best places to do your reference checking:

- ✔ **Check academic references.** A surprising number of people exaggerate or tell outright lies when reporting their educational experience. Start your reference check here. If your candidates didn't tell the truth about their education, you can bet that the rest of their experience is suspect, too, and you can toss the candidate into the discard pile before you proceed.

- ✔ **Call current and former supervisors.** Getting information from employers is getting harder. Many business people are rightfully concerned that they may be sued for libel or defamation of character if they say anything negative about current or former subordinates. Still, it doesn't hurt to try. You get a much better picture of your candidates if you speak directly to their current and former supervisors instead of to their firms' human resources department — especially if the supervisors you speak to have left their firms. The most you are likely to get from the human resources folks is a confirmation that the candidate worked at the firm during a specific period of time.

- ✔ **Check your network of associates.** If you belong to a professional association, union, or similar group of like-minded careerists, you have the opportunity to tap into the rest of the membership to get the word on your candidates. For example, if you're a certified public accountant (CPA) and want to find out about a few candidates for your open accounting position, you can check with the members of your professional accounting association to see whether anyone knows anything about them.

- ✔ **Do some surfing.** On the Web, that is. Plug your candidate's name into a search engine such as Google (`www.google.com`), perhaps along with the name of the company where he or she last worked or the city in which he or she lives. You never know what can turn up!

✔ **Enlist the aid of a professional psychic.** Just joking here, although, to listen to the raving testimonials on the late-night TV psychic hotline infomercials, you'd think that you should never make a step without first consulting your psychic or astrologer. And you can simply charge your call to your Visa or MasterCard.

Reviewing your notes

You did take interview notes, didn't you? Now's the time to drag them back out and look them over. Review the information package for each candidate — one by one — and compare your findings against your predetermined criteria. Take a look at the candidates' resumes, your notes, and the results of your reference checks. How do they stack up against the standards that you set for the position? Do you see any clear winners at this point? Any clear losers? Organize your candidate packages into the following stacks:

✔ **Winners:** These candidates are clearly the best choices for the position. You have no hesitation in hiring any one of them.

✔ **Potential winners:** These candidates are questionable for one reason or another. Maybe their experience isn't as strong as that of other candidates, or perhaps you weren't impressed with their presentation skills. Neither clear winners nor clear losers, you hire these candidates only after further investigation or if you can't hire anyone from your pool of winners.

✔ **Losers:** These candidates are clearly unacceptable for the position. You simply don't consider hiring any of them.

Conducting a second (or third) round

When you're a busy manager, you have pressure to get things done as quickly as possible, and you're tempted to take shortcuts to achieving your goals. It seems that everything has to be done yesterday — or maybe the day before. When do you have the opportunity to really spend as much time as you want to complete a task or project? Time is precious when you have ten other projects crying for your attention. Time is even more valuable when you're hiring for a vacant position that's critical to your organization and needs to be filled right now.

Hiring is one area of business where you can't take shortcuts. Remember: Hire slowly, fire quickly. Finding the best candidates for your vacancies requires a very real investment of time and resources to be successful. Your company's future depends on it.

Depending on your organization's policies or culture, or because you're undecided as to the best candidate, you may decide to bring candidates in for several rounds of interviews. In this kind of system, lower-level supervisors, managers, or interview panels conduct initial screening interviews. Candidates who pass this round are invited back for another interview with a higher-level manager. Finally, the best two or three candidates interview with the organization's top manager.

But, keep in mind, the timeline for an offer is very different depending on the job you're interviewing for. Lower-level job hunters cannot afford to be unemployed (if they are) for long, and they often get and accept job offers quickly. A higher-level position — say, a general manager — gives you more time.

The ultimate decision on how many rounds and levels of interviews to conduct depends on the nature of the job itself, the size of your company, and your policies and procedures. If the job is simple or at a relatively low level in the company, a single phone interview may be sufficient to determine the best candidate for a job. However, to determine the best candidate, you may need several rounds of testing and personal interviews if the job is complex or at a relatively high level in the organization.

Hiring the Best (And Leaving the Rest)

The first step in making a hiring decision is to rank your candidates within the groups of winners and potential winners that you established during the evaluation phase of the hiring process. You don't need to bother ranking the losers because you wouldn't hire them anyway — no matter what. The best candidate in your group of winners is first, the next best is second, and so on. If you have done your job thoroughly and well, the best candidates for the job should be readily apparent at this point.

The next step is to get on the phone and offer your first choice the job. Don't waste any time — you never know whether your candidate has interviewed with other employers. It would be a shame to invest all this time in the hiring process only to find out that she just accepted a job with one of your competitors. If you can't come to terms with your first choice in a reasonable amount of time, then go on to your second choice. Keep going through your pool of winners until you either make a hire or exhaust the list of candidates.

The following sections give you a few tips to keep in mind as you rank your candidates and make your final decision.

Being objective

In some cases, you may prefer certain candidates because of their personalities or personal charisma — regardless of their abilities or work experience. Sometimes the desire to like these candidates can obscure their shortcomings, while a better qualified, albeit less socially adept, candidate may fade in your estimation.

Be objective. Consider the job to be done and consider the skills and qualifications that being successful requires. Do your candidates have these skills and qualifications? What would it take for your candidates to be considered fully qualified for the position?

Don't allow yourself to be unduly influenced by your candidates' looks, champagne-like personalities, high-priced hairstyles, or dangerously named colognes. None of these characteristics can tell you how well your candidates will perform the job. The facts are present for you to see in your candidates' resumes, interview notes, and reference checks. If you stick to the facts, you can still go wrong, but the chances are diminished.

And one more thing: Diversity in hiring is positive for any organization — both for the business and for society in general. Check your bias at the door!

Trusting your gut

Sometimes you're faced with a decision between two equally qualified candidates, or with a decision about a candidate who is marginal but shows promise. In such cases, you have weighed all the objective data, and you have given the analytical side of your being free rein, but you still have no clear winner. What do you do in this kind of situation?

Listen to yourself. Unlock your heart, your feeling, and your intuition. What do you feel in your gut? Not nausea, we hope. Although two candidates may seem equal in skills and abilities, do you have a feeling that one is better suited to the job than the other? If so, go with it. As much as you may want your hiring decision to be as objective as possible, whenever you introduce the human element into the decision-making process, a certain amount of subjectivity is naturally present.

In reality, rarely are two candidates equally qualified, although often one or more people seem to have more to bring to the job than anticipated (for example, industry focus, fresh ideas, previous contacts, and so forth). This is again where your pre-work can be so valuable in keeping you focused. Can they both do the job? If so, the bonus traits can tip the scale.

Top five hiring Web sites

Wondering where to find the best information on the Web about the topics addressed in this chapter? Well, you've come to the right place! Here are our top five favorites:

✔ Wall Street Journal Career Journal: www. careerjournal.com

✔ Monster.com: www.monster.com

✔ BusinessTown.com: www.businesstown.com/hiring/index.asp

✔ CCH Business Owner's Toolkit: www."toolkit.cch.com/text/P05_0001.asp

✔ HRZone: www.hrzone.com/topics/hiring.html

Other options:

✔ Give them each a non-paid assignment and see how they do.

✔ Try them each on a paid project.

When Bob recently hired a bookkeeper for his business, his hiring team narrowed the applicants down to two candidates, both of whom looked like they could do the job. As a result, secondary information became more relevant. The top pick was a little less flexible, lived farther away from the office, and wanted $7 more an hour than the company was offering for the position. The second pick therefore got the offer.

One more thing: Be sure to keep in touch with other top candidates as additional needs arise in case your first choice doesn't work out.

Adjusting after the offer

What do you do if, heaven forbid, you can't hire anyone from your group of winners? This unfortunate occurrence is a tough call, but no one said that management is an easy task. Take a look at your stack of potential winners. What would it take to make your top potential winners into winners? If the answer is as simple as a training course or two, then give these candidates serious consideration — with the understanding that you can schedule them for the necessary training soon after hire. Perhaps they just need a little more experience before you can put them in the ranks of the winners. You can make a judgment call as to whether you feel that their current experience is sufficient to carry them through until they gain the experience you are looking for. If not, you may want to keep looking for the right candidate. After all, this person may be working with you for a long time — waiting for the best candidate only makes sense.

If you're forced to go to your group of almost winners, and no candidate really seems up to the task, then don't hire someone simply to fill the position. If you do, you probably are making a big mistake. Hiring employees is far easier than unhiring them. The damage that an inappropriate hire can wreak — on coworkers, your customers, and your organization (not to mention the person you hired!) — can take years and a considerable amount of money to undo. Not only that, but it also can be a really big pain in your neck! Other options are to redefine the job, reevaluate other current employees, or hire on a temporary basis to see whether a risky hire works out.

Chapter 5

Inspiring Employees to Better Performance

The question of how to motivate employees has loomed large over managers ever since management was first invented. (Substantial anthropologic evidence indicates that it was invented at about the time of Fred Flintstone and Barney Rubble.) Most of management comes down to mastering skills and techniques for motivating people — to make them better, more productive employees who love their jobs more than anything else in the world. Okay, maybe you'd be happy if they just liked their jobs and didn't complain so much.

You have two ways to motivate employees: rewards and punishments. If employees do what you want them to do, reward them with incentives that they desire: awards, recognition, important titles, money, and so on. We often call these *positive consequences*. Alternatively, if employees don't do what you want, punish them with what they don't desire: warnings, reprimands, demotions, firings, and so on — often known as *negative consequences*. By nature, employees are drawn toward positive consequences and shy away from negative consequences.

Increasingly, however, with today's employees, to be an effective manager you have to work harder at providing a greater number of positive consequences on an ongoing basis when employees perform well (they expect it!) and to be more selective as to when and how you use negative consequences. (Today's employees feel the sting of the negative more deeply.)

This chapter deals with the positive side of employee motivation: positive consequences, especially recognition and rewards. (We're sorry if you're eager to read about the punishment side, but we cover that in Chapter 15.) Besides, 100 years of research in behavioral science and extensive studies at Ohio State University show that you have a much greater impact on getting the performance you want from your employees when you use positive consequences rather than negative ones.

We aren't saying that negative consequences don't have a place; sometimes you have no choice but to punish, reprimand, or even terminate employees. However, first give your employees the benefit of the doubt that they do want to do a good job and acknowledge them when they do so. Make every effort to use positive recognition, praise, and rewards to encourage the behaviors you seek, and catch people doing things right. As a result, your employees will be more motivated to want to excel in their jobs, performance and morale will improve, and your company will be considered a much better place to work.

By leading with *positive reinforcers,* not only can you inspire your employees to do what you want, but you can also develop happier, more productive employees in the process — and that combination is tough to beat!

The Greatest Management Principle in the World

We're about to let you in on the Greatest Management Principle in the World. This simple rule can save you countless hours of frustration and extra work, and it can save your company many thousands or perhaps even millions of dollars. Sounds pretty awe inspiring, doesn't it? Are you ready? Okay, the statement is:

You get what you reward.

Recognition isn't as simple as it looks

Now don't let the seeming simplicity of the statement fool you — great depth is hiding behind the two dimensions of this printed page. You may think that you're rewarding your employees to do what you want them to do — but are you really?

Consider the following example. You have two employees: Employee A is incredibly talented and Employee B is a marginal performer. You give similar assignments to both employees. Employee A completes the assignment before the due date and turns it in with no errors. Because Employee A is already done, you give him two additional assignments. Meanwhile, Employee B is not only late, but when he finally turns in the report you requested, it is full of errors. Because you're now under a time crunch, you accept Employee B's report and then correct it yourself.

What's wrong with this picture? Who's actually being rewarded: Employee A or Employee B?

If you answered Employee B, you're right! This employee has discovered that submitting work that is substandard and late is okay. Furthermore, he also sees that you'll personally fix it! That's quite a nice reward for an employee who clearly doesn't deserve one. (Another way to put it is Employee B certainly has you well trained!)

On the other hand, by giving Employee A more work for being a diligent, outstanding worker, you're actually punishing him. Even though you may think nothing of assigning more work to Employee A, he knows the score. When Employee A sees that all he gets for being an outstanding performer is more work (while you let Employee B get away with doing less work), he's not going to like it one little bit. And if you end up giving both employees basically the same raise (and don't think they won't find out), you make the problem even worse. You will lose Employee A, either literally, as he takes another job, or in spirit, as he stops working so hard.

If you let the situation continue, all your top performers eventually realize that doing their best work is not in their best interest. As a result, they leave their position to find an organization that values their contribution, or they simply kick back and forget about doing their best work. Why bother? No one (that means you, the manager) seems to care anyway!

Jellybean motivation

Whenever you give everyone the same incentive — the same salary increase, equal recognition, or even equal amounts of your time — we call that *jellybean motivation*. Although this treatment may initially sound fair, it isn't.

Nothing is as unfair at work as the equal treatment of unequal performers.

Bob tells a great story about a large California aerospace manufacturer that decided to be nice and thank all its employees at Christmas with a turkey to take home for the holidays. Sounds good so far, doesn't it? However, some employees noticed that their turkeys were smaller than their coworkers' turkeys. Soon, the complaints reached the executive suites — employees with the smaller turkeys thought that they were being punished for poor performance.

Of course, management couldn't continue to have this misconception. The order went out to the supplier of the Christmas turkeys the next year — all turkeys must have the same weight. Unfortunately, the turkey supplier had to inform the aerospace manufacturer that, despite rumors to the contrary, the Lord didn't create all turkeys equal and supplying thousands of identical-weight turkeys would be impossible. Faced with this dilemma, management did what only management could do — it accompanied each Christmas turkey with a printed note that stated, "The weight of your turkey does not necessarily reflect your performance over the last year." Hmmm.

Complaints continued and the situation only worsened. Some employees said that they wanted a choice between turkey and ham; others wanted a fruit basket, and so on. As the years went by, management found it necessary to hire a full-time turkey administrator! Finally, the annual Christmas turkey program came to a crashing halt when management discovered that certain employees were so disillusioned that they were dumping the turkeys out of their boxes, filling the boxes with company-owned tools, and then sneaking them past security.

Did the company achieve its goal of equal reward for all? Obviously not. Even though the Christmas turkey program cost quite a bit of money, it didn't boost employee performance or morale, but instead, it caused a new set of management problems.

Don't forget the Greatest Management Principle in the World — you get what you reward. Before you set up a system to reward your employees, make sure that you know exactly what behaviors you want to reward and then align the rewards with those behaviors.

After you put your employee-reward system into place, you need to check periodically to see that the system has the results that you want. Check with those you're trying to motivate and see if the program is still working. If it isn't, change it!

Figuring Out What Employees Want

In today's tight, stressful, changing times, what things are most important to employees? Bob recently conducted a survey of about 1,500 employees from across seven industries to answer that question. The top ten items he found employees said were most important are listed, along with some thoughts on how you can better provide each of these things to your own employees.

- **A learning activity (No. 1) and choice of assignment (No. 9):** Today's employees most value learning opportunities in which they can gain skills that can enhance their worth and marketability in their current job as well as future positions. Find out what your employees want to find out, how they want to grow and develop, and where they want to be in five years. Give them opportunities as opportunities arise and the ability to choose work assignments whenever possible. When you give employees the choice, more often than not they'll rise to meet or exceed your expectations.

- **Flexible working hours (No. 2) and time off from work (No. 7):** Today's employees value their time — and their time off. Be sensitive to their off-schedule needs, whether they involve family or friends, charity or church, education or hobbies, and provide flexibility whenever you can so they can meet those obligations. Time off may range from an occasional afternoon off to attend a child's play at school or the ability to start the workday an hour early so they can leave an hour early. By allowing work to fit best with an employee's life schedule, you increase the chances that they'll be motivated to work harder while they are at work, and to do their best to make their schedule work. As long as the job gets done, what difference does it matter what hours they work?

- **Personal praise — verbal (No. 3), public (No. 8), or written (No. 10):** Although you can thank someone in 10–15 seconds, most employees report that they're never thanked for the job they do — especially not by their manager. Systematically start to thank your employees when they do good work, whether one-on-one in person, in the hallway, in a group meeting, on voice mail, in a written thank-you note, on e-mail, or at the end of each day at work. Better yet, go out of your way to act on and share and amplify good news when it occurs — even if it means interrupting someone to thank them for a great job they've done. By taking the time to say you noticed and appreciate their efforts, those efforts — and results — will continue.

- **Increased autonomy (No. 5) and authority (No. 4) in their job:** The ultimate form of recognition for many employees is to have increased autonomy and authority to get their job done, including the ability to spend or allocate resources, make decisions, or manage others. Greater autonomy and authority means, "I trust you to act in the best interests of the company, to do so independently and without approval of myself or others." Increased autonomy and authority should be awarded to employees as a form of recognition itself for the past results they have achieved. Autonomy and authority are privileges, not rights, which should be granted to those employees who have most earned them, based on past performance, and not based on tenure or seniority.

✔ **Time with their manager (No. 6):** In today's fast-paced world of work in which everyone is expected to get more done faster, personal time with one's manager is in itself also a form of recognition. As managers are busier, taking time with employees is even more important. The action says: "Of all the things I have to do, one of the most important is to take time to be with you, the person or persons I most depend upon for us to be successful." Especially for younger employees, time spent with one's manager is a valued form of validation and inspiration, as well as serving a practical purpose of learning and communication, answering questions, discussing possibilities, or just listening to an employee's ideas, concerns, and opinions.

By the way, you may wonder where money ranked in importance in this survey. A "cash reward" ranked 13th in importance to employees. (We say more about the topic of money as a motivator later in this chapter.) Everyone needs money to live, but work today involves more than what anyone gets paid.

Employees report that the most important aspects at work today are primarily the intangible aspects of the job that any manager can easily provide — if they make it a priority to do so. Now we're going to tell you a big secret. This secret is the key to motivating your employees. You don't need to attend an all-day seminar or join the management-video-of-the-week club to discover this secret: We are letting you in on it right here and right now at no extra charge!

Ask your employees what they want.

This statement may sound silly, but you can take a lot of the guesswork out of your job by simply getting clear about what your employees most value in their jobs. It may be one or more of the items mentioned earlier in this section, or it may be something entirely different. The simplest way to find out how to motivate your employees is to ask them. Often managers assume that their employees want only money. These same managers are surprised when their employees tell them that other things — such as being recognized for doing a good job, being allowed greater autonomy in decision making, or having a more flexible work schedule — may be much more motivating than cash. Regardless of what preferences your employees have, you'll be much better off knowing those preferences explicitly rather than guessing or ignoring them. So,

✔ **Plan to provide employees more of what they value.** Look for opportunities to recognize employees for having done good work and act on those opportunities as they arise, realizing that what motivates some employees doesn't motivate other employees.

✔ **Stick with it over time.** Motivation is a moving target and you need to constantly be looking to meet your employees' needs in order to have them be motivated to help you meet your needs.

Consider the following as you begin setting the stage for your efforts:

1. **Create a supportive environment for your employees by first finding out what they most value.**

2. **Design ways to implement recognition to thank and acknowledge them when they do good work.**

3. **Be prepared to make changes to your plan, based on what works and what doesn't.**

Creating a supportive environment

The new business realities of the 21st century bring a need to find different ways to motivate employees. Motivation is no longer an absolute, my-way-or-the-highway proposition. The incredible acceleration of change in business and technology today is coupled with greatly expanded global competitive forces. With these forces pressing in from all sides, managers can have difficulty keeping up with what employees need to do, much less figure out what to tell them to do. In fact, a growing trend is for managers to manage individuals who are doing work that the managers themselves have never done. (Fortunately, given a little time and a little trust, most employees can figure out what needs to be done by themselves.)

Inspiring managers must embrace these changing business forces and management trends. Instead of using the power of their positions to motivate workers, managers must use the power of their ideas. Instead of using threats and intimidation to get things done, managers must create environments that support their employees and allow creativity to flourish.

You, as a manager, can create a supportive workplace in the following ways:

✔ **Build and maintain trust and respect.** Employees who are trusted and respected by their managers are motivated to perform their best. By including employees in the decision-making process, today's managers get better ideas (that are easier to implement), and at the same time, they improve employee morale, loyalty, and commitment. "I'll bet our sales clerks can come up with the best way to handle this problem."

✔ **Open the channels of communication.** The ability of all your employees to communicate openly and honestly with one another is critical to the ultimate success of your organization and has a major role in employee motivation. Today, quick and efficient communication of information throughout your organization can be what differentiates you from your competition. Encourage your employees to speak up, to make suggestions, and to break down the organizational barriers — the rampant departmentalization, protecting one's turf, and similar roadblocks — that separate them from one another, where and whenever they find them.

✔ **Make your employees feel safe.** Are your employees as comfortable telling you the bad news as they are telling you the good news? If the answer is no, you haven't created a safe environment for your employees. Everyone makes mistakes; people discover valuable lessons from their mistakes. If you want employees who are motivated, make it safe for them to take chances and to let you know the bad along with the good. Avoid the urge to punish them when they make a mistake. At least be thankful that they are doing something!

✔ **Develop your greatest asset — your employees.** By helping to meet your employees' needs, you are also achieving your organization's needs. Challenge your employees to improve their skills and knowledge and provide them with the support and training that they need to do so. Concentrate on the positive progress that they make and recognize and reward it whenever possible.

Having a good game plan

Motivated employees don't happen by accident. You must have a plan to reinforce the behavior that you want. In general, employees are more strongly motivated by the potential to earn rewards than they are by the fear of punishment. Clearly, a well thought-out and planned rewards system is important to creating a motivated, effective workforce. Here are some simple guidelines for setting up a system of low-cost rewards in your organization:

✔ **Link rewards to organizational goals.** To be effective, rewards need to reinforce the behavior that leads to an organization's goals. Use rewards to increase the frequency of desired behavior and decrease the frequency of undesired behavior.

✔ **Define parameters and mechanics.** After you identify the behaviors that you want to reinforce, develop the specifics of your reward system and create rules that are clear and easily understood by all employees. Make sure that targets are attainable and that all employees have a chance to obtain rewards. For example, your clerks also should have a shot at the rewards, not just salespeople or assemblers.

✔ **Obtain commitment and support.** Of course, communicate your new rewards program to your employees. Many organizations publicize their programs in group meetings. They present the programs as positive and fun activities that benefit both the employees and the companies. To get the best results, plan and implement your rewards program with your employees' direct involvement.

✔ **Monitor effectiveness.** Is your rewards system getting the results that you want? If not, take another look at the behaviors you want to reinforce and make sure that your rewards are closely linked. Even the most successful rewards programs tend to lose their effectiveness over time as employees begin to take them for granted. Keep your program fresh by discontinuing rewards that have lost their luster and bringing in new ones from time to time.

Deciding What to Reward

Most managers reward the wrong things, if they reward their employees at all. This tendency has led to a crisis of epic proportions in the traditional system of incentives and motivation in business. Consider these statistics quoted in the *Management Accounting* journal:

✔ Only 3 percent of base salary separates average from outstanding employees in American companies.

✔ 81 percent of American workers report that they would not receive rewards for increasing their productivity.

✔ 60 percent of American managers say that they would not receive increases in their compensation for increasing their performance.

Yikes! *Houston, we have a problem here!* If managers and workers aren't being rewarded for increasing their productivity and performance, what are they being rewarded for? As we point out in our prior example of the Christmas turkey program (see the section, "Jellybean motivation" earlier in the chapter for info), employees are often rewarded just for showing up for work. Isn't that why you give your employees their paychecks?

For an incentive program to have meaningful and lasting effects, it must be contingent, that is, it must focus on performance — nothing less and nothing more.

"But wait a second," you say, "that isn't fair to the employees who aren't as talented as my top performers." If that's what you think, we'll straighten out that particular misunderstanding right now. Everyone, regardless of how smart, talented, or productive they are, has the potential to be a top performer.

Praising guidelines

A basic foundation for a positive relationship is the ability to give a good praising. Bob uses ASAP-cubed to give a good praising, which means:

- **As soon** — Timing is very important when using positive reinforcement. Give praise as soon as the desired behavior is displayed.

- **As sincere** — Words alone can fall flat if you're not sincere in why you're praising someone. Praise someone because you are truly appreciative and excited about the other person's success. Otherwise, it may come across as a manipulative tactic.

- **As specific** — Avoid generalities in favor of details of the achievement. For example, "You really turned that angry customer around by focusing on what you could do for him, not on what you could not do for him."

- **As personal** — A key to conveying your message is praising in person, face-to-face. This shows that the activity is important enough to you to put aside everything else you have to do and just focus on the other person.

- **As positive** — Too many managers undercut praise with a concluding note of criticism. When you say something like, "You did a great job on this report, but there were quite a few typos," the "but" becomes a verbal erasure of all that came before.

- **As proactive** — Lead with praising and "catch people doing things right" or else you will tend to be reactive — typically about mistakes — in your interactions with others.

A good praising is given directly with the employee, in front of another person (in public), or when the person isn't around (via letter, e-mail, voice mail, and so forth). Praising employees only takes a moment, but the benefits — to your employees and to your organization — will last for years.

Suppose that Employee A produces 100 widgets an hour and stays at that level of performance day in and day out. On the other hand, Employee B produces 75 widgets an hour but improves output to 85 widgets an hour. Who should you reward? Employee B! This example embodies what you want to reward: the efforts that your employees make to improve their performance, not just to maintain a certain level (no matter how good that level is).

The following are examples of *performance-based measures* that any manager must recognize and reward. What measures should you be monitoring, measuring, and rewarding in your organization? Don't forget, just showing up for work doesn't count!

- Defects decrease from 25 per 1,000 to 10 per 1,000.

- Annual sales increase by 20 percent.

✔ The department records system is reorganized and color-coded to make filing and retrieval more efficient.

✔ Administrative expenses are held to 90 percent of the authorized budget.

✔ The organization's mail is distributed in 1 hour instead of 1½ hours.

Some managers break incentives into two categories: "results measures," where measures are linked to the bottom line, and "process measures," where the link to the bottom line isn't as clear. Both categories need to be recognized.

Starting with the Positive

As we note at the beginning of this chapter, you're more likely to lead your employees to great results by focusing on their positive accomplishments rather than by finding fault with and punishing their negative outcomes. Despite this fact, many managers' primary mode of operation is correcting their employees' mistakes instead of complimenting their successes.

In a recent study, 58 percent of employees reported that they seldom received a personal thank-you from their managers for doing a good job even though they ranked such recognition as their most motivating incentive. They ranked a written thank-you for doing a good job as motivating incentive No. 2, while 76 percent said that they seldom received thanks from their managers. Perhaps these statistics show why a lack of praise and recognition is one of the leading reasons why people leave their jobs.

American Express recognizes great performers

If you could increase your organization's net income by 500 percent in a decade's time, would you take the time to recognize your great performers? The Travel Related Services division of American Express did by creating its Great Performers program to recognize and reward exceptional employee performance. The program accepted nominations from employees, supervisors, and even customers. Winners of the Great Performers award were eligible for selection by a worldwide governing committee to become Grand Award recipients. In addition to an all-expenses-paid trip for two to New York City, Grand award winners received $4,000 in American Express traveler's checks, a platinum award pin, and a certificate.

(Source: Bob Nelson, *1001 Ways to Reward Employees*.)

Years of psychological research have clearly shown that positive reinforcement works better than negative reinforcement for several reasons. Without getting too technical, the reasons are that positive reinforcement:

✔ Increases the frequency of the desired behavior

✔ Creates good feelings within employees

On the other hand, negative reinforcement may decrease the frequency of undesired behavior, but doesn't necessarily result in the expression of desired behavior. Instead of being motivated to do better, employees who receive only criticism from their managers eventually come to avoid their managers whenever possible. Furthermore, negative reinforcement (particularly when manifested in ways that degrade employees and their personal sense of worth) can create tremendously bad feelings with employees. And employees who are unhappy with their employers have a much more difficult time doing a good job than the employees who are happy with their employers.

The following ideas can help you seek out the positive in your employees and reinforce the behaviors that you want:

✔ **Have high expectations for your employees' abilities.** If you believe that your employees can be outstanding, soon they will believe it, too. When Peter was growing up, his parents rarely needed to punish him when he did something wrong. He needed only the words "we know that you can do better" to get him back on course.

✔ **Give your employees the benefit of the doubt.** Do you really think that your employees want to do a bad job? Unless they are consciously trying to sabotage your firm, no one wants to do a bad job. Your job is to figure out what you can do to help them do a good job. Additional training, encouragement, and support should be among your first choices — not reprimands and punishment.

✔ **Catch your employees doing things right.** Although most employees do a good job in most of their work, managers naturally tend to focus on what employees do wrong. Instead of constantly catching your employees doing things wrong, catch them doing things right. Not only can you reinforce the behaviors that you want, but you can also make your employees feel good about working for you and for your firm.

Making a Big Deal about Something Little

Okay, here's a question for you: "Should you reward your employees for their little day-to-day successes, or should you save up rewards for when they accomplish something really major?" The answer to this question lies in the way that most people get their work done on a daily basis.

The simple fact is for most people in business, work is not a string of dazzling successes that come one after another without fail. Instead, the majority of work consists of routine, daily activities; employees perform most of these duties quietly and with little fanfare. A manager's typical work day, for example, may consist of an hour or two of reading memos and e-mail messages, listening to voice-mail messages, and talking to others on the phone. The manager spends another couple of hours in meetings and perhaps another hour in one-on-one discussions with staff members and coworkers, much of which involves dealing with problems as they occur. With additional time spent on preparing reports or filling out forms, the manager actually devotes precious little time to decision making — the activity that has the greatest impact on an organization.

For a line worker, this dearth of opportunities for dazzling success is even more pronounced. If the employee's job is assembling lawnmower engines all day (and she does a good, steady job), when does she have an opportunity to be outstanding in the eyes of her supervisor?

We've taken the long way around to say that major accomplishments are usually few and far between, regardless of your place in the organizational chart. Work is a series of small accomplishments that eventually add up to big ones. If you wait to reward your employees for their big successes, you may be waiting a long time.

Therefore, reward your employees for their small successes as well as for their big successes. You may set a lofty goal for your employees to achieve — one that stretches their abilities and tests their resolve — but remember that praising your employees' progress toward the goal is perhaps even more important than praising them when they finally reach it.

Money Isn't Important (No, Really!)

You may think that money is the ultimate incentive for your employees. After all, who isn't excited when they receive a cash bonus or pay raise? *As visions of riches beyond her wildest dreams danced through her head, she pledged her eternal devotion to the firm.* The problem is that money really isn't the top motivator for employees — at least not in the way that most managers think. And it can be a huge demotivator if you manage it badly!

Compensation is a right

Money is clearly important to your employees. They need money to pay bills, buy food and clothes, put gas in their cars, and afford the other necessities of life.

Most employees consider the money that they receive on the job (whether it comes in the form of pay or cash bonuses) to be a fair exchange for the labor that they contribute to their organizations. Today's employees view compensation as a right. Recognition, on the other hand, is a gift. Using recognition, however, helps you get the best effort from each employee.

When incentives become entitlements

In particular, employees who receive annual bonuses and other periodic, money-based rewards quickly come to consider them part of their basic pay. Peter once worked at a company where he received an annual bonus that amounted to approximately 10 percent of his annual pay. The first time he received the bonus, he was very excited by it. His motivation skyrocketed, and he pledged his eternal loyalty to the firm.

However, after Peter realized that receiving the bonus was going to be an annual event, he quickly took it for granted. In his mind, he converted the reward (for work above and beyond his basic job description) into a part of his basic compensation package. As far as Peter was concerned, his annual salary was really the amount of his base pay plus the annual bonus. He even centered his holiday-spending plans on the assumption that the bonus would arrive on or about a certain date — and it always did.

Of course, if a year had ever passed and he didn't receive the bonus, disappointment and open hostility would erupt in its absence.

Management expert Peter Drucker hit the nail on the head when he pointed out in his book *Management: Tasks, Responsibilities, Practices,* "Economic incentives are becoming rights rather than rewards. Merit raises are always introduced as rewards for exceptional performance. In no time at all, they become a right. To deny a merit raise or to grant only a small one becomes punishment. The increasing demand for material rewards is rapidly destroying their usefulness as incentives and managerial tools." In other words, money becomes an expectation, then an entitlement, for many if not most workers.

The ineffectiveness of money as a motivator for employees is a good news/bad news kind of thing. We start with the bad news first. Many managers have thrown lots of money into cash-reward programs, and for the most part, these programs really didn't have the positive effect on motivation that the managers expected. Although we don't want to say that you waste your money on these programs, you can use it more effectively. In fact, with other programs, you may achieve better results with far fewer dollars!

Now you get the good news: Because you know that money is not the most effective motivation tool, you can focus on using tools that are more effective — and the best forms of recognition cost little or no money!

Figuring out what motivates today's employees

According to Dr. Gerald Graham of Wichita State University, the most motivating incentives (as reported by employees today) are

- **Manager-initiated incentives:** Instead of coming from some nebulous ad-hoc committee, corporate bigwig, or completely out of the blue, the most valuable recognition comes directly from one's supervisor or manager.

- **Performance-based incentives:** Employees want to be recognized for the jobs they are hired to do. The most effective incentives are therefore based on job performance and not on nonperformance-related things such as attendance, attire, or drawing the lucky number out of a hat at the monthly sales meeting.

So you're a busy manager. Cash rewards are convenient because you simply fill out a check request once a year to take care of all your motivation for the year. This manager-initiated, based-on-performance stuff sounds like a lot of work! To be frank, running an effective rewards program does take more work on your part than running a simple, but ineffective one. But as we show you, the best rewards can be quite simple. After you get the hang of using them, you can easily integrate them into your daily routine. Doing so is part of managing today.

Don't save up recognition for special occasions only — and don't just use them with the top performers! Every employee needs to be recognized when they do good work in their job. Your employees are doing good things — things that you want them to do every day. Catch them doing something right and recognize their successes regularly and often!

The following incentives are simple to execute, take little time, and are the most motivating for employees:

✔ Personal or written congratulations from you for a job well done

✔ Public recognition, given visibly by you for good job performance

✔ Morale-building meetings to celebrate successes

✔ Time off or flexibility in one's working hours

✔ Asking employees their opinions and involving them in decision making

For unbelievably comprehensive listings of incentive ideas that really work, check out Bob's best-selling books *1001 Ways to Reward Employees*, *1001 Ways to Energize Employees*, and *The 1001 Rewards & Recognition Fieldbook*.

Ten ways to motivate employees

Here are some easy, no-cost things you can do to create a motivating workplace:

1. Personally thank employees for doing a good job — one-on-one, in writing, or both. Do it timely, often, and sincerely.

2. Take the time to meet with and listen to employees — as much as they need or want.

3. Provide employees specific and frequent feedback about their performance. Support them in improving performance.

4. Recognize, reward, and promote high performers; deal with low and marginal performers so that they improve or leave.

5. Provide information on how the company makes and loses money, upcoming products, and services and strategies for competing. Explain the employee's role in the overall plan.

6. Involve employees in decisions, especially those decisions that affect them. Involvement equals commitment.

7. Give employees a chance to grow and develop new skills; encourage them to be their best. Show them how you can help them meet their goals while achieving the organization's goals. Create a partnership with each employee.

8. Provide employees with a sense of ownership in their work and their work environment. This ownership can be symbolic (for example, business cards for all employees, whether they need them to do their jobs or not).

9. Strive to create a work environment that is open, trusting, and fun. Encourage new ideas, suggestions, and initiative. Learn from, rather than punish for, mistakes.

10. Celebrate successes — of the company, of the department, and of individuals in it. Take time for team- and morale-building meetings and activities. Be creative and fresh.

Top five motivation Web sites

Wondering where to find the best information on the Web about the topics addressed in this chapter? Well, you've come to the right place! Here are our top five favorites:

✔ Nelson Motivation, Inc.: www.nelson-motivation.com

✔ National Association for Employee Recognition (NAER): www.recognition.org

✔ Aubrey Daniels International: www.aubreydaniels.com

✔ Watson Wyatt Worldwide: www.watsonwyatt.com

✔ U-inspire: www.uinspire.com

Realizing you hold the key to your employees' motivation

In our experience, most managers believe that their employees determine how motivated they choose to be. Managers tend to think that some employees naturally have good attitudes, that others naturally have bad attitudes, and that they (as managers) can't do much to change these attitudes. "If only we could unleash the same passion and energy people have for their families and hobbies," these managers think, "then we could really get something done around here!"

As convenient as blaming your employees for their bad attitudes may be, looking in a mirror may be a more honest approach. Studies show that managers have the biggest influence on how motivated their employees are, and even more so, how demotivated they are! Do managers recognize their employees for doing a good job? Do they provide a pleasant and supportive working environment? Do they create a sense of joint mission and teamwork in the organization? Do they treat their employees as equals? Do they avoid favoritism? Do they make time to listen when employees need to talk?

For the most part, you determine how motivated (and demotivated) your employees are. Managers create a motivating environment that makes it easier for employees to be motivated. When the time comes, recognize and reward them fairly and equitably for the work they do well.

When you give out rewards, keep in mind that employees don't want hand-outs, and they hate favoritism. Don't give recognition when none is warranted. Don't give it just to be nice or with the hope that people will like you better. Provide them for the performance that helps you be mutually successful. Not only do you cheapen the value of the incentive with the employee who received it, but also you lose credibility in the eyes of your other employees. Trust and credibility with your employees are some of the most important qualities that you can build in your relationship with your employees; if you lose these qualities, you risk losing the employee.

Chapter 6

When in Doubt, Coach

As you refer to various parts of this book, you may notice common themes. These themes are the heart and soul of today's new management reality.

One recurring theme is the new role of managers as people who support and encourage their employees, instead of telling them what to do (or worse, simply expecting them to perform). The best managers are *coaches* — that is, individuals who guide, discuss, and encourage others on their journey. With the help of coaches, employees can achieve outstanding results, organizations can perform better than ever, and you can sleep well at night, knowing that everything is A-Okay.

Coaching plays a critical part in the learning process for employees who are developing their skills, knowledge, and self-confidence. Your employees don't learn effectively when you simply tell them what to do. In fact, they usually don't learn at all.

As the maxim goes . . .

> Tell me . . . I forget.
>
> Show me . . . I remember.
>
> Involve me . . . I learn.

Neither do your employees learn effectively when you throw a new task at them with no instruction or support whatsoever. Sure, good employees can eventually figure things out, but they waste a lot of time and energy in the process. "What the heck is this all about? I guess I'll just stumble along until I get the hang of it!"

Between these two extremes — being told what to do and being given no support whatsoever — is a happy medium where employees can thrive and the organization can prosper. This is happy land where everyone lives in peace and harmony. *[Offstage, the chorus swells: "I'd like to sing the world a song in perfect harmony . . ."]* This happy medium happens with coaching.

Who's a Coach?

Even if you have a pretty good sense of what it means to be a manager, do you really know what it means to be a coach? A coach is a colleague, counselor, and cheerleader, all rolled into one. Based on that definition, are you a coach? How about your boss? Or your boss's boss? Why or why not?

We bet that you're familiar with the role of coaches in other nonbusiness activities. A drama coach, for example, is almost always an accomplished actor or actress. The drama coach's job is to conduct tryouts for parts, assign roles, schedule rehearsals, train and direct cast members throughout rehearsals, and support and encourage the actors and actresses during the final stage production. These roles aren't all that different from the roles that managers perform in a business, are they?

Coaching a team of individuals isn't easy, and certain characteristics make some coaches better than others. Fortunately, as with most other business skills, you can discover, practice, and improve the traits of good coaches. You can always find room for improvement, and good coaches are the first to admit it. The list that follows highlights important characteristics of coaching:

- **Coaches set goals.** Whether an organization's vision is to become the leading provider of wireless telephones in the world, to increase revenues by 20 percent a year, or simply to get the break room walls painted this year, coaches work with their employees to set goals and deadlines for completion. They then go away and allow their employees to determine how to accomplish the goals.

- **Coaches support and encourage.** Employees — even the best and most experienced — can easily become discouraged from time to time. When employees are learning new tasks, when a long-term account is lost, or when business is down, coaches are there — ready to step in and help the team members through the worst of it. "That's okay, Kim. You've learned from your mistake, and I know that you'll get it right next time!"

- **Coaches emphasize team success over individual success.** The team's overall performance is the most important concern, not the stellar abilities of a particular team member. Coaches know that no one person can carry an entire team to success; winning takes the combined efforts of all team members. The development of teamwork skills is a vital step in an employee's progress in an organization.

✔ **Coaches can quickly assess the talents and shortfalls of team members.** The most successful coaches can quickly determine their team members' strengths and weaknesses and, as a result, tailor their approach to each. For example, if one team member has strong analytical skills but poor presentation skills, a coach can concentrate on providing support for the employee's development of better presentation skills. "You know, Mark, I want to spend some time with you to work on making your viewgraph presentations more effective."

✔ **Coaches inspire their team members.** Through their support and guidance, coaches are skilled at inspiring their team members to the highest levels of human performance. Teams of inspired individuals are willing to do whatever it takes to achieve their organization's goals.

✔ **Coaches create environments that allow individuals to be successful.** Great coaches ensure that their workplaces are structured to let team members take risks and stretch their limits without fear of retribution if they fail.

Coaches are always available to advise their employees or just to listen to their problems if need be. "Carol, do you have a minute to discuss a personal problem?"

✔ **Coaches provide feedback.** Communication and feedback between coach and employee is a critical element of the coaching process. Employees must know where they stand in the organization — what they're doing right, and what they're doing wrong. Equally important, employees must let their coaches know when they need help or assistance. And both parties need this dialog in a timely manner, on an ongoing basis — not just once a year in a performance review.

Firing someone doesn't constitute effective feedback. Unless an employee has engaged in some sort of intolerable offense (such as physical violence, theft, intoxication on the job — see Chapter 16 for more details), then a manager needs to give the employee plenty of verbal and written feedback before termination is even considered. Giving your employee several warnings provides your employee an opportunity to correct deficiencies that he or she may not be able to see.

Coaching: The Short Lesson

Besides the obvious coaching roles of supporting and encouraging employees in their quest to achieve an organization's goals, coaches also teach their employees how to achieve an organization's goals. Drawing from their experience, coaches lead their workers step by step through work processes or procedures. After the workers discover how to perform a task, the coach delegates full authority and responsibility for its performance to them.

For the transfer of specific skills, you can find no better way of teaching, and no better way of learning, than the *show-and-tell* method. Developed by a post-World War II American industrial society desperate to quickly train new workers in manufacturing processes, show and tell is beautiful in its simplicity and effectiveness.

Show-and-tell coaching has three steps:

1. *You do, you say.* **Sit down with your employees and explain the procedure in general terms while you perform the task.** Most businesses today use computers as a critical tool for getting work done. When a manager needs to coach a new employee in the use of an obscure word processing or spreadsheet technique, the first thing she needs to do is to explain the technique to the employee while she demonstrates it. "I click my left mouse button on the Insert command on the toolbar and pull down the menu. Then I point the arrow to Symbol and click again. I choose the symbol I want from the menu, point my arrow to it, and click to select it. I then point my arrow to Insert and click to place the symbol in the document; then I point my arrow to Close and click again to finish the job."

2. *They do, you say.* **Now, have the employee do the same procedure as you explain each step in the procedure.** "Click your left mouse button on the Insert command on the toolbar and pull down the menu. Okay, good. Now point your arrow to Symbol and click again. Super! Choose the symbol you want from the menu and point your arrow to it. Now click to select it. All right — point your arrow to Insert and click to place the symbol in the document. Okay, you're almost done now. Point your arrow to Close and click again to finish the job. There you are!"

3. *They do, they say.* **Finally, as you observe, have your employees perform the task again as they explain to you what they are doing.** "Okay, Yinka, now it's your turn. I want you to insert a symbol in your document and tell me what you're doing."

   "All right, Susan. First, I click my left mouse button on the Insert command on the toolbar and pull down the menu. Then I point the arrow to Symbol and click again. I decide the symbol I want from the menu, point my arrow to it, and click to select it. Next, I point the arrow to Insert and click to place the symbol in the document. Finally, I point my arrow to Close and click again to finish the job. I did it!"

It also never hurts to have employees create a "cheat sheet" of the new steps to refer to until they become habit.

Coaching Metaphors for Success in Business

In business, Bob and Peter are often reminded that, when it comes to coaching and teamwork, the metaphor of a company as a winning sports team is strong. In many organizations, CEOs hire professional athletes and coaches to lecture their employees on the importance of team play and winning; managers are given the label of *coaches* or *team leaders;* and workers are given the labels of *players* or *team members.*

This being the case, ignoring the obvious parallels between coaching in sports and in business is difficult. So we're going to get this out of our system once and for all and refrain from linking coaching in sports and business anyplace else in this book after the following list of quotes from Gerald Tomlinson's book, *Speaker's Treasury of Sports Anecdotes, Stories, and Humor.* We promise.

- Lou Holtz, head coach of the South Carolina football team, said about coaching: "I don't think discipline is forcing someone to do something. It's showing them how this is going to help them in the long run."

- According to former Dartmouth lacrosse coach Whitey Burnham, "Good judgment comes from experience, and experience comes from bad judgment."

- Former Houston Oilers head coach Bum Phillips's theory of football coaching may apply equally well in business: "Two kinds of football players ain't worth a damn: the one that never does what he's told, and the other that never does anything *except* what he's told."

- The phenomenally successful UCLA basketball coach John Wooden once said, "If you're not making mistakes, then you're not doing anything. I'm positive that a doer makes mistakes."

- Former head coach of the Oakland Raiders football team John Madden summed up his coaching philosophy as this: "I didn't want a big play once in a while, I wanted solid play every time."

One last point: In sports as in business, *everybody* needs a coach. Who's the greatest golfer of all time? Tiger Woods, right? Most people don't realize that even Tiger Woods has a coach to help him stay sharp and to improve.

Eyeing Turning Points

Despite popular impressions to the contrary, 90 percent of management isn't the big event — the blinding flash of brilliance that creates markets where none previously existed, the magnificent negotiation that results in unheard of levels of union-management cooperation, or the masterful stroke that catapults the firm into the big leagues. No, 90 percent of a manager's job consists of the daily chipping away at problems and the shaping of talents.

The best coaches are constantly on the lookout for *turning points* — the daily opportunities to succeed that are available to all employees.

Making turning points into big successes

The big successes — the victories against competitors, the dramatic surges in revenues or profits, the astounding new products — are typically the result of building a foundation of countless small successes along the way. Making a voice-mail system more responsive to your customers' needs, sending an employee to a seminar on time management, writing a great sales agreement, conducting a meaningful performance appraisal with an employee, meeting a prospective client for lunch — all are turning points in the average business day. Although each event may not be particularly spectacular on its own, when aggregated over time, they can add up to big things.

This is the job of a coach. Instead of using dynamite to transform the organization in one fell swoop (and taking the chance of destroying it, their employees, or themselves in the process), coaches are like the ancient stonemasons who built the great pyramids of Egypt. The movement and placement of each individual stone may not have seemed like a big deal when considered as a separate activity. However, each was an important step in the achievement of the ultimate result — the construction of awe-inspiring structures that have withstood thousands of years of war, weather, and tourists.

Incorporating coaching in your day-to-day interactions

Coaches focus daily on spending time with employees to help them succeed — to assess their progress and to find out what they can do to help the employees capitalize on the turning points that present themselves every day. Coaches complement and supplement the abilities and experience of their employees by bringing their own abilities and experience to the table. They reward positive performance and they help their employees learn important lessons from making mistakes — lessons that, in turn, help the employees to improve their future performance.

For example, suppose that you have a young and inexperienced, but bright and energetic, sales trainee on your staff. Your employee has done a great job contacting customers and making sales calls, but she has yet to close her first deal. When you talk to her about this, she confesses that she is very nervous about her own personal turning point: She's worried that she may become confused in front of the customer and blow the deal at the last minute. She needs your coaching.

The following guidelines can help you, the coach, handle any employee's concerns:

- **Meet with your employee.** Make an appointment with your employee as soon as possible for a relaxed discussion of the concerns. Find a place that is quiet and free of distractions and put your phone on hold or forward it to voice mail.

- **Listen!** One of the most motivating things one person can do for another is to listen. Avoid instant solutions or lectures. Before you say a word, ask your employee to bring you up to date with the situation, her concerns, and any possible approaches or solutions she's considered. Let her do the talking while you do the listening.

- **Reinforce the positive.** Begin by pointing out the things that your employee did right in the particular situation. Let your employee know when she is on the right track. Give her positive feedback on her performance.

- **Highlight areas for improvement.** Point out the things that your employee needs to do to improve and tell her what you can do to help. Agree on the assistance that you can provide, whether your employee needs further training, an increased budget, more time, or whatever is necessary. Be enthusiastic about your confidence in the employee's ability to do a great job.

- **Follow through.** After you determine what you can do to support your employee, do it! Notice when she improves! Periodically check up on the progress that your employee is making and offer your support as necessary.

Above all, be patient. Coaching is something that you can't accomplish on your terms alone. At the outset, understand that everyone is different. Some employees catch on sooner than others, and some employees need more time to develop. Differences in ability don't make certain employees any better or worse than their coworkers — they just make them different. Just as you need time to build relationships and trust in business, your employees need time to develop skills and experience.

When the coach needs a coach

Sometimes even coaches need to be coached. Scott McNealy, chairman, president, and CEO of Sun Microsystems, has used a combination of drive, passion, and tough financial controls to shepherd his company from $39 million in sales in 1984, when he took over, to more than $18 billion in sales in fiscal year 2001. Calling the stand-alone personal computer a "hairball on the desktop," McNealy has pushed the concept of network computing for years — long before the Internet became the "in" place to be. Sun is the leading maker of UNIX-based servers used to power corporate computer networks and Web sites, and Sun's Internet-ready networks have been adopted for internal use by an increasing number of companies, including Gap, Federal Express, and AT&T Universal Card Services.

However, despite his success, Scott McNealy hired a "CEO coach" to help him become even more effective. The coach, Chuck Raben of Delta Consulting Group, Inc., asked McNealy's managers to report areas where they thought their boss could improve. Raben compiled the surveys and summarized the responses. According to Sun's management team, the result: McNealy needs to become a better listener. So McNealy now carries with him a reminder to respond to the points that his managers raise in meetings.

(Source: *Business Week*)

Identifying a Coach's Tools

Coaching is not a one-dimensional activity. Because every person is different, the best coaches tailor their approach to their team members' specific, individualized needs. If one team member is independent and needs only occasional guidance, recognize where the employee stands and provide that level of support. This support may consist of an occasional, informal progress check while making the rounds of the office. If, on the other hand, another team member is insecure and needs more guidance, the coach recognizes this employee's position and assists as needed. In this case, support may consist of frequent, formal meetings with the employee to assess progress and to provide advice and direction as needed.

Although every coach has his or her own style, the best coaches employ certain techniques to elicit the greatest performance from their team members:

- **Make time for team members.** Managing is primarily a people job. Part of being a good manager and coach is being available to your employees when they need your help. If you're not available, your employees may seek out other avenues to meet their needs — or simply stop trying to work with you. Always keep your door open to your employees and remember that they are your No.1 priority. Manage by walking around. Regularly get out of your office and visit your employees at their workstations. "Do I have a minute, Elaine? Of course, I always have time for you and the other members of my staff."

✔ **Provide context and vision.** Instead of simply telling employees what to do, effective coaches explain the why. Coaches provide their employees with context and a big picture perspective. Instead of spouting long lists of do's and don'ts, they explain how a system or procedure works and then define their employees' parts in the scheme of things. "Chris, you have a very important part in the financial health and vitality of our company. By ensuring that our customers pay their invoices within 30 days after we ship their products, we're able to keep our cash flow on the plus side, and we can pay our obligations such as rent, electricity, and your paycheck on time."

✔ **Transfer knowledge and perspective.** A great benefit of having a good coach is the opportunity to discover from someone who has more experience than you do. In response to the unique needs of each team member, coaches transfer their personal knowledge and perspective. "We faced the exact situation about five years ago, Dwight. I'm going to tell you what we did then, and I want you to tell me whether you think that it still makes sense today."

✔ **Be a sounding board.** Coaches talk through new ideas and approaches to solving problems with their employees. Coaches and employees can consider the implications of different approaches to solving a problem and role-play customer or client reactions before trying them out for real. By using active listening skills, coaches can often help their employees work through issues and come up with the best solutions themselves. "Okay, David, you've told me that you don't think your customer will buy off on a 20 percent price increase. What options do you have to present the price increase, and are some more palatable than others?"

✔ **Obtain needed resources.** Sometimes, coaches can help their employees make the jump from marginal to outstanding performance simply by providing the resources that their employees need. These resources can take many forms: money, time, staff, equipment, or other tangible assets. "So, Gene, you're confident that we can improve our cash flow if we throw a couple more clerks into collections? Okay, how about giving it a try."

✔ **Offer a helping hand.** For an employee who is learning a new job and is still responsible for performing his or her current job, the total workload can be overwhelming. Coaches can help workers through this transitional phase by reassigning current duties to other employees, authorizing overtime, or taking other measures to relieve the pressure. "John, while you're learning how to troubleshoot that new network server, I'm going to assign your maintenance workload to Rachel. We can get back together at the end of the week to see how you're doing."

Top five coaching Web sites

Wondering where to find the best information on the Web about the topics addressed in this chapter? Well, you've come to the right place! Here are our top five favorites:

✔ The Coaching and Mentoring Network: `www.coachingnetwork.org.uk/`

✔ International Coach Federation: `www.coach federation.org/`

✔ The Coaching Connection: `www.leader ship.gc.ca/static/coaching/`

✔ Fast Company Magazine: `www.fast company.com/online/05/coach2. html`

✔ About.com: `www.humanresources. about.com/cs/coachingmentoring/`

Part III
Making Things Happen

The 5th Wave   By Rich Tennant

"The next part of your performance evaluation will test your ability to handle a sudden crisis."

In this part . . .

Employees without goals are employees without direction. And after you set goals with employees, you have to measure employee progress to their goals. In this part, we address setting goals with employees, measuring employee performance, and conducting performance evaluations the right way.

Chapter 7

Goal Setting Made Easy

. . . .

In This Chapter

▶ Linking goals to your vision

▶ Creating SMART goals

▶ Concentrating on fewer goals

▶ Publicizing your goals

▶ Following through with your employees

▶ Determining sources of power

. . . .

Ask any group of workers, "What is the primary duty of management?" The answer "setting goals" is likely to be near the top of the list. If setting goals appears near the bottom of the list, you know there's a problem! In most companies, top management sets the overall purpose — the vision — of the organization. Middle managers then have the job of developing goals and plans for achieving the vision set by top management. Managers and employees work together to set goals and develop schedules for attaining them.

As a manager, you're probably immersed in goals — not only for yourself but also for your employees, your department, and your organization. This flood of goals can overwhelm you as you try to balance the relative importance of each one.

Should I tackle my department's goal of improving turnaround time first, or should I get to work on my boss's goal of finishing the budget? Or maybe the company's goal of improving customer service is more important. Well, I think I'll just try to achieve my own personal goal of setting aside some time to eat lunch today.

As you discover in this chapter, sometimes having too many goals is as bad as not having any goals at all.

Goals provide direction and purpose. Don't forget: If you can see it, you can achieve it. Goals help you see where you're going and how you can get there. And the *way* that you set goals can impact how motivating they are to others.

If You Don't Know Where You're Going, How Do You Know When You Get There?

Did you realize that Lewis Carroll's classic book *Alice in Wonderland* offers lessons that can enhance your business life? If you read this book when you were a child, you may recall the exchange between Alice and the Cheshire Cat about the importance of setting goals. Consider the following passage from Carroll's book, in which Alice asks the Cheshire Cat for advice on which direction to go.

"Would you tell me please, which way I ought to go from here?"

"That depends a good deal on where you want to go," said the Cat.

"I don't much care where — " said Alice.

"Then it doesn't matter which way you go," said the Cat.

" — so long as I get *somewhere*," Alice added as an explanation.

"Oh, you're sure to do that," said the Cat, "if you only walk long enough."

It takes no effort at all to get *somewhere*. Just do nothing, and you're there. (In fact, everywhere you go, there you are!) However, if you want to get somewhere meaningful, you first have to know where you want to go. And after you decide where you want to go, you need to make plans on how to get there. This practice is as true in business as in your everyday life.

For example, suppose that you have a vision of starting up a new sales office in Prague so that you can better service your Eastern European accounts. How do go about achieving this vision? You have three choices:

- ✔ An unplanned, non-goal-oriented approach
- ✔ A planned, goal-oriented approach
- ✔ A hope and a prayer.

Which choice do you think is most likely to get you to your goal? Go ahead; take a wild guess!

If you guessed the unplanned, non-goal-oriented approach to reaching your vision, shame on you! Please report to study hall. Your assignment is to write 500 times: "A goal is a dream with a deadline." Now, no talking to your classmates and no goofing off. We've got our eyes on you!

If you guessed the planned, goal-oriented approach, you've earned a big gold star and a place in the *Managing For Dummies* Hall of Fame! Congratulations!

Following are the main reasons to set goals whenever you want to accomplish something significant:

- ✔ **Goals provide direction.** For our preceding example (starting up a new sales office in Prague), you can probably find a million different ways to better service your Eastern European business accounts. However, to get something done, you have to set a definite vision — a target to aim for and to guide the efforts of you and your organization. You can then translate this vision into goals that take you where you want to go. Without goals, you're doomed to waste countless hours going nowhere. With goals, you can focus your efforts and your staff's efforts on only the activities that move you toward where you're going — in this case, opening a new sales office.

- ✔ **Goals tell you how far you've traveled.** Goals provide milestones along the road to accomplishing your vision. If you determine that you must accomplish several specific milestones to reach your final destination and you complete a few of them, you know exactly how many remain. That is, you know exactly where you stand and how far you have yet to go.

- ✔ **Goals help to make your overall vision attainable.** You can't reach your vision in one big step — you need many small steps to get there. If, again, your vision is to open a new sales office in Prague, you can't expect to proclaim your vision on Friday and walk into a fully staffed, and functioning office on Monday. You must accomplish many goals — from shopping for office space, to hiring and relocating staff, to printing stationery and business cards — before you can attain your vision. Goals enable you to achieve your overall vision by dividing your efforts into smaller pieces that, when accomplished individually, add up to big results.

- ✔ **Goals clarify everyone's role.** When you discuss your vision with your employees, they may have some idea of where you want to go but no idea of how to go about getting there. As your well-intentioned employees head off to help you achieve your vision, some employees may duplicate the efforts of others, some employees may ignore some tasks, and some employees may simply do something else altogether (and hope that you don't notice the difference). Setting goals with employees clarifies what the tasks are, who does which tasks, and what is expected from each employee.

- ✔ **Goals give people something to strive for.** People are typically more motivated when challenged to attain a goal that's beyond their normal level of performance — this is what's known as a *stretch goal*. Not only do goals give people a sense of purpose, but they also relieve the boredom that can come from performing a routine job day after day. Be sure to discuss the goal with them and gain their commitment.

For goals to be useful, they have to link directly to the final vision. To stay ahead of the competition, or simply to remain in business, organizations create compelling visions and then management and employees work together to set and achieve the goals to reach those visions. Look over these examples of compelling visions that drive the development of goals at several successful enterprises (which are, perhaps, even more important as they fight to thrive in the face of depressed telecommunications and technology sectors):

✔ Samsung is the $35 billion, Korean-based manufacturer of electronics, chemicals, and heavy machinery, as well as architectural and construction services. At Samsung, management created a clear and compelling vision that drives the goals of the organization. Samsung's vision is to become one of the world's ten largest "technological powerhouses."

✔ Motorola, long known for its obsession with quality, has set a truly incredible vision for where it wants to be in the next decade. Motorola has set a target of no more than two manufacturing defects per billion.

✔ Almost a century ago, the chairman of AT&T created this vision for the organization: the dream of good, cheap, and fast worldwide telephone service. Now, with the explosion of information technology creating incredible new opportunities for the telecommunications industry, AT&T has had to create a new vision. AT&T's new vision is to be a "major factor in the worldwide movement and management of information."

When it comes to goals, the best ones

✔ Are few in number, specific in purpose.

✔ Are stretch goals — not too easy, not too hard.

✔ Involve people — when you involve others, you get buy-in so it becomes their goal, not just yours.

Identifying SMART Goals

You can find all kinds of goals in all types of organizations. Some goals are short-term and specific ("starting next month, we will increase production by two units per employee per hour"), and others are long-term and nebulous ("within the next five years, we will become a learning organization"). Employees easily understand some goals ("line employees will have no more than 20 rejects per month"), but others can be difficult to fathom and subject to much interpretation ("all employees are expected to show more respect to each other in the next fiscal year"). Still others can be accomplished relatively easily ("reception staff will always answer the phone by the third ring"), but others are virtually impossible to attain ("all employees will master the five languages that our customers speak before the end of the fiscal year").

How do you know what kind of goals to set? The whole point of setting goals, after all, is to achieve them. It does you no good to go to the trouble of calling meetings, hacking through the needs of your organization, and burning up precious time, only to end up with goals that aren't acted on or completed. Unfortunately, this scenario describes what far too many managers do with their time.

The best goals are *smart* goals — well, actually *SMART* goals is more like it. SMART refers to a handy checklist for the five characteristics of well-designed goals.

- ✔ **Specific:** Goals must be clear and unambiguous; broad and fuzzy thinking has no place in goal setting. When goals are specific, they tell employees exactly what's expected, when, and how much. Because the goals are specific, you can easily measure your employees' progress toward their completion.

- ✔ **Measurable:** What good is a goal that you can't measure? If your goals aren't measurable, you never know whether your employees are making progress toward their successful completion. Not only that, but your employees may have a tough time staying motivated to complete their goals when they have no milestones to indicate their progress.

- ✔ **Attainable:** Goals must be realistic and attainable by average employees. The best goals require employees to stretch a bit to achieve them, but they aren't extreme. That is, the goals are neither out of reach nor below standard performance. Goals that are set too high or too low become meaningless, and employees naturally come to ignore them.

- ✔ **Relevant:** Goals must be an important tool in the grand scheme of reaching your company's vision and mission. We've heard that 80 percent of workers' productivity comes from only 20 percent of their activities. You can guess where the other 80 percent of work activity ends up! This relationship comes from Italian economist Vilfredo Pareto's 80/20 rule. This rule, which states that 80 percent of the wealth of most countries is held by only 20 percent of the population, has been applied to many other fields since its discovery. Relevant goals address the 20 percent of workers' activities that has such a great impact on performance and brings your organization closer to its vision.

- ✔ **Time-bound:** Goals must have starting points, ending points, and fixed durations. Commitment to deadlines helps employees to focus their efforts on completion of the goal on or before the due date. Goals without deadlines or schedules for completion tend to be overtaken by the day-to-day crises that invariably arise in an organization.

SMART goals make for smart organizations. In our experience, many supervisors and managers neglect to work with their employees to set goals together. And in the ones that do, goals are often unclear, ambiguous, unrealistic, immeasurable, demotivating, and unrelated to the organization's vision. By developing SMART goals with your employees, you can avoid these traps while ensuring the progress of your organization and its employees.

Although the SMART system of goal setting provides guidelines to help you frame effective goals, you have additional considerations to keep in mind. These considerations (explained in the following list) help you ensure that the goals, which you and your employees agree to, can be easily understood and acted on by anyone in your organization.

- ✔ **Ensure that goals are related to your employees' role in the organization.** Pursuing an organization's goals is far easier for employees when those goals are a regular part of their jobs. For example, suppose you set a goal for employees who solder circuit boards to "Raise production by 2 percent per quarter." These employees spend almost every working moment pursuing this goal, because the goal is an integral part of their job. If, however, you give the same employees a goal of "Improving the diversity of the organization," what exactly does that have to do with your line employees' role? Nothing. The goal may sound lofty and may be important to your organization, but because your line employees don't make the hiring decisions, you're wasting your time and their time with that particular goal.

- ✔ **Whenever possible, use values to guide behavior.** What is the most important value in your organization? Honesty? Fairness? Respect? Whatever it is, ensure that leaders model this behavior, and reward employees who live it.

- ✔ **Simple goals are better goals.** The easier your goals are to understand, the more likely the employees are to work to achieve them. Goals should be no longer than one sentence; make them concise, compelling, and easy to read and understand.

Goals that take more than a sentence to describe are actually multiple goals. When you find multiple-goal statements, break them into single, one-sentence goals. Goals that take a page or more to describe aren't really goals; they are books. File them away and try again.

Setting Goals: Less Is More

Peter remembers the scene as if it were yesterday. His organization had determined that it needed to develop a long-range, strategic plan. (Strategic planning was "in" at the time and seemed like a good thing to do.) The entire management team was marshaled for this effort — the team scheduled several all-day planning sessions, retained a high-priced consultant, and pronounced to the workers that something major was brewing at the top.

The management team threw itself wholeheartedly into the planning effort. The managers wanted to answer questions like:

- ✔ Why did the organization exist?
- ✔ Who were its customers?
- ✔ What were its values?
- ✔ What was its mission?
- ✔ What were its goals?
- ✔ How can the organization know when it achieves the goals?

Session after session, they had great idea after great idea. Before long, they had more than 12 poster-sized flip chart pages taped to the walls of the meeting room, each brimming with goals for the organization. "Improve customer service." "Provide quicker project turnaround." "Fix the heating and air conditioning system at corporate headquarters." And many more — in all, more than 200!

When the last planning meeting ended, the managers congratulated each other over their collective accomplishment and went back to their regular office routines. Before long, the goals were forgotten — the pages on which they were recorded neatly folded and stored away in someone's file cabinet. Meanwhile, business went on as usual, and the long-range planning effort went into long-term hibernation. Soon, the organization's employees who knew that the management team had embarked on a momentous process of strategic planning finally tired of asking about it.

Don't let all your hard work go for naught. When you go through the trouble of setting goals, keep them to a manageable number that can realistically be followed up on. And, when you finish one goal, move on to the next.

When it comes to goal setting, less is more.

The following guidelines can help you select the right goals — and the right number of goals — for your organization:

- ✔ **Pick two to three goals to focus on.** You can't do everything at once, and you can't expect your employees to either. A few goals are the most you should attempt to conquer at any one time. Picking too many goals dilutes the efforts of you and your staff and can result in a complete breakdown in the process.

- ✔ **Pick the goals with the greatest relevance.** Certain goals take you a lot farther down the road to attaining your vision than do other goals. Because you have only so many hours in your workday, it clearly makes sense to concentrate your efforts on a few goals that have the biggest payoff — rather than on a boatload of goals with relatively less payoff.

✔ **Focus on the goals that tie most closely to your organization's mission.** You can be tempted to take on goals that are challenging, interesting, and fun to accomplish but that are far removed from your organization's mission. Don't.

✔ **Periodically revisit the goals and update them as necessary.** Business is anything but static, and periodically assessing your goals is important to making sure that they're still relevant to the vision you want to achieve. If so, great — carry on. If not, meet with your employees to revise the goals and the schedules for attaining them.

The power of the annual goal at Marmot Mountain

When Steve Crisafulli was brought on a number of years ago as president of Marmot Mountain Ltd., a California-based producer of super high-quality outdoor clothing, he quickly discovered that Marmot was in big trouble. According to Crisafulli, Marmot "had no credit records, an unusable computer inventory system, and financial statements that were six months late. I had never before seen a company this screwed up from an operational standpoint." Crisafulli planned to develop specific goals to lead the company to his vision of profitability. However, the job wasn't done immediately, but one step at a time. "The way to run a small business is to concentrate on one or two small things," Crisafulli said.

The first problem to receive Crisafulli's attention was the firm's traditional difficulties making deliveries to customers on time. In one particularly bad example of Marmot's problems in this area, the entire winter clothing line — due to stores by Labor Day — was not delivered until January of the next year. As a result, business dropped precipitously. Soon, Crisafulli made timely delivery of Marmot products the firm's No.1 priority. Employees agreed to a goal of getting the next winter clothing line out no later than mid-September. To meet the goal, the management team implemented daily meetings, managers began to communicate with each other and with workers, quality control inspectors went out to check on key suppliers, and marketing budgets were increased.

"Most of what you lack in a small business is resources. People often say, 'I don't have enough money,' but the real thing you lack is time. People are doing a once-over-lightly on too many things. Trying to advance on too broad a front, they don't go anywhere," Crisafulli said.

To make a long story short, not only did Marmot achieve its goal, but also the entire winter clothing line was shipped out two weeks ahead of the mid-September deadline. Even today, the company and its president retain the single-mindedness that delivered it from the brink of disaster years ago. At its annual strategic meeting, Marmot's management team decides on one goal for the following year. According to Crisafulli, "It hasn't failed to work yet. That's the beauty of the system: If you focus on only one thing, it's not difficult to achieve. It's much easier than trying to meet 20 different goals." Amen.

(Source: *Inc. Magazine*)

Avoid taking on too many goals in your zeal to get as many things done as quickly as you can. Too many goals can overwhelm you, and they can overwhelm your employees, too. You're far better off if you set a few, significant goals and then concentrate your efforts on attaining them. Don't forget that management isn't a game of huge success after huge success. Instead, it's a daily meeting of challenges and opportunities — gradually, but inevitably, improving the organization in the process. Remember that too many goals can overwhelm you so set your goals accordingly.

Communicating Your Goals to Your Team

Having goals is great, but how do you get the word out to your employees? As you know, goals grow out of an organization's vision. Establishing goals helps you ensure that employees focus on achieving the vision in the desired time frame. You have many possible ways to communicate goals to your employees, but some ways are better than others. In every case, you must communicate goals clearly, the receiver must understand the goals, and the goals must be followed through on.

Communicating your organization's vision is as important as communicating specific goals. You can communicate the vision in every way possible, as often as possible, throughout your organization and to significant others such as clients, customers, suppliers, and so forth. And you need to be aware of possible obstacles: Often an organization's vision is pounded out in a series of grueling management meetings that leave the participants (you, the managers!) beaten and tired. By the time the managers reach their final goal of developing a company's vision, they are sick of it and ready to go on to the next challenge.

Many organizations drop the ball at this crucial point and are thereby slow to communicate the vision. Also, each succeeding layer of an organization has the natural tendency to draw some of the energy from the vision so that, by the time it filters down to the frontline employees, the vision has become dull and lifeless.

When you communicate vision and goals, do it with energy and with a sense of urgency and importance. You are talking about the future of your organization and your employees — not chopped liver! If your employees don't think that you care about the vision, why should they? Simply put, they won't.

Companies usually announce their visions with much pomp and fanfare. The following are different ways that companies commonly announce and communicate their vision:

✔ By conducting huge employee rallies where the vision is unveiled in inspirational presentations.

✔ By printing their vision on anything possible — business cards, letterhead stationery, massive posters hung in the office, newsletters, employee name tags, and more.

✔ By encouraging managers to "talk up" the vision in staff meetings or other verbal interactions.

To avoid a cynical "fad" reaction from employees who are suspicious of management's motives when unveiling a new initiative, consistent, casual reference to it is much more effective than a huge, impersonal event. Again, in this case, less is often better.

Goals, on the other hand, are much more personal, and the methods you use to communicate them must be much more formal and direct. The following guidelines can help you out:

✔ Make sure that the goals are written down.

✔ Always conduct one-on-one, face-to-face meetings with your employees to introduce, discuss, and assign goals.

If physical distance prohibits, or for any reason you can't conduct, a face-to-face meeting, conduct your meeting over the phone. The point is to make sure that your employees receive the goals, understand them, and have the opportunity to ask for clarifications.

✔ Call your team together to introduce team-related goals.

You can assign goals to teams instead of to individuals. If this is the case, get the team together and explain the role of the team and each individual in the successful completion of the goal. Make sure that all team members understand exactly what they are to do. Get them fired up and then let them have at it. We discuss the function of teams in more detail in Chapter 11.

✔ Gain the commitment of your employees, whether individually or on teams, to the successful accomplishment of their goals.

Ask your employees to prepare and present plans and milestone schedules explaining how they can accomplish the assigned goals by the deadlines that you agreed to. After your employees embark on the pursuit of their goals, regularly monitor their progress to ensure that they're on track and meet with them to help them overcome any problems.

Juggling Priorities: Keeping Your Eye on the Ball

After you've decided the goals that are important to you and to your organization, you come to the difficult part. How do you maintain the focus of your employees — and your own focus, for that matter — on achievement of the goals that you've set?

The process of goal setting often generates a lot of excitement and energy within employees — whether the goals are set in large group meetings or in one-on-one encounters. This excitement and energy can quickly dissipate as soon as everyone gets back to his or her desk. You, the manager, must take steps to ensure that the organization's focus remains centered on the goals and not on other matters (which are less important but momentarily more pressing). Of course, this task is much easier said than done.

Staying focused on goals can be extremely difficult — particularly when you're a busy person and the goals are added on top of your regular responsibilities. Think about situations that fight for your attention during a typical day at work:

✔ How often do you sit down at your desk in the morning to plot out your priorities for the day only to have them pushed aside five minutes later when you get a call from your boss?

Mike, I need you to drop everything and get to work on a report for the general manager right away! She has to have it on her desk by 3:00 p.m. today.

✔ How many times has an employee come to you with a problem?

Sorry, Mike, but I think you had better hear about this problem before it gets any worse. Jenny and Tony just had a fight and Jenny says she's going to quit. We can't afford to lose Jenny — especially not right now. She's the key to the development project. What are we going to do?

✔ Do you remember getting caught in a 15-minute meeting that drags on for several hours?

Are there any questions on steps 1 through 14 of the new recruitment process? Fine, now let's get started on steps 15 through 35.

In unlimited ways, you or your employees can fall off track and lose the focus that you need to get your organization's goals accomplished. One of the biggest problems that employees face is confusing activity with results. Do you know anyone who works incredibly long hours — late into the night and on weekends — but never seems to get anything done? Although this employee always seems to be busy, the problem is that he or she is working on the wrong things. This is called the *activity trap,* and it's very easy for you and your employees to fall into. "Help, I've fallen and I can't get out!"

Hallmark communicates its goals in many different ways

The management of Hallmark Cards, Inc., the world's largest producer of greeting cards, firmly believes in the value of communicating the organization's vision, goals, and vital business information to its employees. According to former Hallmark president and CEO, Irvine O. Hockaday, Jr., "The only sustainable edge for a corporation is the energy and cleverness of its people. To tap that, a chief executive must craft a vision, empower employees, encourage teamwork, and kindle the competitive fires."

To back up its commitment to getting the word out to employees, Hallmark developed an elaborate portfolio of formal employee publications. In addition to distributing a daily newsletter, *Noon News,* for all employees, Hallmark publishes *Crown,* a bimonthly magazine for employees, and a newsletter for managers titled *Directions.* However, Hallmark's commitment to communicating doesn't end with newsletters and magazines — when Hockaday worked at Hallmark, he regularly invited workers from throughout the organization to join him for a meal to share information.

We previously mentioned the general rule that says that 80 percent of workers' productivity comes from 20 percent of their activity. The flip side of this rule is that only 20 percent of workers' productivity comes from 80 percent of their activity. This statistic illustrates the activity trap at work. What do you do in an average day? More important, what do you do with the 80 percent of your time that produces so few results? You can get out of the activity trap and take control of your schedules and priorities. However, you have to be tough, and you have to be single-minded in pursuit of your goals.

Achieving your goals is all up to you. No one, not even your boss (perhaps especially not your boss), can make it any easier for you to concentrate on achieving your goals. You have to take charge, and you have to take charge now! If you aren't controlling your own schedule, you're simply letting everyone else control your schedule for you.

Following are some tips to help you and your employees get out of the activity trap:

- **Do your No. 1 priority first!** With all the distractions that compete for your attention, with the constant temptation to work on the easy stuff first and save the tough stuff for last, and with people dropping into your office just to chat or to unload their problems on you, concentrating on your No. 1 priority is always a challenge. However, if you don't do your No. 1 priority first, you're almost guaranteed to find yourself in the activity trap. That is, you're almost guaranteed to find the same priorities on your list of tasks to do day after day, week after week, and month after month. If your No. 1 priority is too big, divide it into smaller chunks and focus on the most important one of those.

✔ **Get organized!** Getting organized and managing your time effectively are incredibly important pursuits for anyone in business. If you're organized, you can spend less time trying to figure out what you should be doing and more time doing what you should be doing.

✔ **Just say no!** If someone tries to make his or her problems your problems, just say no! If you're a manager, you probably like nothing more than taking on new challenges and solving problems. The conflict arises when solving somebody else's problems interferes with solving your own. You have to constantly be on guard and fight the temptation to fritter your day away with meaningless activities. Always ask yourself, "How does this help me achieve my goals?" Focus on your own goals and refuse to let others make their problems your own.

Using Your Power for Good: Making Your Goals Happen

After you create a wonderful set of goals with your employees, how do you make sure that they get done? How do you turn your priorities into your employees' priorities? The best goals in the world mean nothing if they aren't achieved. You can choose to leave this critical step in the process to chance, or you can choose to get involved.

You have the power to make your goals happen.

Power has gotten a bad rap lately. In reaction to the autocratic leadership styles that often ruled the roost in many American corporations, employees have increasingly demanded, and organizations have increasingly provided, management that is principle-centered and that has a more compassionate, human face.

We believe that nothing is inherently wrong with power — everyone has many sources of power within them. And not only do you have power but you also exercise power to control or influence people and events around you on a daily basis. Generally, power is a positive thing. However, power can be a negative thing when abused. Manipulation, exploitation, and coercion have no place in the modern workplace.

You can use the positive power within you to your advantage — and to the advantage of the people around you — by tapping into it to help achieve your organization's goals. People and systems often fall into ruts or into nonproductive patterns of behavior that are hard to break. Power properly applied can jump-start these people and systems and move them in the right direction — the direction that leads to the accomplishment of goals.

Everyone has five primary sources of power, and each of you has specific strengths and weaknesses related to these sources. Recognize your strengths and weaknesses and use them to your advantage. As you review the five sources of power that follow, consider your own personal strengths and weaknesses.

- ✓ **Personal power:** This is the power that comes from within your character. Your passion for greatness, the strength of your convictions, your ability to communicate and inspire, your personal charisma, and your leadership skills all add up to personal power.

- ✓ **Relationship power:** Everyone has relationships with others at work. These interactions contribute to the relationship power that you wield in your offices. Sources of relationship power include close friendships with top executives, partners, or owners, people who owe you favors, and coworkers who provide you with information and insights that you would normally not get through your formal business relationships.

- ✓ **Knowledge power:** To see knowledge power in action, just see what happens the next time your organization's computer network goes down! Then you'll see who really has the power in an organization (in this case, your computer network administrator). Knowledge power comes from the special expertise and knowledge that you have gained during the course of your career. Knowledge power also comes from obtaining academic degrees (think MBA) or special training.

- ✓ **Task power:** Task power is the power that comes from the job or process that you perform at work. As you have undoubtedly witnessed on many occasions, people can facilitate or impede the efforts of their coworkers and others through the application of task power. For example, when you submit a claim for payment to your insurance company and months pass with no action ("Gee, we don't seem to have your claim in our computer — are you sure you submitted one? Maybe you should send us another one just to be safe!"), you are on the receiving end of task power.

- ✓ **Position power:** This kind of power derives strictly from your rank or title in the organization and is a function of the authority that you wield to command human and financial resources. Although the position power of the receptionist in your organization is probably quite low, the position power of the president or owner is at the top of the chart. The best leaders seldom rely on position power to get things done today.

If you're weak in certain sources of power, you can increase them if you want. For example, work on your weakness in relationship power by making a concerted effort to know your coworkers better and to cultivate relationships with higher ranking managers or executives. Instead of passing on the invitations to get together with your coworkers after work, join them — have fun and strengthen your relationship power at the same time.

Top five goal Web sites

Wondering where to find the best information on the Web about the topics addressed in this chapter? Well, you've come to the right place! Here are our top five favorites:

✔ Personal Goal Setting: `www.mindtools.com/page6.html`

✔ OPEN Small Business Network: `www10.americanexpress.com/sif/cda/page/0,1641,6259,00.asp`

✔ The Awesome Power of Goal Setting: `www.humanresources.about.com/library/weekly/aa121000a.htm`

✔ Goal Setting with Employees: `www.mapnp.org/library/emp_perf/goal_set/goal_set.htm`

✔ myGoals.com: `www.mygoals.com`

Be aware of the sources of your power and use it in a positive way to help you and your employees accomplish the goals of your organization. For getting things done, a little power can go a long way.

Chapter 8

Measuring and Monitoring Individual and Project Performance

*I*n Chapter 7, we discuss the whys and wherefores of setting goals. Setting goals — for individuals, for teams, and for the overall organization — is extremely important. However, ensuring that the organization is making progress toward the successful completion of goals (in the manner and time frames agreed to) is equally important. The organization's performance depends on each individual who works within it. Achieving goals is what this chapter is all about.

Measuring and monitoring the performance of individuals in your organization is like walking a tightrope: You don't want to overmeasure or overmonitor your employees. Doing so only leads to needless bureaucracy and red tape, which can negatively affect your employees' ability to perform their tasks. Neither do you want to undermeasure nor undermonitor your employees. This lack of watchfulness can lead to nasty surprises when a task is completed late, over budget, or not at all. "What? The customer database conversion isn't completed yet? I promised the VP of sales that we would have that job done two weeks ago!"

Please keep in mind that, as a manager, your primary goal in measuring and monitoring your employees' performance is not to punish them for making a mistake or missing a milestone. Instead you help your employees stay on schedule and find out whether they need additional assistance or resources to do so. Few employees like to admit that they need help getting an assignment done — whatever the reason. Because of their reluctance, you must systematically check on the progress of your employees and regularly give them feedback on how they're doing.

If you don't monitor desired performance, you won't achieve desired performance. Don't leave achieving your goals to chance; develop systems to monitor progress and ensure that your goals are achieved.

Keeping Your Eye on the Ball

The first step in checking your employees' progress is to determine the key indicators of a goal's success. If you follow the advice in Chapter 7, you set goals with your employees that are few in number and *SMART* (specific, measurable, attainable, relevant, and time-bound).

When you quantify a goal in precise numerical terms, your employees have no confusion over how their performance is measured and when their job performance is adequate (or less than adequate). If you measure performance in terms of the quantity of sprockets produced per hour, your workers know exactly what you mean. If the goal is to produce 100 sprockets per hour, with a reject rate of one or less, your employees clearly understand that producing only 75 sprockets per hour with 10 rejects is unacceptable performance. Nothing is left to the imagination, and the goals aren't subject to individual interpretation or to the whims of individual supervisors or managers.

How you measure and monitor the progress of your employees toward completion of their goals depends on the nature of the goals. You can measure some goals, for example, in terms of time, others in terms of units of production, and others in terms of delivery of a particular work product (such as a report or a sales proposal).

The following are examples of different goals and the ways you can measure them:

- ✔ **Goal:** Plan and implement a company newsletter before the end of the second quarter of the current fiscal year.

   Measurement: The specific date (for example, June 30) that the newsletter is mailed out (time).

- ✔ **Goal:** Increase the number of mountain bike frames produced by each employee from 20 to 25 per day.

   Measurement: The exact number of mountain bike frames produced by the employee each day (quantity).

> ✔ **Goal:** Increase profit on the project by 20 percent in fiscal year 2009.
>
> **Measurement:** The total percentage increase in profit from January 1 through December 31, 2009 (percentage increase).

Although noting when your employees attain their goals is obviously important, recognizing your employees' incremental progress toward attaining their goals is just as important. For example:

> ✔ The goal for your drivers is to maintain an accident-free record. This goal is ongoing with no deadline. To encourage them in their efforts, you prominently post a huge banner in the middle of the garage that reads "153 Accident-Free Days." And you increase the number for each day of accident-free driving.
>
> ✔ The goal of your fiscal clerks is to increase the average number of transactions from 150 per day to 175 per day. To track their progress, you publicly post a summary of each employee's daily production counts at the end of each week. As production increases, you praise the progress of your employees toward the final goal.
>
> ✔ The goal set for your reception staff is to improve the percentage of "excellent" responses on customer feedback cards by 10 percent. You tabulate the monthly counts for each receptionist and announce the results at department staff meetings. The department manager buys lunch for the receptionist with the highest total each month.

The secret to performance measuring and monitoring is the power of positive feedback. When you give positive feedback (increased number of units produced, percentage increase in sales, and so on), you encourage the behavior that you want. However, when you give negative feedback (number of errors, number of work days lost, and so on), you aren't encouraging the behavior you want; you're only discouraging the behavior that you don't want. Consider the following examples:

> ✔ **Instead of measuring this:** Number of defective cartridges
>
> **Measure this:** Number of correctly assembled cartridges
>
> ✔ **Instead of measuring this:** Number of days late
>
> **Measure this:** Number of days on time
>
> ✔ **Instead of measuring this:** Quantity of backlogged transactions
>
> **Measure this:** Quantity of completed transactions

You may wonder whether the feedback that you provide to employees regarding their performance should be public or private. What do you think? Do you put the information out for everyone to see, or do you get a better response by making the information confidential?

From our experience as managers, we find that you're much more likely to get the results you want when you put group performance measures (total revenues, average days sick, and so on) out in the open for everyone to see, but keep individual performance measures (sales performance by employee, tardiness rankings by employee, and so on) private. The intent is to get a team to work together to improve its performance — tracking and publicizing group measures, and then rewarding improvement can lead to dramatic advances in the performance you seek. What you do *not* want to do is to embarrass your employees or subject them to ridicule by other employees when their individual performance is not up to par. Instead, counsel them privately, and coach them (and provide additional training and support, as necessary) to improve performance.

Developing a System for Providing Immediate Performance Feedback

You can measure an infinite number of behaviors or performance characteristics. What you measure and the values that you measure against are up to you and your employees. In any case, keep certain points in mind when you design a system for measuring and monitoring your employees' performance. Build your system on the *MARS* system. MARS is an acronym for *milestones, actions, relationships,* and *schedules.* We describe each element of the MARS system in the following sections.

Setting your checkpoints: The milestones

Every goal needs a starting point, an ending point, and points in between to measure progress along the continuum. *Milestones* are the checkpoints, events, and markers that tell you and your employees how far along you are on the road to reaching the goals that you've set together.

For example, suppose that you establish a goal of finalizing corporate budgets in three months time. The third milestone along the way to your ultimate goal is that draft department budgets be submitted to division managers no later than June 1. If you check with the division managers on June 1 and they haven't submitted the draft budgets, you quickly and unambiguously know that the project is behind schedule. If, however, all the budgets are in on May 15, you know that the project is ahead of schedule and that you may reach the final goal of completing the corporate budgets sooner than you originally estimated.

Reaching your checkpoints: The actions

Actions are the individual activities that your employees perform to get from one milestone to the next. To reach the third milestone in your budgeting project, your employees must undertake and complete several actions after they reach the second milestone in the project. In this example, these actions may include the following:

- ✔ Review prior year expenditure reports and determine the relationship, if any, to current activities.

- ✔ Review current year-to-date expenditure reports and project final, year-end numbers.

- ✔ Meet with department staff to determine their training, travel, and capital equipment requirements for the new fiscal year.

- ✔ Review possible new hires, terminations, and pay raises to determine the impact on payroll cost.

- ✔ Create a computerized draft budget spreadsheet using numbers developed in the preceding actions.

- ✔ Print the draft budget and manually double-check the results. Correct entries and reprint if necessary.

- ✔ Submit the draft budget to the division manager.

Each action gets your employees a little farther along the way toward reaching the third milestone in the project — completion of draft corporate budgets by June 1 — and is therefore a critical element in your employees' performance. When developing a plan for completion of a project, note each action in writing. By taking notes, you make focusing easier for your employees because they know exactly what they must do to reach a milestone, how far they have gone, and how much farther they have to go.

Sequencing your activity: The relationships

Relationships are how milestones and actions interact with one another. Relationships shape the proper sequencing of activities that lead you to the successful, effective accomplishment of your goals. Although sequence doesn't always matter, it usually can be more effective to perform certain actions before others and to attain certain milestones before others.

For example, in the prior list of actions needed to achieve the third project milestone, trying to perform the fifth action before the first, second, third, or fourth is not going to work! If you haven't figured out the right numbers to put into your spreadsheet before you fill in the blanks, your results will be meaningless.

Learning to measure instead of count

According to management guru Peter Drucker, most business people spend too much time counting and too little time actually measuring the performance of their organizations. What does Drucker mean by this? Drucker is talking about the tendency of managers to be short-sighted in their application of management controls such as budgets. For example, most budgets are meant to ensure that company funds are spent only where authorized. They are control mechanisms that prevent spending from going out of control unnoticed by counting the number of dollars spent for a particular activity. However, Drucker suggests that, instead of using budgets only to count, managers can use them to measure things that are even more important to the future of the business. Managers can relate proposed expenditures to future results, for example, and provide follow-up information to show whether the desired results were achieved.

Drucker likens counting to a doctor using an X-ray machine to diagnose an ill patient. Although some ailments — broken bones, pneumonia, and such — show up on an X-ray, other, more life-threatening illnesses such as leukemia, hypertension, and AIDS don't. Similarly, most managers use accounting systems to X-ray their organization's financial performance. However, accounting systems don't measure a catastrophic loss of market share or a failure of the firm to innovate until it's already too late and the "patient" has been damaged — perhaps irretrievably.

However, keep in mind that you may have more than one way to reach a milestone and give your employees the latitude to find their own ways to reach their goals. Doing so empowers your employees to take responsibility for their work and to learn from their mistakes and successes. The results are successful performance and happy, productive employees.

Establishing your time frame: The schedules

How do you determine how far apart your milestones should be and how long project completion should take? You can plan better by estimating the *schedule* of each individual action in your project plan. How long does it take to review current year-to-date expenditure reports and project final, year-end numbers? A day? A week? How long does it take you to meet with all your staff members to assess their needs?

Using your experience and training to develop schedules that are realistic and useful is important. For example, you may know that if everything goes perfectly, meeting with all your employees will take exactly four days.

However, you also know that if you run into problems, the process can take as long as six days. Therefore, for planning purposes, you decide that five days is an appropriate schedule to apply to this particular action. This schedule allows for some variability in performance while ensuring that you meet the milestone on time.

Application of each characteristic — milestones, actions, relationships, and schedules — results in goals that you can measure and monitor. If you can't measure and monitor your goals, chances are that your employees will never achieve them and you won't know the difference. And wouldn't that be a shame?

Putting Performance Measuring and Monitoring into Practice

Theory is nice, but practice is better. So far we've discussed the theory of measuring and monitoring employee performance, but now how does measuring and monitoring really happen? Following are a couple of real-life cases for your reading pleasure. Each case takes a different path to achieve the same end: successful employee performance.

Case 1: World-class performance

Several years ago, before Bob started his own company, he took over his previous employer's product customization department. At the time, the department was in shambles — project management was haphazard at best, with no clear system of organization, and customers had to wait weeks or even months to receive their customized products, which often came to them with countless errors. Clearly, a change was needed, and Bob was given the task of straightening the mess out.

After reviewing the department's operations and collecting data from internal and external customers, Bob developed a checklist of tasks to do to bring the organization up to a world-class level of performance. At the heart of Bob's plan was a complete revamping of the department's system of measuring and monitoring performance.

Step 1: Setting goals with employees

The first two steps that Bob took after drafting a checklist of what he wanted to accomplish were to talk to the employees in his new department and to interview users. And everyone talked! By the time he finished collecting everyone's feedback, Bob had filled seven pages with negative comments about the department, work processes, finished products, and more. An example of the kind of problems that Bob's employees talked about was vividly illustrated on his first day in the office when a company salesperson called in some urgently needed changes to one of the projects completed the day before only to find out that the software version of that product was lost! Ouch!

All performance starts with clear goals. After Bob figured out exactly what was interfering with his employees' ability to do a good job, he discussed department needs and changes with them. Bob and the department agreed on a set of mutually acceptable goals and a game plan. Together, Bob and the employees set the stage for the next step in achieving world-class performance.

Step 2: Changing the performance-monitoring system

When he reviewed the department's systems for measuring and monitoring employee performance, Bob quickly noticed that the measurements were all negative. All the talk was about problems: late projects, the number of mistakes, backlogged orders, and so on. The department had no tracking of any positive performance measure.

Bob wanted to start some positive tracking to establish a baseline for performance and to build a positive momentum. He installed a new system that focused on only one performance measure — a positive one — the number of on-time projects. From only a few on-time projects when Bob took over, the department racked up an amazing 2,700 on-time projects (in a row!) by the end of two years. Not only did this tremendous increase in performance make Bob happy, but also the difference in the morale of his employees was like night and day. Instead of dreading the requests for customized products — and never having their efforts appreciated or "good enough" — they looked forward to the challenge of exceeding the high standards of performance that they'd set for themselves.

Step 3: Revising the plan

As project performance improved, Bob pushed for other improvements: 24-hour project quotes, project indexing, software storage, streamlining of royalty and invoicing systems, and more. At the same time that the improvements were planned and implemented, Bob walked a tightrope between balancing the long-term needs of system improvements with the short-term needs of getting the work done.

Before long, top management noticed what was going on in Bob's department. As the department's performance continued to improve, their work went from being a liability to the firm (that many salespeople refused to use) to being a major competitive advantage in the marketplace. By this time, the department completed 80 percent of its projects within two weeks after receipt, and the customization function became a leading competitive advantage — and revived products — for the company.

Case 2: Helping your employees give 100 percent

You may not always measure the results you want for your organization in terms of the number of widgets produced or the percentage increase in an employee's contributions to profitability. Sometimes you simply want your employees to show up on time and to at least seem to enjoy the eight or nine hours that they spend at work each day. If your employees' morale is poor, their productivity is likely to be poor, too.

A survey of employees at Cascades Diamond, Inc. that's cited in Bob's *1001 Ways to Reward Employees* showed that 79 percent of employees felt they weren't being rewarded for a job well done, 65 percent felt that management treated them disrespectfully, and 56 percent were pessimistic about their work. Not exactly the formula for a great company! Fortunately, company managers recognized that they had a problem (to say the least) and what follows is what they did to fix it.

Step 1: Create a program based on the behaviors you want

The first step the management of Cascades Diamond took was to create a brand new club in the company. They developed the 100 Club to reinforce the behaviors that management wanted to promote throughout the organization. These behaviors were

- Attendance
- Punctuality
- Safety

The plan was to award points to employees based on certain measurable criteria related to these behaviors. Any employee who attained a total of 100 points received an award — in this case, a nylon jacket with the Diamond Fiber logo and the words "The 100 Club" imprinted on it.

Step 2: Assign points to the desired behaviors

The next step was to assign points to each desired behavior. Depending on whether employees exhibit the desired behavior (or not), they can either receive points or have them taken away. For example, employees receive 25 points for a year of perfect attendance. However, for each full or partial day of absence, they have points deducted from their totals. Employees who go an entire year without formal disciplinary actions receive 20 points, and employees who work for a year without injuries resulting in lost time receive 15 points. Employees can also receive points for making cost-saving suggestions, safety suggestions, or participating in community service projects such as Red Cross blood drives or the United Way.

In assigning points to each behavior, management made sure that the number of points was proportionate to the behavior's importance to the organization. Furthermore, management ensured that, although the numeric goals weren't too easy to attain — that is, employees had to stretch themselves to reach them — they weren't impossible to reach and thereby weren't demotivating.

Step 3: Measure and reward employee performance

Measurement and reward of the desired employee behavior are the heart of Diamond Fiber's program. Supervisors and managers closely track the performance of their employees and assign points for each of the factors. When employees reach the coveted 100-point level, they're inducted into the 100 Club, and the jacket — and all the pride that goes along with it — is theirs.

You may think that this program is trivial — who really cares about getting a jacket with a company logo and three words, "The 100 Club," printed on it? Your employees, that's who! A local bank teller tells a story about a Diamond Fiber employee who once visited the bank to proudly model her new 100 Club jacket to bank customers and employees. According to the woman, "My employer gave this to me for doing a good job. It's the first time in the 18 years that I've been there that they've recognized the things I do every day."

Even more telling, in the first year of the program, Diamond Fiber saved $5.2 million, increased productivity by nearly 15 percent, and reduced quality-related mistakes by 40 percent. Not only that, but also 79 percent of employees said that their work quality concerned them more now than before the program started; 73 percent reported that the company showed concern for them as people; and an amazing 86 percent of employees said that the company and management considered them to be either "important" or "very important." Not bad results at all for a $40 baby blue jacket!

Gantts, PERTs, and Other Yardsticks

In some cases, measuring your employees' progress toward achieving a goal doesn't really take much. For example, if the goal is to increase the number of widgets produced from 100 per hour to 125 per hour, a simple count can tell you whether your employees have achieved that goal. "Sorry Stella, you're still averaging only 120 widgets per hour!" However, if the goal is to fabricate a prototype electric-powered vehicle in six months' time, the job of measuring and monitoring individual performance gets much more complicated and confusing.

Although you may decide to write out all the different milestones and actions (as we did in the corporate budgeting example earlier in this chapter), reading and understanding a graphical representation of the project is often much easier for complex projects. *Gantts, PERTs,* and other yardsticks perform this vital service for businesspeople around the world 24 hours a day, 7 days a week. *[Offstage, the music swells as cannons fire a 21-gun salute, troops pass in review, and high-octane fighter planes thunder over the throng.]*

Bar charts

Bar charts, also known as *Gantt charts* (named for that famous [*who?*] industrial engineer, Henry L. Gantt), are probably one of the simplest and most common means for illustrating and monitoring project progress. With a quick glance, a manager can easily see exactly where the project is at any given date and can compare actual progress against planned progress.

The three key elements of bar charts are the following:

- ✔ **Timeline:** The timeline provides a scale with which you measure progress. You can express the timeline in any units you want: Days, weeks, months, or whatever is most useful for managing the project. In most bar charts, the timeline appears along the horizontal axis (the *x-axis* for you math majors).

- ✔ **Actions:** Actions are the individual activities that your employees perform to get from one milestone to the next. In a bar chart, each action is listed — usually in chronological order — vertically along the left side of the chart (that's the *y-axis,* math experts!).

- ✔ **Bars:** Now, what would a bar chart be without bars? An "unbar" chart perhaps? Bars are the open blocks that you draw on your bar chart to indicate the length of time that a particular action is estimated to take. Short bars mean short periods of time; long bars mean long periods of time. What's really neat about bars is that, as an action is completed, you can fill in the bar — providing a quick visual reference of complete and incomplete actions.

We use our prior example again to illustrate the use of a bar chart. Figure 8-1 shows a typical bar chart; in this case, the chart illustrates the actions that lead up to the third milestone in the corporate budgeting example.

As Figure 8-1 shows, the timeline is along the top of the bar chart — just as we said it would be. In this example, the timeline stretches from April 15 to June 1, with each increment representing one week. The six actions necessary to reach the third milestone are listed vertically along the left side of the bar chart. Finally, you see those neat little bars that are really the heart and soul of the bar chart. Leave the bars unfilled until an action is completed; you may color them in now if you like.

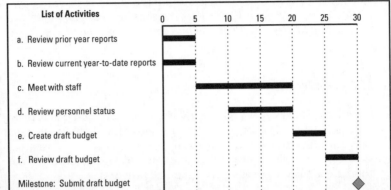

Figure 8-1:
A bar chart
illustrating
actions
leading up
to the third
milestone.

If all actions are completed according to the bar chart, the third milestone will be reached on June 1. If some actions take longer to complete than estimated, you may not reach the milestone on time and someone may end up in hot water. Conversely, if some actions take less time than estimated, the milestone can be reached early (sounds like a bonus is in order!).

The advantages of the Gantt chart are its simplicity, ease of preparation and use, and low cost. Although fine for a simple project such as preparing a budget, Gantt charts are generally unsuitable for large, complex projects such as building a space shuttle or doing your taxes.

Flowcharts

When the going gets tough, the tough get going — and they reach for their flowcharts. Although bar charts are useful for simple projects, they don't illustrate the sequential flow of actions in a project (and, therefore, aren't as useful for complex projects). On the other hand, *flowcharts* do a good job of illustrating this sequential flow. Although flowcharts look completely different than bar charts, they also have three key elements:

- ✔ **Actions:** In the case of flowcharts, arrows indicate actions. Arrows lead from one event to the next on a flowchart until the project is completed. The length of the arrows doesn't necessarily indicate the duration of an action. The arrows' primary purpose in a flow chart is to illustrate the sequential relationship of actions to one another.

- ✔ **Events:** Events, represented in flowcharts by numbered circles, signify the completion of a particular action.

- ✔ **Time:** Time estimates are inserted alongside each action (arrow) in the flowchart. By adding the number of time units along a particular path, you can estimate the total time for the completion of an action.

Figure 8-2 shows a flowchart of the corporate budgeting example illustrated in Figure 8-1. As you can see, the flowchart shows exactly how each action relates to the others. By following the longest path in terms of time, you can determine the *critical path* of the project. This kind of analysis is called the *critical path method (CPM)* and assumes that the time to complete individual actions can be estimated with a high degree of certainty. The CPM highlights the actions that determine the soonest that a project can be completed — in this case, 30 days.

PERT, short for *program evaluation and review technique,* is a variation of CPM used when the time to complete individual actions can't be estimated with a high degree of certainty. Using some very interesting statistical techniques (zzzzz . . .), PERT averages a range of possible times to arrive at an estimate for each action.

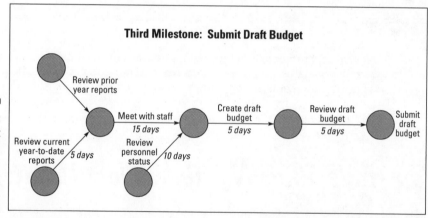

Figure 8-2:
A flowchart
for the
corporate
budgeting
example.

Software

Fortunately for those of you who missed out on taking calculus in 12th grade, the wonderful world of computers and software has now touched project monitoring and measurement. What you used to do with hours of drawing, erasing, redrawing, and so on, you can now accomplish with only a few well-placed keystrokes.

Microsoft Project, one of the foremost project-planning software packages on the market today, enables you to create and revise project schedules quickly and easily. Setting up a project with Microsoft Project is as easy as 1, 2, 3:

1. **Enter the actions to be completed.**

2. **Enter the sequence of the actions and their dependencies on other actions.**

3. **Enter the resources (people and money) required to complete the action.**

A project's six phases

Some management techniques are so popular that they're photocopied and passed from employee to employee and from company to company in an informal system of communication that outperforms the formal communication system of many organizations. These tongue-in-cheek lists, diagrams, and cartoons help many employees find humor in their own workplaces and brighten up their days. The following six phases of a project list has been floating around for years — our copy looks like it's at least fifth generation:

1. Enthusiasm

2. Disillusionment

3. Panic

4. Search for the guilty

5. Punishment of the innocent

6. Praise and honors for the nonparticipants

As a project progresses, you can input data such as actual start and completion dates, actual expenditures, and more to get a realistic picture of where the project is at any time. You can print out these results in the form of tables, charts, or graphs — whatever your preference — and then save them for future reference.

You Have Their Number: Now What?

You've set up your goals, you've set performance measures, and you've obtained pages of data for each of your employees. Now what? Now you determine whether the expected results were achieved, as follows.

- ✔ **Compare results to expectations:** What is the expected goal? Suppose that the goal is to complete the budget by June 1. When was the budget completed? It was completed on May 17 — well ahead of the deadline. Super! The mission was accomplished with time to spare.

- ✔ **Record the results:** Make note of the results — perhaps put them in the files that you maintain for each employee or print them out on your computer and post them in the work area.

- ✔ **Praise, coach, or counsel your employees:** If the job was done right, on time, and within budget, congratulate your employees for a job well done and reward them appropriately: A written note of appreciation, a day off with pay, a formal awards presentation — whatever you decide.

However, if the expected results were not achieved, find out why and what you can do to ensure that the expected results are achieved the next time. If the employees need only additional support or encouragement, coach them for a better performance. You can listen to your employees, refer them to other employees, or provide your own personal examples. If the poor results stem from a more serious shortcoming, counsel or discipline your employees. (More on this subject in Chapter 15.)

Top five project management Web sites

Wondering where to find the best information on the Web about the topics addressed in this chapter? Well, you've come to the right place! Here are our top five favorites:

- The PM Forum: www.pmforum.org/
- Gantt Chart and Timeline Center: www.smartdraw.com/resources/centers/gantt/
- The Balanced Scorecard Institute: www.balancedscorecard.org/
- American Productivity and Quality Center: www.apqc.org/
- Performance Measurement Association: www.som.cranfield.ac.uk/som/cbp/pma/

Chapter 9

The Fine Art of Performance Evaluations

In This Chapter

▶ Considering the importance of performance evaluations

▶ Developing performance evaluations

▶ Avoiding evaluation mistakes

▶ Making evaluations better

Timely and accurate performance evaluations are an extremely important tool for every business manager or supervisor. So if performance evaluations are so important to the successful management of employees, why do most managers and supervisors dread doing them, and why do so many employees dread receiving them? According to studies on the topic, an estimated 40 percent of all workers never receive performance evaluations. And for the 60 percent of the workers who do receive performance evaluations, most are poorly done. Very few employees actually receive regular, formal performance evaluations that are thoughtful, complete, and beneficial to the employee.

Ask any human resources manager: Are formal performance evaluations really necessary? The answer you get will likely be a resounding yes! However, if you look a little below the surface, the reality may echo something quite different. Although most managers consider performance evaluations a necessary tool in developing their employees, reinforcing good performance, and correcting poor performance, these evaluations are often too little, too late. They often miss the mark as tools for developing employees. If performance evaluations are done poorly, managers are better off not doing them at all — especially if by not doing evaluations, the alternative is more frequent coaching.

In this chapter, we consider the benefits of performance evaluations and explore the right and wrong ways to do them.

Evaluating Performance: Why Bother?

You can find many good reasons for conducting regular formal performance evaluations with your employees. Formal performance evaluations are just one part of an organization's system of delegation, goal setting, coaching, motivating, and ongoing informal and formal feedback on employee performance. If you don't believe us, try a few of these positive elements of performance evaluations on for size:

- ✔ **A chance to summarize past performance and establish new performance goals:** All employees want to know whether they're doing a good job. Formal performance evaluations force managers to communicate performance results — both good and bad — to their employees and to set new goals. In many organizations, the annual performance evaluation is the only occasion when supervisors and managers speak to their employees about performance expectations and the results of employee efforts for the preceding evaluation period.

- ✔ **An opportunity for clarification and communication:** You need to constantly compare expectations. In fact, try this exercise with your manager. List your ten most important activities. Then ask your manager to list what he or she considers to be your ten most important activities. Surprise! Chances are, your lists are quite different. On average, business people who do this exercise find that their lists overlap only 40 percent at best. Performance evaluations help the employer and employee to compare notes and make sure that assignments and priorities are in order.

- ✔ **A forum for learning goals and career development:** In many organizations, career development takes place as a part of the formal performance evaluation process. Managers and employees are all busy folks and often have difficulty setting aside the time to sit down and chart out the steps that they must take to progress in an organization or career. Although career development discussions should generally take place in a forum separate from the performance evaluation process, combining the activities does afford the opportunity to kill both birds with the same stone, or something like that.

- ✔ **A formal documentation to promote advancement or dismissal:** Most employees get plenty of informal performance feedback — at least of the negative kind. "You did what? Are you nuts?" Most informal feedback is verbal and, as such, undocumented. If you're trying to build a case to give your employee a promotion, you can support your case much easier if you have plenty of written documentation (including formal performance evaluations) to justify your decision.

The preceding list gives very important reasons for conducting regular formal performance evaluations. However, consider this statement: Many companies have paid a lot of money to employees and former employees who have successfully sued them for wrongful termination or for other, biased employment decisions. Imagine how lonely you'd feel on the witness stand in the following scene, a scene that's replayed for real time and again in courts of law around the world:

> **Lawyer:** So, Manager Framus, would you please tell the court exactly why you terminated Employee Dingdong?

> **Manager Framus (You):** Certainly, I'll be glad to. Employee Dingdong was a very poor performer — clearly the worst in my department.

> **Lawyer:** During the five years that my client was with your firm, did you ever conduct formal performance evaluations with Employee Dingdong?

> **Manager Framus (You):** Uhhh . . . well, no. I meant to, but I'm a very busy person. I was never quite able to get around to it.

> **Lawyer:** Manager Framus, do you mean to say that, in all the time with your firm, Employee Dingdong never received a formal performance evaluation? Exactly how was my client supposed to correct the alleged poor performance when you failed to provide Employee Dingdong with the feedback needed to do so?

> **Manager Framus (You):** Uhhhhh. . . .

Spelling Out the Performance Evaluation Process

Believe it or not, one of the very most important things you can do as a manager is conduct accurate and timely performance evaluations of your employees. As the old saying goes, feedback is the breakfast of champions — make it a regular part of your management diet!

Many managers, however, tend to see the performance evaluation process in very narrow terms: How can I get this thing done as quickly as possible so I can get back to my real job? (Whatever their "real" job is as managers.) In their haste to get the evaluation done and behind them, many managers merely consider a few examples of recent performance and base their entire evaluation on them. And because few managers give their employees the kind of meaningful, ongoing performance feedback that they need to do their jobs better, the performance evaluation can become a dreaded event — full of surprises and dismay. Or it can be so sugar coated that it becomes a meaningless exercise in management. This scenario isn't the right way to evaluate your employees!

The performance appraisal process is much broader than just the formal, written part of it. Here are five steps that help you encompass the broader scope of the process. Follow them when you evaluate your employees' performance:

1. **Set goals, expectations, and standards.**

   Before your employees can achieve your goals, or perform to your expectations, you have to set goals and expectations with them and develop standards to measure their performance. And after you've done all this, you have to communicate the goals and expectations before you evaluate your employees — not after. In fact, the performance review really starts on the first day of work! Tell your employees right then how you evaluate them, show them the forms to be used, and explain the process.

   Make sure that job descriptions are clear and unambiguous, and that you and your employees understand and agree to the standards you've set for them. This is a two-way process. Make sure that employees have a voice in setting their goals and standards.

2. **Give continuous and specific feedback.**

   Catch your employees doing things right — every day of the week — and tell them about it then and there. And if you catch them doing wrong (nobody's perfect!), then let them know about that, too. Feedback is much more effective when you give it regularly and often than when you save it up for a special occasion (known as *gunnysacking*, if the feedback is negative). The best formal performance evaluations contain the fewest surprises.

   Not only does gunnysacking have little effect on getting the performance that you want out of your employees, but also it can cost you their respect in the process.

3. **Prepare a formal, written performance evaluation with your employee.**

   Every organization has different requirements for the formal performance evaluation. Some evaluations are simple, one-page forms that only require checking off a few boxes — others are multipage extravaganzas that require extensive narrative support. The form often varies by organization, and by the level of the employee being evaluated (the ones you can buy at an office supply store are worthless!). Regardless of the requirements of your particular organization, the formal performance evaluation should be a summary of the goals and expectations for the evaluation period — events that you have discussed previously (and frequently!) with your employees. Support your words with examples and make evaluations meaningful to your employees by keeping your discussion relevant to the goals, expectations, and standards that you developed in Step 1.

As a collaborative process, have the employee complete his or her own performance evaluation. Then compare your (the manager's) comments with the employee's comments; the differences that you find become topics of discussion and mutual goal setting.

4. **Meet personally with your employees to discuss the performance evaluation.**

   Most employees appreciate the personal touch when you give the evaluation. Set aside some quality time to meet with them to discuss their performance evaluation. This doesn't mean five or ten minutes, but at least an hour or maybe more! When you plan performance appraisal meetings, less is definitely not more. Pick a place that's comfortable and free of distractions. Make the meeting positive and upbeat. Even when you have to discuss performance problems, center your discussions on ways that you and your employees can work together to solve them.

   Often performance appraisals and discussions can become defensive as negative elements are raised and the employee starts to feel that he or she will get little or no raise. Start with letting the employee share how his or her job is going, what's working — and what's not — then share your version, starting with the positive.

5. **Set new goals, expectations, and standards.**

   The performance evaluation meeting gives you and your employees the opportunity to step back from the inevitable daily issues for a moment and to take a look at the big picture. You both have an opportunity to review and discuss the things that worked well and the things that, perhaps, didn't work so well. Based on this assessment, you can then set new goals, expectations, and standards for the next review period. The last step of the performance evaluation process becomes the first step, and you start all over again.

When it comes to conducting performance appraisals, managers have plenty of things to remember; here are a few more:

- ✔ Communication with employees should be frequent so there are no surprises (okay, *fewer* surprises). You should give your employees informal feedback on their performance early and often.

- ✔ The primary focus of performance appraisals should be on going forward — setting new goals, improving future performance — rather than on looking back.

- ✔ Learning and development should always be included as a part of the performance appraisal process (although sometimes a discussion about pay raises can be separate).

Avoiding Common Mistakes That Evaluators Make

Evaluators can easily fall into certain traps in the evaluation process. To avoid making a misstep that may result in getting your foot stuck in one of these traps (ouch!), keep in mind these common mistakes that evaluators make:

✔ **The halo effect:** This happens when an employee is so good in a particular area of their performance that you ignore problems in other areas of their performance. For example, you may give your star salesperson (whom your firm desperately needs to ensure continued revenue growth) a high rating (a halo) despite the fact that she refuses to complete and submit paperwork within required time limits.

✔ **The recency effect:** The opposite of the halo effect, the recency effect happens when you allow an instance of poor performance to adversely affect your assessment of an employee's overall performance. For example, your administrative assistant has done a very good job for you in the months preceding his evaluation, but last week he missed a customer's deadline for submission of a proposal to continue with their advertising account. Your firm lost the account and you gave your assistant a scathing performance evaluation as a result.

✔ **Stereotyping:** This occurs when you allow preconceived notions about your employees to dictate how you rate them. For example, you may be convinced that women make better electronic parts assemblers than do men. As a result, your stereotyping automatically gives female employees the benefit of the doubt and higher ratings, while men have to prove themselves before you take them seriously.

✔ **Comparing:** Often, when you rate two employees at the same time, you can be tempted to compare their performances. If one of the employees is a particularly high performer, your other employee may look bad in comparison — despite his or her individual level of performance. Conversely, if one of the employees is a particularly low performer, the other employee may look really good in comparison. Make your assessment of an individual employee's performance and allow it to stand on its own two feet and not be subject to how good or bad your other employees are.

✔ **Mirroring:** Everyone naturally likes people who are most like themselves. That's why you can easily fall into the trap of rating highly those employees who are most like you (same likes, dislikes, interests, hobbies, and so forth) and rating lowly those employees who are least like you. Although this is great for the employees who you favor, the employees you don't favor won't like it. Take some advice. Don't do it.

Turning the tables: Upward and 360-degree evaluations

In recent years, a new kind of performance evaluation has emerged. Instead of the typical downward evaluation where managers review their workers' performance, the upward evaluation process stands this convention on its head by requiring workers to evaluate their managers' performance. If you think that getting a performance evaluation from your manager is uncomfortable, you haven't seen anything yet. There's nothing quite like the feeling you get when a group of your employees gives you direct and honest feedback about the things you do that make it hard for them to do a good job. Ouch!

However, despite the discomfort that you may feel, the upward evaluation is invaluable — who better to assess your real impact on the organization than your employees? The system works so well that Fortune 500 companies such as Federal Express and others have institutionalized the upward evaluation and made it a part of their corporate cultures. In a recent survey, almost 15 percent of American firms are using some form of the upward performance evaluation to assess the performance of their managers.

Also popular is the 360-degree evaluation, which companies such as Levi Strauss & Co. and Boeing Co use. Levi's 360-degree evaluation process dictates that all employees are evaluated by their supervisors and by their underlings and peers. The results can be quite a surprise to the lucky employee who is the subject of the evaluation who may find that other employees see him or her as less caring and visionary than he or she thought.

✔ **Nice guy/gal:** One reason that many managers dread doing performance evaluations is that it forces them to acknowledge the failings of their employees and then talk to their employees about them. Few managers enjoy giving their employees bad news, but employees need to receive the bad news as well as the good (just be ready to duck when you give them the bad news). Otherwise, they won't know where they need to improve. And if they don't know where they need to improve, you can bet they won't.

Realizing Why Evaluations Go Bad

From our experience, few employee evaluations are done well. Not only do managers write evaluations that lack any meaningful examples and insights, but they also fail to give the main process of the performance evaluation — the discussion — the time and attention that it deserves. And, further, performance evaluation meetings often become one-way presentations from manager to employee, rather than two-way discussions or conversations. As a result, performance evaluations often fail to have the kind of impact that the managers and supervisors who gave them intended.

Real apprehension can surround the evaluation process from both sides of the equation. Often, managers don't feel adequate to the task, and workers don't get the kind of timely and quality feedback that they need to do the best job possible. In addition, an underlying tension often accompanies the performance evaluation process and comes from the fact that most companies tie money and pay raises to performance evaluations. Evaluations that focus on the pay instead of on the performance, or the lack thereof, are not uncommon.

Why do so many performance evaluations go bad?

Don't drop the ball

To begin, although the performance evaluation process itself is pretty simple, a lot more goes into it than filling out a three-page form you get once a year to justify a salary action and then meeting with your employees for 15 minutes to give them the results of your assessment. The performance evaluation process begins on the day that your employees are hired, continues each and every day that they report to you, and doesn't end until, through transfer, promotion, or termination, they move out of your sphere of responsibility.

The entire process consists of setting goals with your employees, monitoring their performance, coaching them, supporting them, counseling them, and providing continuous feedback on their performance — both good and bad. If you've been doing these things before you sit down for your annual or semi-annual performance evaluation session with your employees, you're going to find reviews a pleasant wrap up and look at the past accomplishments instead of a disappointment for both you and your employees.

Don't be among the many managers who fail to give their employees ongoing performance feedback and, instead, wait for the scheduled review. Despite your best intentions, and the best efforts of your employees, assignments can easily go astray. Schedules can stretch, roadblocks can stop progress, and confusion can wrap its ugly tentacles around a project. However, if you haven't set up systems to track the progress of your employees, you may not figure this oversight out until too late. You end up mad, and your employees get black eyes because of their mistakes.

Call 911: I've been mugged!

Peter remembers one particularly large gunnysack that a manager dropped on him one bright and sunny morning. One day — a day that started out like any other — Peter picked up a folder from his inbox. The folder was stapled tightly shut, not uncommon in this organization, where all personnel actions were routed in folders. Still, the extra five or ten staples securing this particular folder did seem a bit much. Peter eagerly tore the folder apart to get to the pages that were nestled within its crimson leaves. Inside was a memo listing numerous examples of Peter's alleged dereliction of duty: projects completed late, errors that had brought the organization to a screeching halt, and other serious transgressions of his manager's expectations. Horrors!

After Peter recovered from the initial shock of getting mugged by the memo (all the while refraining from the overwhelming urge to dial 911), he noticed an interesting pattern. This pattern illustrates the shortcomings of the gunnysack method:

- First, the memo neglected to mention — even in passing — the 99 percent of the things that Peter and his department did right and on time day in and day out.

- Second, in the cases where projects were not completed to his manager's expectations, Peter's manager had not spelled out any expectations — either in advance or during the projects' course. It was the old "I'll let you know if that's not what I wanted" approach to management. Peter didn't know that he hadn't met his manager's expectations until after the fact, when it was too late to do anything about it. The body was already cold, and all that was left to do was bury it.

- Third, Peter's manager dropped the bomb and then went on to other things. The manager didn't schedule a follow-up meeting. Peter's manager didn't set any expectations. Nothing. Nada. The die was cast for the next round of unfulfilled expectations. Here we go again: *Management by ambush!*

Instead of checking up on Peter's progress along the way and coaching and supporting his efforts, Peter's manager instead chose to save up these alleged misdeeds and dump them squarely on Peter's lap all at once. Although this ambush clearly took a lot less time to accomplish than would setting up and administering an ongoing system of performance monitoring, evaluation, and feedback — or even a discussion, for that matter — the results were likely not what Peter's manager intended. Not only were the manager's expectations unmet (how could they be met if they weren't communicated?), but also no changes were made to ensure that the expectations would be met in the future.

Preparing for the No-Surprises Evaluation

If you're doing your job as a manager, the evaluation holds no surprises for your employees. Follow the lead of the best managers: Keep in touch with your employees and give them continuous feedback on their progress. Then, when you do sit down with them for their formal performance evaluation, the session is a recap of the things that you've already discussed during the

The Net speaks

In the following comments, conducted within the Managing People board of *Inc.* magazine's service on America Online, participants consider the pluses and minuses of different kinds of performance evaluations.

Bizzwriter (Peter Economy): "What is your opinion on that necessary evil of management, performance appraisals?"

Fizza (Arthur Manuel, Industrial Engineering/ Assembly Manager, Keithley Metrabyte Division of Keithley Instruments): "I must say that the type of review that has had the biggest impact on me was a review system called "Managing for Performance" (MFP). This type of review was done by getting input from my peers. Getting input from people on the same level is eye opening to say the least. You get a real feel for what kind of manager you are and what people think of your performance. The biggest problem with this type of review system is that it takes time to do."

Abben (James Dierberger, Owner, Synergetics): "As a project engineer, I once asked my supervisor why we didn't have subordinates evaluate their manager's skills at leadership. He said

there wouldn't be anything to learn by doing such a 'reverse' appraisal. Time marched on. I began having my staff do self-appraisals about three years before it was required. I did one and each of them did one. Then we went one-on-one and compared the two reviews. It was excellent! This isn't rocket science. All it takes is a little ingenuity and creativity and the interest in getting the best from your people."

MWEISBURGH (Mitchell Weisburgh, President, Personal Computer Learning Centers): "A few things to watch out for, though, are that sometimes there is a popularity contest. A manager may go out of the way to get employees to give him or her a good rating. Also, no matter how well you spell things out, each person grades on their own scale, so one group of people may think a 3 is really good, while another may regard anything less than a 4 as being poor. Finally, we tried having managers evaluated by other managers. This was a disaster. The responses indicated a real hidden agenda. More like, 'How will my career benefit if I rate this person well, or how if I rate this person poorly?'"

evaluation period, instead of an ambush. Keeping up a continuous dialog lets you use the formal evaluation to focus on the positive things that you and your employees can work on together to get the best possible performance.

Above all, be prepared for your employee evaluations!

Like interviews, many managers leave their preparation for performance evaluation meetings for the last possible minute — often just before the employee is scheduled to meet with them. "Oh, no. Cathy is going to be here in five minutes. Now, what did I do with her file? I know it's here somewhere!" The average manager spends about one hour preparing for an employee review that required an entire year of performance.

Performance evaluation is a year-round job. Whenever you recognize a problem with your employees' performance, mention it to them, make a note of it, and drop it in your employees' files. Similarly, whenever your employees do something great, mention it to them, make a note of it, and drop it in their files. Then, when you're ready to do your employees' periodic performance evaluations, you can pull their files and have plenty of documentation available on which to base the evaluations. Not only does this practice make the process easier for you, but also it makes the evaluation a lot more meaningful and productive for your employees.

Top five performance evaluation Web sites

Wondering where to find the best information on the Web about the topics addressed in this chapter? Well, you've come to the right place! Here are our top five favorites:

- Guide to Performance Management: www. hr.ucsd.edu/~staffeducation/ guide

- ZPG Performance Measurement Resources: www.zigonperf.com/performance. html

- Linkage, Inc.: www.linkageinc.com

- Introduction to Performance Appraisal: www. performanceappraisal.com/intro. htm

- Work911: www.work911.com/perfor mance/

Part IV
Working with (Other) People

The 5th Wave   By Rich Tennant

"I assume everyone on your team is on board with the proposed changes to the office layout."

In this part . . .

No manager is an island. Managers work with other people — clients, teams, coworkers, and higher-ups, to name a few — all the time. In this part, we introduce some key skills for communicating effectively with others, working with teams, managing virtual employees, and navigating the shifting waters of ethics and office politics.

Chapter 10

Getting Your Message Across

*H*ow important is getting your message across to your employees, peers, boss, clients, and customers? Very! You can't be a manager today without being able to communicate, and communicate effectively (well, at least not a very good manager).

You have more ways to communicate today than ever before, and many more are on the way. Only a couple of decades ago (yes, we do vaguely recall that ancient time), you had only a few different communications skills to master. Telephones, letters, face-to-face conversations, and the occasional speech or presentation were about it.

Now, however, you have all kinds of exciting and new ways to tell your counterpart on the other side of the world to take a hike. You have e-mail — both on local networks within companies and on the Internet — voice mail, voice pagers, conference calls, teleconferencing, faxes, wireless phones, satellite uplinks, satellite downlinks, and on and on. In fact, certain airlines now allow you to make telephone calls to individuals at their seats!

This chapter is about communicating with others and, in particular, the way in which you do it.

Understanding Communication: The Cornerstone of Business

Communication is all-important for the growth and survival of today's organizations. How big or how small the organization is doesn't matter — communication must be the cornerstone of every organization.

In business, communication takes place in a variety of formats. Table 10-1 shows you the order in which the bulk of business communication occurs. However, the formal training that most Americans receive in school reverses this order. Table 10-2 illustrates the focus of formal communication training.

Table 10-1	The Format of Business Communications
Communication Format	**Frequency of Use**
Listening	Most frequent
Speaking/Presentation	Next most frequent
Writing	Next most frequent
Reading	Least frequent

Table 10-2	Formal Education Provided in Communications
Communication Format	**Training Provided**
Reading	4 years English
Writing	4 years English
Speaking/Presentation	Optional class
Listening	Little formal training offered

As you can see, *informal* communication — not *formal* communication — is most important in business. Many managers fail because they don't understand this critical point. The occasional speeches you make, the beautifully crafted memos you write, and the many articles on chaos theory that you read don't have any effect on how you really communicate with your employees. You can make a difference when you talk to your employees one-on-one, face-to-face, day in and day out. Listening to them and really hearing what they have to say is vital.

Over the past couple of decades, a fundamental change in the style of business communication has occurred. Long ago, most business communication — whether verbal or in writing — was very formal and constrained. This style came out of the old view of business where workers were little more than cogs in a vast machine. In this obsolete view of business, the formal hierarchy — with bosses ruling strictly over workers — was everything. If a line worker had an idea that could make life better for a company's customers and save some money to boot, that worker had a right way and a wrong way to communicate the idea.

The right way was to write a formal memorandum to your boss. If your boss liked the idea, then he or she passed it up to the next level, and so on until it found its way to the top of the organization. If the big boss liked the idea, then the memo — probably rewritten several times by each manager along the way — received the stamp of approval and was passed back down the line for implementation. The process was slow and the procedure "proper."

The wrong way was to jump any of the steps in the formal hierarchy or to make the change without the explicit approval of the powers that be. Woe to the employees who strayed outside the approved lines of communication. They were renegades who were bucking the status quo.

Today, the way that businesspeople communicate has changed. In fact, the wrong way is now the right way. Business communication today is, above anything else, informal and nonhierarchical. Fast and furious. Quick and dirty. Sure, formal communication still has its place — contracts, licensing agreements, and nasty letters to wayward suppliers, for example. After all, three-quarters of a million American lawyers can't be wrong! (Or can they?)

The Cutting Edge of Communication

The explosion in information technology has brought with it numerous, often surprising and powerful new ways to communicate. Whether you like them or not, they're here, and they're here to stay. Not only are they here to stay, but also more are on the way. You can choose to ignore them and be left behind, or you can choose to leverage these new technologies to your advantage. What's it going to be for you? (See Chapter 19 on ways to harness the power of technology.)

Today's manager no longer needs to be in an office to communicate with clients and coworkers. You can be anywhere — using your wireless phone while at a restaurant or in your car, or dialing into the Internet while in bed at a remote cabin in the woods. All it takes is the right tools. The future is here and now.

You can communicate not only anywhere you want but anytime you want. Regular business hours used to be just that — regular. The office opened at 9:00 a.m., and it closed at 5:00 p.m., Monday through Friday. Until the introduction of the answering machine and voice mail, if you called outside those regular business hours, an answering service or a phone that rang and rang greeted you.

With the advent of e-mail, voice mail, fax machines, wireless phones, pagers, and overnight air delivery services, business is rapidly becoming a 24-hour-a-day, 7-days-a-week affair. You can leave a message at any time of the day or night at almost any business across the nation. If you're a voice mail user, you can access your date- and time-stamped messages remotely — from anywhere in the world that you can make a phone call. Then you can reply to them, forward them to coworkers, or archive them for future reference.

Although many corporations outfit their employees with wireless phones, pagers, portable computers, and such, they aren't doing so just to make life more convenient for their employees. Employers know that employees who have such equipment spend more of their personal time doing work. A study of individuals whose company provides them with telecommunications equipment indicates that these individuals work 20 to 25 percent more hours on their own time (whether or not this is a good thing for overworked employees is a different question altogether).

Hotels, airlines, and even car rental agencies have jumped on the bandwagon of universal communication, providing the tools and facilities for business travelers to stay connected with their clients. An example is the Hyatt Business Plan offered by the Hyatt Hotel chain. For a nominal charge over the standard room rate, the well-connected businessperson gets a personal work space and desk phone with no phone access charges, a computer hookup, and an in-room all-in-one fax/copier/printer. To sweeten the deal, Hyatt even throws in an express breakfast and morning newspaper.

Faster, more flexible, and more competitive

The 21st-century manager is a master of time and space. You know the old saying: "You can't be in two places at once." Although this statement may have been true years ago, the Information Revolution has brought about changes that have turned this worn-out cliché on its head. A manager, by using readily available, microprocessor-based tools, can be anywhere, anytime he or she wants.

Want to schedule meetings with customers in five different states, confirm their attendance, enter the meetings into your personal calendar, check all your notes, and then be reminded half an hour before each meeting — all while you relax in your hotel room in Miami? Piece of cake. Just tap out a message on your personal digital assistant (PDA), touch the on-screen icon, and you're on your way.

According to *Business Week,* technological innovation gives small businesses the edge over their larger competitors. As we show you, many of these advantages are a direct result of the innate ability of small firms to work faster than larger firms.

- ✔ Unfettered by bureaucracy and expensive existing information systems, small companies can implement new technologies more rapidly and effectively than their larger counterparts.

- ✔ As companies become electronically linked, outsourcing of functions, from accounting to product development by large companies creates many opportunities for highly skilled small shops.

- ✔ Electronic bulletin boards and online data services give small companies access to more market data and business opportunities than ever before, allowing them to quickly attack new opportunities.

- ✔ Cheap computer-aided design, manufacturing software, and flexible factories let small companies crank out multiple prototypes quickly and cheaply without large product development labs.

- ✔ Groups of small companies can easily use information links to form "virtual corporations," gaining market heft while enabling them to concentrate on what they do best.

- ✔ Mobile computing lets small companies compete around the world without setting up expensive branch offices.

Use the latest advances in computing and telecommunications technology to make your organization faster and more flexible. The faster that information is distributed and acted on within your organization, the more competitive and successful your business is.

Faxes and electronic mail

The *facsimile machine,* also known as a *fax,* has become a necessity for every serious business enterprise. A fax machine digitally transmits documents such as letters, reports, and photographs to another fax machine that then prints out a copy of the original document. The two communicating fax machines can be across the hall or halfway around the world from each other — it doesn't matter. Fax technology has now migrated to personal computers. Instead of printing a document first and then faxing it, you can now transmit and receive documents directly from personal computer to personal computer.

That Internet thing

On September 2, 1969, the group of 40-plus people crowded in a lab in Boelter Hall at UCLA had no idea that they were witnessing the birth of a vast communications network that would some 25 years later span all the continents and consist of millions of individual computers worldwide.

The Internet is a network of millions of host computers located in educational institutions, businesses, and research laboratories worldwide. Without question the largest computer network in the world, the Internet is used by an ever-growing number of individuals to send e-mail, weather maps, video clips, photographs, and a wide variety of other information to each other. What makes the Internet unique is that no one person or entity owns it. Rather, it exists because of the investment in computer resources of numerous organizations and the volunteer efforts of thousands of individuals and organizations that act as system managers.

Despite all the media attention, the Internet is not the be-all, end-all of the Information Superhighway. Other computer networks exist (accessible through their own dedicated telecommunications connections, or through Internet portals), and have for some time. CompuServe, America Online, and The Well are all commercial networks, also known as *online services* that allow users to tap into vast databases of information and chat live with other users worldwide. Each service has its own distinct personality. For example, The Well is known for its stimulating and uninhibited discussions on a variety of topics.

Each service is vying to offer the most attractive package of services for its users. As such, online services are quickly becoming essential to today's businesspeople. America Online, for example offers a wide variety of topics, electronic magazines, reference materials, and bulletin boards of interest to businesspeople, including a complete area dedicated to small businesses. This area contains information about starting a business, obtaining financing and assistance from the Small Business Administration, and bulletin boards to share information and advice with other small business owners.

Electronic mail, also known as *e-mail,* is similar to voice mail but is a text-driven message system instead of a voice-driven message system. With e-mail, users on a computer network can send and receive messages to and from each other and can attach document files to their e-mail messages. For example, if you're working on a draft report on product sales for your boss, you can attach a copy for her to review to an e-mail message that informs her of your progress. She can then make changes to the text file and return it to you along with a note thanking you for your hard work.

E-mail allows business people to be much more responsive than they ever dreamed possible by using the Postal Service. Not surprisingly, the online community refers to old-fashioned letters in an envelope with a stamp as *snail* mail. Although it may take several days for a standard letter to be delivered by the Postal Service from a city on the west coast of the United States to a city on the east coast, it takes only the push of a button, and a few seconds, for an e-mail message to be delivered to its destination.

Use fax machines and e-mail to make the transmission of information instantaneous. Your organization operates faster and is more responsive to client needs as a result.

According to Andrew S. Grove, chairman of Intel, "Companies that use e-mail are much faster, much less hierarchical. There are two companies — one that operates this way and one that doesn't . . . you're either going to do it or you disappear" (*Business Week*).

Portable computers and personal digital assistants

Personal digital assistants, or *PDAs,* combine the features of a computer, a fax machine, a modem, wireless communication, and handwriting recognition into a small (about the size of a thin paperback book) battery-operated package. Instead of having to deal with the standard typewriter keyboard of most computers, PDAs allow you to write your input on the work surface with a special stylus or through nifty little keyboards that unfold and attach to the bottom of the PDA. As the first digital tool to combine all the best elements of the Information Age along with true portability, the PDA has opened new avenues for the businessperson on the move.

What is bringing the ultimate communication device even closer is the continued integration of all the aforementioned systems — personal computers, fax, e-mail, wireless phones, and so on — into a coherent business system where the whole is much greater than the sum of its parts. The *connectivity* of computers and other digital devices is bringing business to a new level of sophistication as information can be generated, edited, transmitted, reviewed, and acted upon — through a wide variety of platforms — without ever being printed onto paper. Connectivity is the capability of using different electronic devices to interface and communicate with each other. The clearly defined distinctions that separated different platforms (like computers from phones) are blurring and become increasingly meaningless — today, you can even make phone calls from your PC over the Internet.

For example, Peter's Sony Vaio laptop computer combines all the following functions into a 5-pound battery-operated package that's about the same size as a paper-based personal planner: computer, fax machine, telephone, voice mail center, word processor, e-mail box, personal calendar/scheduler, contact manager, and (Peter's personal favorite) 3-D pinball machine. If Peter needs to fax a document or connect to the Internet, he simply plugs in a phone cord, touches a button or two, and the computer does the rest. Anywhere, anytime. Having lugged it all over Europe while he was working on his book *Leadership Ensemble: Lessons in Collaborative Management from the World's Only Conductorless Orchestra,* Peter definitely knows this to be the case.

With portable computers and PDAs, you can take your office with you — anywhere you want it to be. Use portable computers and PDAs to get your employees out of their offices and into your customers' offices, where they can have the greatest impact on your organization's bottom line.

Voice mail and pagers

Answering machines are such a ubiquitous part of our culture that, although having one was once considered a novelty, not having an answering machine is now the novelty. The Information Revolution has taken the basic idea of the answering machine and increased its power a thousand fold. The result is *voice mail.* Voice mail is a computer-based digital system that allows a telephone caller to leave messages and allows the user to extensively manage those messages. For example, the user of a voice mail system has the ability to take a phone message and forward it, along with a personal message, to another voice mail user. If the caller is also on the voice mail system, the user can send a verbal response directly to the caller's own mailbox, and even record and broadcast messages to lists of selected voice mailboxes.

Most of the recent excitement in the new era of telecommunications has centered on *wireless communications.* Wireless communications systems work by utilizing radio, infrared, or other electromagnetic frequencies to transmit and receive information. Although wireless communication isn't a new concept — radio and television have been around for decades — the conversion of devices such as telephones, computers, and other business staples into digital wireless communications tools has generated the most excitement.

The *pager* is one of the first digital wireless communications devices to gain widespread acceptance in the business world. A pager is a small radio receiver — smaller than a deck of playing cards — that displays the phone number of a caller. To complete the communication, the pager owner then calls the phone number displayed on the pager. More advanced (and more expensive) models can also display a caller's message or record voice messages. Pagers are very portable, and with the use of an array of satellites circling the earth, can receive messages almost anywhere. Particularly interesting are the latest generation of pagers that can both receive and send messages.

Voice mail and pagers allow you to send and receive messages anywhere, anytime, and be notified when you receive messages. Use these systems to keep your employees in better touch with their coworkers and your clients.

Wireless phones

Increasingly, communication between devices is being conducted without wires. According to AT&T product manager Lisa Pierce, "Right now we have a physical wire from phone company to house, and that wire does one thing at a time. It does that one thing at a relatively low speed." Wireless communication bypasses the physical limitations of wires and allows for a brave new world of offerings by service providers."

The *wireless telephone* advanced the progress of wireless communications considerably. A wireless telephone is a portable, battery-operated device that broadcasts on a special high frequency radio band. Although wireless phones were once little more than expensive status symbols, prices have plunged, and wireless phones are now essential tools to the mobile businessperson.

The wireless phone brought more than just another gadget into the lives of the modern businessperson — it brought freedom, too. It created freedom to conduct business outside of the constraints of the normal office environment — unchained from desks, phones, and old, worn-out paradigms. Says Mark Adler, a Washington, D.C. publishing agent, "It lets me have my office anywhere I happen to be" (*Business Week*). According to Adler, he once used a wireless telephone to close a publishing deal while watching his daughter play at a local playground.

Wireless phones can make you more accessible to your coworkers and clients. Make sure that your employees have these tools so that they can communicate easily and affordably with business associates.

Videoconferencing and electronic meetings

Not too many years ago, if you wanted to have a meeting with your design team members in Boston, production engineers in Toronto, and vendors scattered all about the countryside, you had to all fly or drive to a central location for the meeting. Hours of travel and thousands of dollars later, you all gathered in the same place at the same time. Heaven help you if you left something important back at the office!

Once again, computers have saved the day. With a computer, a video camera, and some special software, you can create your very own videoconference — live and in living color! Phones are okay for conducting business, but sometimes you need to be able to see what your client is trying to describe to you. And sometimes your counterpart needs to see what the heck you're trying to say. Thus the miracle of videoconferencing. Which do you prefer, Option A or Option B?

> ✔ **Option A:** "Okay, Bob, I just made the changes to the sales figures and printed out a new graph. Now, sales rose 39.5 percent in 2005 to $45.5 million. Our Northwestern sales office led the surge. In the first quarter of 2006 we saw a decline to an annualized figure of $39.1 million in sales, primarily due to weak sales out of the South Central and North Central sales offices that were off target by a combined total of $4.2 million. The second quarter looks a lot better. It looks like we're back on track with an annualized number of $44.7 million. Did you get all that, Bob?"

> ✔ **Option B:** "Okay, Bob, I just made the changes to the sales figures and printed out a new graph — you should be able to see it now on your computer monitor. Do you have any questions?"

Similarly, you can link together large groups of individuals into *virtual* meetings, where everyone can see and speak to each other in real time. Now you never have to get stuck in another airport waiting for your late flight or endure another night on a lumpy mattress in some nameless town in the middle of nowhere. Unless, of course, that's your idea of fun. Just turn on your computer, fire up the video camera, and meet to your heart's content!

Videoconferencing is rapidly becoming more common as computers and telecommunications systems become more powerful. Use it to set up meetings of employees at different locations — whether across town or around the world. You can save substantial amounts of both time and money.

Use technology — don't let it use you! Keep to your purpose of communicating and avoid processing information and people with it.

Listening

The communication equation has two sides. The previous section discussed the side that most people think about when they hear the word "communication" — the doing side. However, just as important is the other side of the equation — the listening side.

You're a busy person. You probably have 10 million things on your mind at any given time: the proposal you have to get out before 5:00 p.m. today; the budget spreadsheets that don't seem to add up; lunch. And if that isn't enough already, someone is in your office gibber jabbering about the latest rumors at corporate. "Did you hear that Sandy is on the way out?" With all the distractions, you sometimes have the habit of tuning out your coworkers. "Huh? Sandy just got promoted?"

Stop!

When you don't give the person on the other side of your desk your full attention, you shortchange both you and the other person. Not only do you miss out on getting the message, but also your inattention sends its own special message: "I don't really care what you have to say." Is that the message that you really want to convey? When you listen actively, you increase the likelihood that you understand what the other person is saying. Depending on what you're talking about, understanding can be quite important.

Don't leave listening to chance. Communication is a two-way street and you have to do your part. Be an active listener. When someone has something to say to you, make a decision to either participate in the communication, or let the other person know that you're busy and have to get back to him or her later. "Sorry, Tony, I've got to get these numbers together before lunch. Can we get together later this afternoon?" If you decide to communicate, then clear your mind of all its distractions. Forget for a moment the proposal that has to go out in a few hours, the spreadsheets, and that growling in the pit of your stomach. Give the other person your full attention.

Of course, making an effort to give your full attention is easier said than done. How can you focus on the other person and not allow all the people and tasks that are vying for your attention distract you? You have a tough job, but someone has to do it. And that someone is you! The following tips may help:

- ✔ **Express your interest:** One of the best listening techniques is to be interested in what your counterpart has to say. For example, give your counterpart your full attention and ask questions that clarify what he or she has to say. You can say, "That's really interesting. What brought you to that particular conclusion?" There is no bigger turn-off to communication than for you to yawn, look around the room aimlessly, or otherwise show that you're not interested in what your coworker is saying. The more interest you show your counterpart, the more interesting he or she becomes.

- ✔ **Maintain your focus:** People speak at the rate of approximately 150 words per minute. However, people think at approximately 500 words per minute. This gap leaves a lot of room for your mind to wander. Make a point of keeping your mind focused on listening to what the other person has to say. If your mind starts to wander, then rein it back in right away.

- ✔ **Ask questions:** If something is unclear or doesn't make sense to you, then ask questions to clarify the subject. Not only does this practice keep communication efficient and accurate, but it also demonstrates to the speaker that you're interested in what he or she has to say. *Reflective listening* — summarizing what the speaker has said and repeating it back to him or her — is a particularly effective way of ensuring accuracy in communication and demonstrating your interest. For example, you can say, "So you mean that it's your belief that we can sell our excess capacity to other firms?"

- ✔ **Seek the key points:** What exactly is your counterpart trying to tell you? Anyone can easily get lost in the forest of details of a conversation and miss seeing the trees as a result. As you listen, make a point of categorizing what your speaker has to say into information that is key to the discussion and information that isn't really relevant. If you need to ask questions to help you decide which is which, then don't be shy — ask away! "What does that have to do with meeting our goals?"

- ✔ **Avoid interruptions:** Although asking clarifying questions or employing reflective listening techniques is okay, constantly interrupting the speaker or allowing others to do so is not okay. When you're having a conversation with an employee, make him or her the most important thing in your life at that moment. If someone telephones you, don't answer it — that's what voice mail is for, after all. If someone knocks on your door and asks whether he or she can interrupt, say no, but that you can talk after you finish your current conversation. If your building is on fire, then you may interrupt the speaker.

✔ **Listen with more than your ears:** Communication involves a lot more than the obvious, verbal component. According to communications experts, up to 90 percent of the communication in a typical conversation is nonverbal! Facial expressions, posture, position of arms and legs, and much more add up to the nonverbal component of communication. Because this is the case, you must use all your senses when you listen — not just your ears.

✔ **Take notes:** Remembering all the details of an important conversation hours, days, or weeks after it took place can be quite difficult. Be sure to take notes when necessary. Jotting down notes can be a terrific aid to listening and remembering what was said. Plus, when you review your notes later, you can take the time to organize what was said and make better sense of it.

By practicing the preceding listening habits, you understand the message, and your coworkers appreciate the fact that you consider them important enough to give them your full attention. So listen early and listen often.

Harnessing the Power of the Written Word

At first glance, you may think that the Information Revolution has made the written word less important. Nothing is farther from the truth. Indeed, instead of making the written word less important, the Information Revolution has merely increased the variety of written media at your beck and call and increased the speed at which the written word travels. Writing well in business is more important than ever — you need to write concisely and with impact.

Regardless of whether you're writing a one-paragraph e-mail message or a 100-page report for your boss, business writing shares common characteristics. Review the list of writing tips that follows and don't forget to practice these tips every opportunity you get. The more you write, the better you get at it. So write, write, and then write some more.

✔ **What's the point? (Get to it!):** Before you set pen to paper (or fingertip to keyboard), think about what you want to achieve. What information are you trying to convey, and what do you want the reader to do as a result? Who is your audience, and how can you best reach it?

✔ **Get organized:** Organize your thoughts before you start to write. Jotting down a few notes or creating a brief outline of your major points may be beneficial. Bounce your ideas off coworkers and business associates or find other ways to refine them and get the all-important reality check.

✔ **Write the same way that you speak:** Written communication and spoken communication have a lot more in common than many people think — the best writing most closely resembles normal, everyday speech. Writing that is too formal or stilted is less accessible and harder to understand than conversational writing. Although this doesn't mean that you should start using slang like "gonna" and "ain't" in your reports and memos, it does mean you should loosen up!

✔ **Make it brief and concise:** Write every word with a purpose. Make your point, support it, and then move on to the next point. Don't, repeat, don't fill your memos, letters, and other correspondence with needless fluff simply to give them more weight or to make them seem more impressive. If you can make your point in three sentences, then don't write three paragraphs or three pages to accomplish the same goal.

✔ **Keep it simple:** Simplicity is a virtue. Avoid the tendency to use a 50-cent word when a simpler one works. Be alert to the proliferation of cryptic acronyms and jargon that mean nothing outside of a small circle of industry insiders and replace them with more common terminology whenever possible.

✔ **Write and then rewrite:** Few writers can get their thoughts into writing perfectly on the first try. The best approach is to write your first draft without worrying too much about whether you've completed it perfectly. Next, read through your draft and edit it for content, flow, grammar, and readability. Keep polishing your work until it shines.

✔ **Convey a positive attitude:** No one likes to read negative memos, letters, reports, or other business writing. Instead of making the intended points with their intended targets, negative writing often only reflects poorly on its author, and the message gets lost in the noise. Be active, committed, and positive in your writing. Even when you convey bad news, your writing can indicate that a silver lining follows even the worst storm.

Those of you who are interested in developing better writing skills can find plenty of books to help. However, Peter still swears by the timeworn 1971-vintage printing of *The Elements of Style,* by William Strunk, Jr. and E.B. White, which he bought in 7th grade. The book's advice is timeless, the writing direct and compelling. Consider Rule 13:

> ***Omit needless words.*** Vigorous writing is concise. A sentence should contain no unnecessary words, a paragraph no unnecessary sentences, for the same reason that a drawing should have no unnecessary lines and a machine no unnecessary parts. This requires not that the writer make all his sentences short, or that he avoid all detail and treat his subjects only in outline, but that every word tell.

Making Presentations

Although many people may dread the idea of standing up in front of a group of people, the ability to give oral presentations, speeches, and the like is a key skill for managers. Of course, some managers already know the value of being able to give effective presentations.

Preparing to present

When you see great speakers or presenters in action, you may think that because of their extraordinary skill, making a presentation takes little preparation on their part. This is kind of like saying that because an Olympic gymnast makes her floor routine look so perfect and so easy, she never has to practice it. What you don't see are the years of almost daily preparation that lead to her 90 seconds of glory.

Preparation is the key to giving a great presentation. The following tips can help you in preparing your presentation:

✔ **Determine what you want to accomplish:** Briefly outline the goals of your presentation. What exactly do you want to accomplish? Are you trying to convince decision makers that they should give you a bigger budget or extend your deadline to design a product that actually works? Are you seeking to educate your audience or to train employees in a new procedure? Are you presenting awards to employees in a formal ceremony? Each kind of presentation requires a different approach; tailor your approach accordingly.

✔ **Develop the heart of your presentation:** Build an outline of the major points that you want to communicate to your audience. Under each point, note any subpoints that are important to support your presentation. Don't try to accomplish too much; keep your major points down to no more than a few. Sketch out any visual aids that you need to reinforce and communicate the ideas that you're presenting verbally.

✔ **Write the introduction and conclusion:** After you finish the heart of your presentation, you can decide on your introduction and conclusion. Make the introduction accomplish three goals:

• Tell your audience what they're going to gain from your presentation.

• Tell your audience why the presentation is important to them.

• Get your audience's attention.

The conclusion is just as important, as is the final punctuation — the period — of your presentation. Write your conclusion to accomplish three objectives:

- Briefly summarize your key points.
- Refer your listeners back to the introduction.
- Inspire your audience.

✔ **Prepare your notes:** Preparing notes to use as an aid in your presentation is always a good idea. Not only do notes help you find your way when you get lost — helping to build your confidence — but they also ensure that you cover all the topics that you planned to cover. Write brief, but specific notes. The idea is for notes to trigger your thoughts on each key point and subpoint, not to be a word-for-word script.

✔ **Practice makes perfect:** After you sketch out your presentation, practice it. Depending on your personal situation, you may be comfortable simply running through your notes a few times the night before the big event. Alternately, you may want to rehearse your presentation in front of a coworker or even a video camera so that you can review it at your leisure. Don't forget: The more presentations you make, the better you get at it.

Make the most of the time that you have before your presentation — doing so pays off in a big way when it comes time to get up in front of your audience and start your performance.

A picture is worth a thousand words

Studies show that approximately 85 percent of all information received by the human brain is received visually. Think about that statistic the next time you make a presentation. Although your spoken remarks may convey a lot of valuable information, your audience is likely to remember more of the information when you present it to them visually.

Consider the following example. Once Peter was called to make a presentation to his company's executive team. Peter's task was to present the most recent financial performance of the company's Western Group. Faced with piles and piles of financial data stacked high to the ceiling, Peter realized that he had to find a way to present the essence of his message without getting himself and his audience lost in the details.

Figure 10-1 illustrates what some of the financial data looked like in a spreadsheet format. As a little extra incentive, Peter had seen what happened to managers who tried to present and explain lots of numbers: They tripped over their tongues and then lost their way. Not a pretty sight!

Western Group Financials

	Past Year	Current Year
Direct Labor	$19,887,000	$21,896,000
Fringe Benefits	$7,504,000	$8,259,000
Overhead Applied	$9,945,000	$10,938,000
Cost of Money	$13,000	$14,000
Travel	$2,801,000	$1,952,000
Other Direct Cost	$278,000	$356,000
G&A Applied	$4,973,000	$5,475,000
Total	$45,401,000	$48,890,000

Figure 10-1: Financial data in spreadsheet format.

Anyway, instead of developing an extensive spoken presentation, Peter had his controller develop a simple bar graph that summarized the piles of financial information visually. Then, he had the bar graph transferred to a transparency for projection onto a screen. The graph compared current year performance against past year performance, and it contained only the information essential to decision makers. Figure 10-2 shows the vastly improved bar graph version of the same financial information.

When Peter made his presentation, he kept his remarks brief, concentrating instead on walking his audience through the bar graphs. Sure, Peter may have given a highly detailed presentation of the numbers, but the results would have been more talk and less communication, a lot of wasted time, and a very numb group of executives! Instead, by using a simple visual presentation, Peter's audience grasped his message quickly and easily, and they concentrated on the message instead of the medium.

Here is the Nelson/Economy axiom of visual learning:

If you don't see it, you can't believe it (and you sure won't remember it!).

So how does this impact your presentations? Whenever possible, think of ways to present your information visually. The following are just a few of your options:

- ✔ Photographs
- ✔ Charts
- ✔ Displays
- ✔ Product samples
- ✔ Prototypes
- ✔ Role plays
- ✔ Graphs
- ✔ Maps

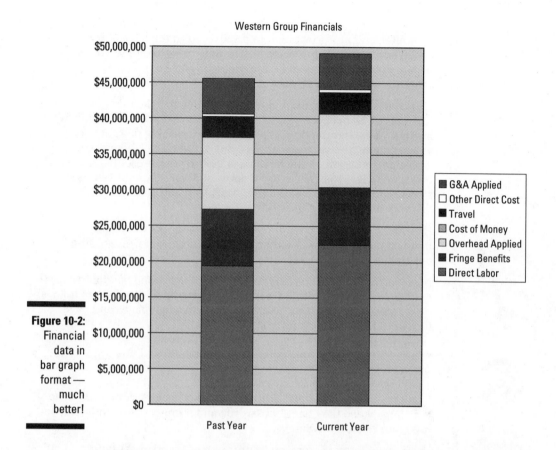

Figure 10-2:
Financial
data in
bar graph
format —
much
better!

Presentation tools, visual aids, and other props serve several purposes. First, they convey your information much more quickly than do your spoken words. Second, people retain visual information longer than other kinds of information. Finally, presentation tools, visual aids, and other such props provide your audience with a welcome break from your oral presentation.

Consider using the following presentation tools and props wherever and whenever possible:

✔ **PowerPoint:** For presentations in front of large groups, computer projections — most often coupling a laptop computer with a high-power liquid crystal display (LCD) projector and the Microsoft PowerPoint software program — are the choice of the pros (just ask Bob!). Not only are presentations crystal clear, but also you can easily fit one or more complete presentations into your laptop computer and carry it around with you anywhere. One danger with computer presentations, however, is that if your computer goes on the fritz, or if your destination has no suitable projector to hook your computer to, your presentation is going to be notably absent. On more than a few occasions, Bob has flown many thousands of miles to make a PowerPoint presentation from his laptop computer, and at the last minute discovered that his client hadn't arranged for an LCD projector in advance. Unfortunately, when this happened, Bob had no way to fix the problem, and he had to make his presentation without his visual aids.

✔ **Flip charts/whiteboards:** If you're presenting to a smaller group — say, up to about 30 people — flip charts and whiteboards are a handy way to present visual information. Flip charts are those big pads of paper that you can hang from an easel at the front of the room. You can set up your whole presentation on the flip charts before your presentation and, like transparencies, you can scribble notes on them for emphasis as you speak. Throw in a dash of fun (oh, boy!) by using different colors of markers throughout! *¡Caramba!*

✔ **Handouts:** Providing your audience with handouts of the information that you plan to cover — either before or after your presentation, depending on your personal preference — is often helpful.

However, don't fall victim to the practice of providing handouts and then reading from them. Nothing is more boring to an audience than following a presenter's handouts as he or she reads through pages and pages of text word for word. *Just say no!*

When using visual aids, keep a couple of points in mind if you want to have a happy audience.

✔ **Don't try to jam too much information into each of your aids.** Keep the type large, keep the quantity of words and numbers to a minimum, and use color to your advantage.

✔ **Have everything ready well in advance of your presentation.** Don't start your presentation by spending five minutes fumbling with setting up your projector or paging through a disorganized stack of transparencies. This flustering doesn't impress your audience and it doesn't enhance your self-confidence.

✔ **Check out everything!** Make sure your electronics, sound, lights, and other tools are working before you find out otherwise at a key point in your presentation.

✔ **Don't forget that you're the center of attention — not your visual aids.** Use visual aids to support your presentation — don't use your presentation to support your visual aids!

Making your presentation

The waiting is over and your audience is gathered — raptly waiting to hear the pearls of wisdom that you're going to fling all about the room. At this point, all your hours of preparation pay off. Follow these steps as you begin your presentation:

✔ **Relax!** What do you have to be nervous about? You're thoroughly prepared for your presentation. Your notes are in order, your visual aids are positioned and ready to go, and your audience is sincerely interested in what you have to say. As you wait for the presentation to start, breathe deeply and stay alert.

✔ **Greet your audience members:** This is one of the pluses of arriving early. As your audience members arrive for your presentation, welcome them personally. Not only does this practice establish an initial level of rapport and interest, but also getting a chance to talk to your audience members before you launch into your presentation helps you feel more at ease in front of the group.

✔ **Listen closely to your introduction:** Make sure that the facts are accurate, and listen for comments that you can incorporate into your initial remarks. For example, if the individual who introduces you mentions that, not only are you a brilliant manager, but that you're also an avid skier, you can work a humorous anecdote about skiing into the beginning of your presentation.

✔ **Wait for your audience's attention:** As a presenter, you must capture the full attention of your audience. One particularly effective technique is to stand in front of your audience and say nothing until everyone's attention is focused on you. Of course, if that doesn't do the trick, you can always resort to the old standbys: threats and intimidation!

✔ **Make your presentation:** Start at the beginning, finish when you're done, and have fun with everything in between! This really is your opportunity to shine — make the most of it!

Top five communication Web sites

Wondering where to find the best information on the Web about the topics addressed in this chapter? Well, you've come to the right place! Here are our top five favorites:

✔ *Business Communication Quarterly* magazine: www.bcq.theabc.org/

✔ Presentations.com: www.presentations. com

✔ Presenters University: www.presenters university.com/

✔ *Busines$:* www.marand.si/business/

✔ AltaVista translation services: babelfish. altavista.com

Chapter 11

It's a Team Thing

A revolution is going on in business today. The revolution is deciding what work to do, how to accomplish it, what goals an organization strives for, and who's responsible for achieving them. The revolution also is touching everyone in an organization — from the very top to the very bottom. What is this revolution? It's wet and wild! It's the ultimate in refreshment. It's the new Vanilla Coke! (Oops! Wrong commercial. We'll try again.) The revolution is called *teams*.

What's a team? A team is two or more people who work together to achieve a common goal.

Why use teams? Teams offer an easy way to tap the knowledge and resources of all employees — not just supervisors and managers — to solve the organization's problems. A well-structured team draws together employees from different functions and levels of the organization to help find the best way to approach an issue. Smart companies have discovered (and not-so-smart companies are just now starting to figure out) that to remain competitive, they can no longer rely solely on management to guide the development of work processes and the accomplishment of organizational goals. The companies need to involve those employees who are closer to the problems and to the organization's customers as well. Guess who those employees are? The front-line workers!

Perhaps management expert Peter Drucker best answers the question "Why use teams?" when he considered the importance of ranking knowledge over ego in the modern organization. According to Drucker, "No knowledge ranks higher than another; each is judged by its contribution to the common task rather than by any inherent superiority or inferiority. Therefore, the modern organization cannot be an organization of boss and subordinate. It must be organized as a team" (*Harvard Business Review*). Wow. We're talking profound here.

This chapter discusses the changes in today's global business environment that set the stage for the movement toward teams, the major kinds of teams and how they work, the impact of the new, computer-based technology on teams, and insights for conducting the best team meetings ever.

Phasing Out the Old Hierarchy

The last couple of decades have seen a fundamental shift in the distribution of power and authority in organizations. Until recently, most organizations were *vertical* — they had many layers of managers and supervisors between top management and front-line workers. The classic model of a vertical organization is the traditional military organization. In the old Army, privates report to corporals, who report to sergeants, who report to captains, and so on, up to the top general. When a general gives an order, it passes down the line from person to person until it reaches the person who is expected to execute it. *Ten hut!*

Until recently, large companies such as Ford, Exxon, and AT&T weren't that different from this rigid, hierarchical model. Employing hundreds of thousands of workers, these companies depended — and in many cases still depend — on legions of supervisors and managers to control the work, the workers that did it, and when and how they did it. (Okay, perhaps today's legions are smaller.) The primary goal of top management was to command and control workers' schedules, assignments, and decision-making processes very closely to ensure that the company met its objectives (and to ensure that workers weren't asleep at their desks!).

The downsizing of organizations

The hierarchical model has one fundamental. Many supervisors and managers made little or no direct contribution to the production of a company's products or services. Instead of producing things, in many cases, managers merely managed other managers or supervisors served as liaisons between levels. They did little more than push paper from one part of their desks to another. In the model's worst scenario, the levels of supervisors and managers actually impeded their organizations' capability to get tasks done — dramatically adding to the cost of doing business and slowing down the response time of decision making. All those company-paid lunches added up. Although this problem was overlooked as the global economy continued to expand in the last half of the 20th century, the economic slowdown in the late

'80s and once again after the dot-com bust that hit full force in 2001 made for quite a wake-up call to those companies (fat, dumb, and happy) with unproductive — or worse, counterproductive — middle management.

Although the downsizing of corporate workforces after economic downturns had obvious negative effects on the employees who lost their jobs — and in many cases, their hopes for comfortable retirement — this dark cloud had a silver lining. In these new, flatter organizations, a new life (and quicker pace) came to the following important areas:

- ✔ **Decision making:** Decisions, which may have taken weeks or even months to make in the old, bloated bureaucracy, are made in hours or minutes.

- ✔ **Communicating:** Instead of being intercepted and possibly distorted by middle managers at numerous points along its path, communication now travels a more direct — and much speedier — route from front-line workers to top management and vice versa, or to whomever the person needs to get information from. There's nothing like cutting six layers of management out of an organization to improve communication!

Also, this transformation from vertical to *horizontal* businesses (organizations with a minimum of levels of management) has had a fundamental impact on financial and organizational elements:

- ✔ **Quantifiable benefits to the bottom line:** By cutting out entire layers of management employees, many companies saved money in the way of substantially reduced costs of personnel, facilities, and company-paid lunches.

- ✔ **Movement of authority and power:** The move happened from the very top of the organization down to the front-line employees who interact with customers on a day-to-day basis. With fewer middle managers to interfere, front-line employees are naturally granted more autonomy and authority.

The move to cooperation

More than ever before, businesses worldwide are rewarding employees for cooperating with each other instead of competing against one another. This innovation in today's business environment is truly amazing! Organizations are no longer measuring employees only by their individual contributions, but also by how effective they are as contributing members of their work teams.

Coupled with this shift of authority is a fundamental change in the way that many businesses structure their organizations. They're moving away from a structure of traditional, functional divisions that once separated departments from each other. In their place are *teams* — made up of employees from different departments — whose members work together to perform tasks and achieve common goals. Of course, most businesses still organize their operations by departments, divisions, and so forth, but smart managers now encourage, rather than discourage, their employees to cross formal organizational lines.

Following are benefits that your organization can reap from promoting cooperation:

- **Reducing unproductive competition:** Promoting a cooperative, team-oriented work environment reduces the chance that your employees can become overcompetitive.

  If allowed to continue unabated, overcompetitiveness results in the shutdown of communication between employees and, ultimately, reduced organizational effectiveness (as overcompetitive employees build and defend private fiefdoms). Besides, overcompetition between employees invariably leads to the release of incredible amounts of bad karma. *(Excuse me, but your dogma just ran over my karma!)*

- **Sharing knowledge:** Knowledge is power. If you're in the know, you have a clear advantage over someone who has been left in the dark — especially if your finger is on the light switch. In a cooperative work environment, team members work together and thereby share their areas of knowledge and expertise.

- **Fostering communication:** The use of teams helps to break down the walls between an organization's departments, divisions, and other formal structures to foster communication between organizational units.

- **Achieving common goals:** The development of teams with members from various departments encourages workers from all levels and all parts of a company to work together to achieve common goals. Not only that, but also they give you someone to hang out with on coffee breaks.

Empowering Your Teams

As we explain in the preceding section, with the flattening of organizational structures that accompanied downsizing, employees gained more authority and autonomy from top management. The result: Employees have a better responsiveness to the customers' needs and the resolution of problems at the lowest possible level in the organization. The transfer of power, responsibility, and authority from higher-level to lower-level employees is called *empowerment.*

By empowering workers, managers place the responsibility for decision making with the employees who are in the best position to make the decision. In the past, many managers felt that they were in the best position to make decisions that affected a company's products or customers. How wrong they were. Although managers may have been right in some cases, their driving need to control workers and processes at all costs often blinded managers — so much so that control became more important than encouraging employee initiative.

The value of an empowered workforce

Effective managers today know the value of empowering their workers. Not only are customers better served, but also by delegating more responsibility and authority to front-line workers, managers are free to pursue other important tasks that only they can do, such as coaching, "big-picture" communicating, long-range planning, walking the walk, and talking the talk. The result is a more efficient, more effective organization. In his book *1001 Ways to Energize Employees,* Bob cites the following stories that demonstrate the clear benefit of empowered teams:

- ✔ Fireman's Fund Insurance Company's personal insurance division in Novato, California, divided its employees into work units organized around its customers. The company cut several levels of management, and whenever possible, the company assigned individuals whole jobs instead of fragmented work tasks. With these changes, employees felt they had a real stake in making customers happy, efficiency increased by 35–40 percent, systems investments declined by $5 million a year, and endorsement turnaround decreased from 21 days to 48 hours.

- ✔ By putting together a small team of workers and encouraging them to take the initiative to solve problems, helicopter parts manufacturer Lord Aerospace Products division of the Lord Corporation in Dayton, Ohio, energized the rest of the company's employees. Productivity went up 30 percent and absenteeism dropped 75 percent.

Empowerment is also a great morale booster in an organization. Managers who empower their workers show that they trust them to make decisions that are important to the company's success.

What about quality?

Today's businesses have discovered a lot from the improvement movement. Taking a cue from successful Japanese businesses — noted for their high-quality automobiles and innovative consumer electronic products — U.S. businesses embarked on a quality quest in the '80s. U.S. managers quickly discovered that the cornerstone of many Japanese programs was the empowerment of workers to make decisions regarding their work processes.

For example, *quality circles* — groups of employees who meet regularly to suggest ways to improve the organization — have become a much-copied Japanese technique of participative decision making. A quality circle's suggestions carry great weight with management.

The management of Motorola considers employee teams to be a crucial part of its strategy for quality improvement. Self-directed teams at its Arlington Heights, Illinois, cellular equipment manufacturing plant not only decide on their own training programs and schedule their own work, but they're also involved in the hiring and firing of coworkers.

Identifying Advantages of Teams

Teams not only have the potential to make better decisions, but they can also make faster decisions as well. Because team members are closest to the problems and to one another, a minimal amount of lag time exists due to communication channels or the need to get approvals from others in the organization.

Smaller and nimbler

Large organizations often have a hard time competing in the marketplace against smaller, more nimble competitors. And, smaller units within a large organization — such as teams — are better able to compete. The rate and scope of change in the global business environment has led to increased competitive pressures on organizations in most every business sector.

As customers can get products and services faster, they demand to have them so (those darn customers!). As they can buy products more cheaply as a result of technology improvements or global competition, they expect lower prices as well (double-darn them!). And the expectation of quality in relation to price has dramatically increased over the years — especially with consumers' experience in obtaining more advanced electronics and computer technology for progressively lower prices. In short, customer values are changing so that they now want products and services "any time, any place." Not only that, but they also want to pay less than they did last year.

Innovative and adaptable

Teams can also lead to increased innovation. According to then-Harvard economist Robert Reich in the *Harvard Business Review,* "As individual skills are integrated into a group, the collective capacity to innovate becomes something greater than the sum of its parts."

Teams are also more adaptive to the external environment as it quickly or constantly changes. Thus, a team's size and flexibility give it a distinct advantage over the more traditional organizational structure of competing organizations. At Xerox and Hewlett-Packard, for example, design, engineering, and manufacturing functions are now closely intertwined in the development of new products — dramatically shortening the time from concept to production.

Teams used to be considered useful only for projects of short duration. However, many companies no longer follow this thought. According to Drucker, "Whereas team design has traditionally been considered applicable only to short-lived, transitory, exceptional task-force assignments, it is equally applicable to some permanent needs, especially to the top-management and innovating tasks" (*Harvard Business Review*). Indeed, the team concept has proved itself to be a workable long-term solution to the needs of many organizations.

Setting Up and Supporting Your Teams

The first point you need to consider when setting up a team is what kind of team to set up. Three major kinds of teams exist: *formal, informal,* and *self-managed.* Each type of team offers advantages and disadvantages depending on the specific situation, timing, and the organization's needs.

Formal teams

A *formal team* is chartered by an organization's management and tasked to achieve specific goals. These goals can range from developing a new product line, determining the system for processing customer invoices, or planning a company picnic. Types of formal teams include

- **Task forces:** Formal teams assembled on a temporary basis to address specific problems or issues. For example, a task force may be assembled to determine why the number of rejects for a machined part has risen from 1 in 10,000 to 1 in 1,000. A task force usually has a deadline for solving the issue and reporting the findings to management.

- **Committees:** Long-term or permanent teams created to perform an ongoing, specific organizational task. For example, some companies have committees that select employees to receive awards for performance or that make recommendations to management for safety improvements. Although committee membership may change from year to year, the committees continue their work regardless of who belongs to them.

✔ **Command teams:** Made up of a manager or supervisor and all the employees who report directly to him or her. Such teams are by nature hierarchical and represent the traditional way that tasks are communicated from managers to workers. Examples of command teams include company sales teams, management teams, and executive teams.

Formal teams are important to most organizations because much of the communication within an establishment traditionally occurs within the team. News, goals, and information pass from employee to employee via formal teams. And they provide the structure for assigning tasks and soliciting feedback from team members on accomplishments, performance data, and so on.

Informal teams

Informal teams are casual associations of employees that spontaneously develop within an organization's formal structure. Such teams include groups of employees who eat lunch together every day, form bowling teams, or simply like to hang out together — both during and after work. The membership of informal teams is in a constant state of flux as members come and go and friendships and other associations between employees change over time.

Although informal teams have no specific tasks or goals assigned by management, they are very important to organizations for the following reasons:

✔ Informal teams provide a way for employees to get information outside formal, management-sanctioned communications channels.

✔ Informal teams provide a (relatively) safe outlet for employees to let off steam about issues that concern them and to find solutions to problems by discussing them with employees from other parts of the organization — unimpeded by the walls of the formal organization.

For example, a group of women employees at NYNEX Corporation, a large telecommunications firm, created *mentoring circles.* The purpose of these informal teams — developed outside the formal NYNEX organization — was to fill the void created by a lack of female top-level managers to serve as mentors for other women in the organization. Organized in groups of 8–12 employees, the circles provide the kind of career networking, support, and encouragement that mentors normally provide to their charges.

Ad hoc groups are informal teams of employees assembled to solve a problem with only those who are most likely to contribute invited. For example, you may form an ad hoc team when you select employees from your human resources and accounting departments to solve a problem with the system for tracking and recording pay changes in the company's payroll system. You don't invite participants from shipping to join this informal team because they probably can't provide meaningful input to the problem.

Self-managed teams

Self-managed teams combine the attributes of both formal and informal teams. Generally chartered by management, self-managed teams often quickly take on lives of their own as members take over responsibility for the day-to-day workings of the team. Self-managed teams usually contain from 3–30 employees whose job is to meet together to find solutions to common worker problems. Self-managed teams are also known as *high performance teams, cross-functional teams,* or *superteams.*

To compress time and gain benefits, an organization's self-managing teams must be

- Made up of people from different parts of the organization.
- Small because large groups create communication problems.
- Self-managing and empowered to act because referring decisions back up the line wastes time and often leads to poorer decisions.
- Multifunctional because that's the best — if not the only — way to keep the actual product and its essential delivery system clearly visible and foremost in everyone's mind.

Self-managed teams of workers at Johnsonville Foods in Wisconsin increased productivity 50 percent between 1986 and 1990 — a much higher rate than chief executive officer Ralph Stayer had imagined possible. As a result of this dramatic productivity gain, Stayer decided to expand the company's sausage production facility.

American automobile manufacturers' management and their union-dominated workforces have a long history of conflict — often violent and disruptive. However, at Saturn Corporation, the innovative subsidiary of General Motors, teams have helped to change this seemingly unchangeable tradition. Teams have led to cooperation between management and workers. Differences of opinion still arise from time to time, according to Michael Bennett, former president of Union Local 1853. Although conflict certainly exists — Saturn is no different in that respect from any other organization — union/management relations are not adversarial as they often are in other unionized workplaces. Each side makes a point of seeking a better solution that benefits everyone.

Being a team member is not optional at Saturn: All employees belong to at least one. On the production floor, employees work in self-managed teams that make decisions regarding training, hiring, budgeting, and scheduling. Each team consists of 5 to 15 workers, and instead of being monitored by outsiders, the teams monitor themselves. As a result, team members gain a better appreciation for what the organization has to do and what it costs to do it.

More and more, where management is willing to let go of the reins of absolute authority and turn them over to workers, self-managing teams are rising to the challenge and are making major contributions to the success of their firms. Indeed, the future success of many businesses lies in the successful implementation of self-managed teams.

The real world

Empowerment is a beautiful thing when it flourishes in an organization. However, real empowerment is still rare. Many plastic substitutes are out there masquerading as empowerment! Although many managers talk a good story about how they empower their employees, few actually do it. When they are real and not pale imitations, empowered teams typically

- ✔ Make the most of the decisions that influence team success.
- ✔ Choose their leaders.
- ✔ Add or remove team members.
- ✔ Set their goals and commitments.
- ✔ Define and perform much of their training.
- ✔ Receive rewards as a team.

Unfortunately, employee empowerment, for the most part, may be only an illusion. A survey of team members showed that plenty of room for change and improvement in the workings of teams still exists. Survey respondents clearly felt that the areas of intragroup trust, group effectiveness, agenda setting/meeting content, and role and idea conformity can use some improvement.

Conducted by management expert Dr. Bob Culver, a recent study of managers, team leaders, and team members at nine different companies discovered that real-world teams are more participative than empowered. Basically, top management is still making the real decisions. Those pesky backsliders! Using Culver's study results as a basis, you can apply the following specific recommendations to counter the ineffectiveness of many teams:

- ✔ **Make your teams empowered, not merely participative:** Instead of just inviting employees to participate in teams, grant team members the authority and power to make independent decisions.

  - Allow your teams to make long-range and strategic decisions, not just procedural ones.
  - Permit the team to choose the team leaders.

- Allow the team to determine its goals and commitments.

- Make sure that all team members have influence by involving them in the decision-making process.

✔ **Remove the source of conflicts:** Despite their attempts to empower employees, managers are often unwilling to live with the results. Be willing to start up a team, and then be prepared to accept the outcome.

- Recognize and work out personality conflicts.

- Fight turf protection and middle-management resistance.

- Work to unify manager and team member views.

- Minimize the stress of downsizing and process improvement tasks.

✔ **Change other significant factors that influence team effectiveness:** Each of these factors indicates that an organization has not yet brought true empowerment to its employees. You have the power to change this situation. Do it!

- Allow the team to discipline poorly performing members.

- Make peer pressure less important in attaining high team performance.

- Train as many team members as you train managers or team leaders.

Although clear examples of companies where management has truly empowered its teams do exist (they're out there somewhere), team empowerment doesn't just happen. Supervisors and managers must make concerted and ongoing efforts to ensure that authority and autonomy pass from management to teams. You can, too!

New technology and teams

According to a *Fortune* magazine article, the three dominant forces shaping 21st-century organizations are the following:

✔ A high-involvement workplace with self-managed teams and other devices for empowering employees.

✔ A new emphasis on managing business processes rather than functional departments.

✔ The evolution of information technology to the point where knowledge, accountability, and results can be distributed rapidly anywhere in the organization.

The integrating ingredient of these three dominant forces is information. Information technology and the way information is handled are increasingly becoming the keys to an organization's success.

But information can be tricky to manage. According to Peter Drucker in *Management: Tasks, Responsibilities, Practices,* "Information activities present a special organizational problem. Unlike most other result-producing activities, they are not concerned with one stage of the process but with the entire process itself. This means that they have to be both centralized and decentralized." Fortunately, information technology has overcome this challenge.

In a team environment, *process management information* moves precisely to where the team needs it, unfiltered by a hierarchy. Raw numbers go straight to those who need them in their jobs because front-line workers, such as salespeople and machinists, have been trained in how to use that information. By letting information flow wherever the team needs it, a horizontal self-managed company isn't only possible, it's also inevitable. Information technology-enabled team support systems include e-mail, computer conferencing, and videoconferencing that coordinate geographically, as well as across time zones, more easily than ever before. The development and use of computer software to support teams also is growing. An example is the expanding body of software called *groupware.* Groupware consists of computer programs specifically designed to support collaborative work groups and processes.

As organizations make better use of information technology, they don't need middle managers as often to make decisions. The result? The number of management levels and the number of managers can be dramatically reduced. Jobs, careers, and knowledge shift constantly. Typical management career paths are eliminated, and workers advance by learning more skills to be of greater value to the organization.

Those managers who remain need to take on new skills and attitudes to be more of a coach, supporter, and facilitator to the front-line employees. Supervisors and managers no longer have the luxury of spending time trying to control the organization — instead, they change it. Their job is to seek out new customers at the same time as they respond to the latest needs of their established customers. Managers still have considerable authority, but instead of commanding workers, their job is to inspire workers.

Meetings: Putting Teams to Work

So what is a discussion about meetings doing in a chapter on teams? The answer is that meetings are the primary forum in which team members conduct business and communicate with one another. And with the proliferation of teams in business today, it pays to master the basic skills of meeting management.

Effective meetings pay off

Teams are clearly an idea whose time has come. As organizations continue to flatten their hierarchies and empower front-line workers with more responsibility and authority, teams are the visible and often inevitable result. This transition is good news to the burgeoning industry of consulting and seminars in business team building. *Cha-ching!* Consider the way the best companies run meetings to respond to this new, team-oriented business environment.

- ✔ Jack Welch, former chairman of General Electric, determined that if the company were going to be successful, it had to move away from the old model of autocratic meetings and direction from top management. Welch's solution was to initiate a town-hall concept of meetings throughout the entire organization. These meetings called *work out* meetings bring workers and managers together in open forums where workers are allowed to ask any question they want and managers are required to respond.

- ✔ The company's core business strategies are shaped in regular meetings of senior executives — each of whom represents one of GE's individual business units. In these high-energy meetings, attendees are encouraged to explore every possible avenue and alternative and to be open to new ideas. GE's recent ventures in Mexico, India, and China are a direct result of these meetings.

- ✔ At GE's Bayamón, Puerto Rico, lightning arrester plant, employees have been organized into teams that are responsible for specific plant functions — shipping, assembly, and so forth. However, for example, instead of tapping only employees from shipping to be on the shipping team, teams consist of employees from all parts of the plant. This process enables representatives from all affected departments to discuss how suggested changes or improvements may affect their part of the operation. Hourly workers run the meetings on their own, and *advisers* — GE's term for salaried employees — participate in meetings only at the team's request.

Results of the Bayamón experiment have produced clear and convincing evidence that General Electric's approach is quite successful. A year after startup, the plant's employees measured 20 percent higher in productivity than their closest counterpart in the mainland United States. And if that weren't enough, management projected a further 20 percent increase in the following year.

Meetings that produce results like these companies don't just happen by accident. Far too many meetings in organizations today are run poorly. Instead of contributing to an organization's efficiency and effectiveness, most meetings actually make employees less efficient and less effective. How many times have you heard someone complain about getting stuck in one more useless meeting? With today's business imperative to get more done with less, making every meeting count is more important than ever.

What's wrong with meetings?

Unfortunately, most meetings are a big waste of time. Meeting experts have determined that approximately 53 percent of all the time spent in meetings — and this means the time that you spend in meetings — is unproductive, worthless, and of little consequence. And when you realize that most business people spend at least 25 percent of their working hours in meetings, with upper management spending more than double that time in meetings, you can begin to gain an appreciation for the importance of learning and applying effective meeting skills.

So what's wrong with meetings, anyway? Why do so many meetings go so wrong, and why can't you ever seem to do anything about it? In our book *Better Business Meetings* (McGraw-Hill), we discuss a few of the reasons:

- ✔ **Too many meetings take place:** When did you last say to yourself, "Gee, I haven't been in any meetings lately. I sure miss them"? Probably never. Indeed, the eternal lament of the manager is something more along the lines of "How am I supposed to get any work done with all these #@!%& meetings?" The problem is not just that too many meetings take place; the problem is that many meetings are unnecessary, unproductive, and a waste of your time.

- ✔ **Attendees are unprepared:** Some meetings happen prematurely, before a real reason to meet arises. Other times, individuals, who have prepared neither themselves nor the participants for the topics to be discussed, lead the meeting. What often results is a long period of time where the participants stumble around blindly trying to figure out why the meeting was called in the first place.

- ✔ **Certain individuals dominate the proceedings:** You may find one or two in every crowd. You know, the people who think that they know it all and who make sure that their opinion is heard loudly and often during the course of a meeting. These folks may be good for occasional comic relief, if nothing else, but they often intimidate the other participants and stifle their contributions.

- ✔ **They last too long:** Yes, yes, yes. Make sure a meeting doesn't last longer than it needs to. No less, no more. Despite this fact, most managers let meetings expand to fill the time allotted to them. So rather than let the participants leave after the business at hand is completed, the meeting drags on and on and on.

- ✔ **The meeting has no focus:** Meeting leadership is not a passive occupation. Many pressures work against keeping meetings on track and on topic, and managers often fail to step up to the challenge. The result is the proliferation of personal agendas, digressions, diversions, off-topic tangents, and worse.

The eight keys to great meetings

Fortunately, you have hope. Although many meetings are a big waste of time, they don't have to be. Your dysfunctional meeting blues have a cure! And good news again: The cure is readily available, inexpensive, and easy to swallow.

- **Be prepared:** You need only a little time to prepare for a meeting, and the payoff is increased meeting effectiveness. Instead of wasting time trying to figure out why you're meeting ("uh, does anyone know why we're here today?"), your preparation gets results as soon as the meeting starts.

- **Have an agenda:** An agenda is your road map, your meeting plan. With it, you and the other participants recognize the meeting goals and know what you're going to discuss. And if you distribute the agenda to participants before the meeting, you multiply its effectiveness many times over because the participants can prepare for the meeting in advance.

- **Start on time and end on time (or sooner):** You go to a meeting on time, and the meeting leader, while muttering about an important phone call or visitor, arrives 15 minutes late. Even worse is when the meeting leader ignores the scheduled ending time and lets the meeting go on and on. Respect your participants by starting and ending your meetings on time. You don't want them spending the entire meeting looking at their watches and worrying about how late you're going to keep them!

- **Have fewer but better meetings:** Call a meeting only when a meeting is absolutely necessary. And when you call a meeting, make the meeting a good one. Do you really have to meet to discuss change in your travel reimbursement policy? Wouldn't an e-mail message to all company travelers do just as well? Or how about the problem you've been having with the financial reports? Instead of calling a meeting, maybe a phone call can do the trick. Whenever you're tempted to call a meeting, make sure that you have a good reason for doing so.

- **Think inclusion, not exclusion:** Be selective with whom you invite to your meetings — select only as many participants as needed to get the job done. But don't exclude people who may have the best insight into your issues simply because of their ranks in the organization or their lifestyles, appearance, or beliefs.

  You never know who in your organization is going to provide the best ideas, and you only hurt your chances of getting those great ideas by excluding people for nonperformance-related reasons.

- **Maintain the focus:** Ruthlessly keep your meetings on topic at all times. Although doing everything but talking about the topic at hand can be a lot of fun, you called the meeting for a specific reason in the first place.

Stick to the topic, and if you finish the meeting early, participants who want to stick around to talk about other topics don't have to hold the other participants hostage to do so.

✔ **Capture action items:** Make sure that you have a system for capturing, summarizing, and assigning action items to individual team members. Flip charts — those big pads of paper that you hang from an easel in front of the group — are great for this purpose. Have you ever come out of a meeting wondering why the meeting took place? You mean a meeting with no purpose, no direction, no assignments or follow-up actions? Make sure that your meetings have purpose and that you assign action items to the appropriate people.

✔ **Get feedback:** Feedback can be a great way to measure the effectiveness of your meetings. Not only can you find out what you did right, but you also can find out what you did wrong and get ideas on how to make your future meetings more effective. Ask the participants to give you their honest and open feedback — verbally or in writing — and then use it. You can never see yourself as others do unless they show you.

Top five teams Web sites

Wondering where to find the best information on the Web about the topics addressed in this chapter? Well, you've come to the right place! Here are our top five favorites:

✔ Self-Directed Work Team: `users.ids.net/~brim/sdwth.html`

✔ Employee Involvement/Teams/Empowerment: `www.humanresources.about.com/cs/involvementteams/`

✔ Teambuildinginc.com: `www.teambuildinginc.com`

✔ Teams and Teamwork: `www.hq.nasa.gov/office/hqlibrary/ppm/ppm5.htm`

✔ Teamwork: `www.fastcompany.com/online/resources/teamwork.html`

Chapter 12

Managing Virtual Employees

- -

In This Chapter

▶ Managing a new flavor of employee

▶ Monitoring far away employees

▶ Leading different shifts

▶ Looking into the future of telecommuting

- -

The past decade has seen a major shift in the attitudes of companies — and in the attitudes of the men and women who run them — toward a more worker-friendly workplace. Today's managers are much more flexible and willing to work with the unique needs of their employees than ever before. Why? Because savvy managers realize that they can get more from employees with a little consideration (and employees increasingly expect this). So, whether employees need to drop their kids off at school in the morning, or work only on certain days of the week, or take an extended leave of absence to care for an ill relative, managers are more likely to do whatever they can to accommodate worker needs.

This shift in attitudes (as well as changes in the nature of work, the improvement of technology, and the reduction of levels of management in many organizations) has led to its eventual conclusion — virtual employees who spend the majority of their work hours away from established company offices and worksites, employees managed from a distance, employees who work a variety of shifts or differing starting and ending times, and employees who telecommute to the office from the comfort of their homes.

Of course, these changes haven't been easy for the managers who are required to implement them. For managers who are used to having employees close by — ready to instantly respond to the needs of customers and clients — managing off-site employees can be a little bit disconcerting.

In this chapter, we consider this new kind of employee and how best to work with him or her. We explore strategies for effectively managing far away employees, as well as those employees working differing shifts, and we take a look at the future of telecommuting.

Making Room for a New Kind of Employee

A new kind of employee is out there — the *virtual* employee. And, exactly what do we mean by virtual employee? A virtual employee simply means someone who regularly works somewhere besides the regular, bricks-and-mortar offices that house a company's business operations. Virtual employees join employees who have accepted (and often clamored for) a variety of alternative working arrangements, including alternate work schedules and flexible work schedules, to name two.

According to a U.S. Labor Department report, approximately one in ten employees today has an alternative work arrangement. These alternative work arrangements can range from something as simple as allowing employees to start and end their workdays at times that are outside the standard, all the way to allowing employees to work full-time from their homes.

Managing people who aren't physically located near you can be particularly challenging, and you must approach it differently than managing employees who work in the same physical location. Perhaps your employees are located at a different facility or even in a different state (remote employees), or maybe they're telecommuting. But regardless of the reason for the separation, these new distance-working relationships make it harder for managers to identify and acknowledge desired behavior and performance. Managers must be more systematic and intentional in determining whether or not employees are fully performing their duties to the same standard as employees housed in a regular office.

Preparing to get virtual

Is your company ready for virtual employees? Are you ready for virtual employees? The following is a quick-and-easy checklist for determining if your organization is ready.

- ❑ Your company has established work standards to measure employee performance.

- ❑ Prospective virtual employees have the equipment they need to properly perform their work off-site.

- ❑ The work can be performed off-site.

- ❑ The work can be completed without ongoing interaction with other employees.

❑ Prospective virtual employees have demonstrated that they can work effectively without day-to-day supervision.

❑ Supervisors can manage and monitor employees by their results rather than by direct observation.

❑ Employee worksites have been examined to ensure that they're adequately equipped.

Do most of the boxes have check marks in them, or are most of them empty? If you have several check marks, then your organization is ready, willing, and able to initiate alternative work arrangements with your employees. If you have several empty boxes, you have your work cut out for you before you can reasonably expect virtual employees to be a viable option in your organization.

Understanding changes to the office culture

One of the key concerns for managers when an increasing number of employees become virtual employees is this: What happens to the company's culture (and employee performance) as more and more workers work outside the office? A company's culture, after all, is mostly defined by the day-to-day interactions of employees. For employees who work outside the mainstream of these interactions — and who are therefore not a part of them — they'll probably have no grounding in an organization's culture, and little attachment to other employees, or to the organization's values and goals.

The result? Employees who are potentially less productive than regular employees, with lowered teamwork and loyalty.

The good news is that you can take a number of steps to help your virtual workers plug into your company's culture, become team players and gain a stake in the organization's goals in the process.

Consider the following ideas:

✔ Schedule regular meetings that everyone attends — in person, or by conference call or Internet chatroom. Discuss current company events and set aside time for the group to tackle and solve at least one pressing organizational issue, or more, if time permits.

✔ Create communication vehicles that everyone can be a part of. Bob recently worked with a limousine company that gives all its drivers a monthly cassette tape, which updates them on current company goings on, policies, questions and answers, and more, to listen to in their cars.

✔ Hire a facilitator and schedule periodic team-building sessions with all your employees — virtual and nonvirtual — to build working relationships and trust among employees.

✔ Initiate regular, inexpensive group events that draw your virtual employees out to mingle and get to know regular employees — and each other. Going out to lunch on the company's tab, volunteering to help a local charity, having a potluck at a local park — the possibilities are endless.

But, as a manager, you need to consider something else: Virtual employees face issues that normal employees don't. These issues include:

✔ Virtual employees may find that they're not fairly compensated by their employers for the home resources (office space, computers, electricity, furniture, and so forth) that they contribute to the job.

✔ Virtual employees may feel that their personal privacy is being violated if management efforts are too intrusive. Remember that your employee is (we assume) not available 24/7. Respect his or her work hours and use work phone numbers and e-mail addresses — not home — when you want to communicate.

✔ Regular employees may become jealous of virtual employees' "special privileges."

✔ Family duties may intrude on work duties much more often for employees who work at home than for employees who work in traditional offices.

These issues don't mean that you just forget about offering your employees alternative working arrangements. Keep these issues in mind and work to ensure that they don't cause problems for your virtual — or regular — employees.

Managing from a Distance

With the changing nature of work today, managers have to adapt to new circumstances for managing employees. How can managers keep up with an employee's performance when an employee may not even have physical contact with his or her manager for weeks or months at a time? Some of the answers may lie in a return to the basics of human interaction.

✔ **Make time for people.** Nothing beats face time when it comes to building trusting relationships. Managing is a people job — you need to take time for people. Not only when taking time is convenient, but also whenever employees are available and need to meet.

✔ **Increase communication as you increase distance.** The greater the distance from one's manager, the greater the effort both parties have to make to keep in touch. And, although some employees want to be as autonomous as possible — minimizing their day-to-day contact with you — other employees quickly feel neglected or ignored if you don't make a routine effort to communicate with them. Increase communication by sending regular updates and/or scheduling meetings and visits more frequently. Also, encourage your employees to contact you (communication is a two-way street, after all), and go out of your way to provide the same types of communication meetings with each work shift or arrange meetings that overlap work shifts or duplicate awards for each facility.

✔ **Use technology.** Don't let technology use you. Use technology as a communication vehicle, and not just to distribute data: Promote the exchange of information and encourage questions. Have problem discussion boards or host chatrooms with managers or executives or create an electronic bulletin board to capture the exchange of individual employee and team progress, problems, and solutions.

Today's managers have to work harder to manage distant employees. If you value strong working relationships and clear communication, you need to seek out others to be sure adequate communication is taking place.

Managing Different Shifts

The challenge of managing today's employees is made harder by the fact that the nature of work is changing so dramatically and so quickly. More and more employers have supplemented traditional work schedules with more flexible scheduling options. Managing employees who work differing shifts is a special challenge for today's managers.

Following are some strategies to consider when making the most of working with shift employees.

✔ **Take time to orient shift employees.** All employees need to get their bearings, and shift employees can often be at a disadvantage because they're working outside a company's normal hours. Be sure to let them know what they can expect about the job and the organization, including work policies you expect them to abide by, and make sure they meet all other individuals that they need to know or work with.

✔ **Give them the resources to be productive.** Giving them the resources can range from the right equipment to do the job, to access to others when they have a question. Other resources also include the right training, especially about company products and services, internal procedures, and administrative requirements.

Long distance recognition

Every employee needs to be recognized by his or her manager for a job well done. Just because an employee is "out of sight" doesn't mean that he or she should be "out of mind." Here are some steps you can take to make sure your virtual employees feel just as appreciated as your regular employees.

- ✔ Ask virtual team members to keep the leader and other team members apprised of their accomplishments, because they can't be as readily seen.

- ✔ Keep a recognition log of remote team members so that they don't fall into the cracks — a particularly important consideration for mixed teams (with both traditional and virtual team members).

- ✔ Make sure that virtual team members are appropriately included in recognition programs (by passing around recognition item catalogs, and by ensuring that remote employees are kept fully in the loop).

- ✔ Provide some "treat" for virtual team members who can't join in face-to-face socials and celebrations.

- ✔ Keep a list of recognition activities and items that are appropriate for a mobile workforce, such as thank-you cards and gift certificates.

- ✔ Become more aware of the recognition capabilities of e-mail, such as virtual flowers or greeting cards.

- ✔ Involve executives in recognition activities by way of conference calls.

- ✔ Make a point of employing a variety of team recognition items (such as coffee mugs, T-shirts, jackets, and so forth) when rewarding members of virtual teams. Such items help remind them of the team membership.

- ✔ **Make an ongoing effort to communicate.** The importance of communication is almost a cliché, but you can't underestimate its value. Many employees prefer to silently suffer through poor directions rather than risk seeming slow to grasp an assignment — and possibly being labeled as difficult to work with. So, you need to constantly check with shift employees to see if they have any questions or need any help. Make every personal interaction count to find out how the employees are doing and how you can better help them. Some managers schedule meetings at shift change to get two shifts at once.

- ✔ **Appreciate employees for the job they do.** If the employee is only at work outside the standard work schedule, their need to be recognized for their hard work and accomplishments is as great as any other employee, although their circumstances make it more inconvenient to thank them. Fortunately, a little appreciation can go a long way. Take the time to find out what may motivate extra performance and then deliver such rewards when you receive the desired performance.

- ✔ **Treat shift employees the way you want them to act.** If you want shift employees to have a long-term perspective, treat them with a long-term perspective. Make them feel a part of the team. Treating shift employees with courtesy and professionalism can help establish your reputation as a desirable employer to work for and thus serve as a draw for additional talent when you need it.

Managing employees who work different shifts is a very achievable task if done with the right effort at the right time. Make the time and the effort and you'll reap the benefits.

Telecommuting: An Idea Whose Time Has (Finally) Come?

With the proliferation of personal computers — both at work and home — and with the availability of fast and inexpensive modems and communications software, the question isn't can your employees telecommute. No, the question is will you let your employees telecommute. The problem that telecommuting presents to managers isn't a problem of technology, but a problem of managing people who aren't working in the office.

In the old-style office, most (if not all) of your employees are just footsteps away from your desk. If you need their help, you can pop your head into their offices to make assignments. Oh, they're away for a break? No problem, you can hunt them down in the breakroom and personally realign their priorities.

Telecommuting has changed all that. When your employees work away from the office, they're no longer at your immediate beck and call. Communication often becomes a long series of voice-mail messages, e-mails, and faxes. Face-to-face communication decreases, as does the feeling of connectedness to the organization. (For more on telecommuting, read *Telecommuting For Dummies* by Minda Zetlin [Wiley].)

Regardless, the benefits of telecommuting are many. According to studies, employee productivity can be increased by 30 percent, less time is lost as people sit in cars or mass transit to and from work, workers are more satisfied with their jobs, and society (and our lungs) benefit from fewer cars on the road every rush hour.

When her fiancé accepted a job in New Mexico, Amy Arnott, an analyst at Chicago-based Morningstar, Inc., was faced with a tough decision. Should she quit her job and move to New Mexico with her husband-to-be, or should she try maintaining a long-distance romance? Fortunately for Arnott, she didn't have to make the choice. Morningstar allows Arnott to telecommute each day from Los Alamos, New Mexico, to Chicago, Illinois — a journey of more than 1,000 miles each way.

Arnott uses her computer and modem to tap into the Morningstar mutual fund database. By using the database, along with off-the-shelf word processing, spreadsheet, and e-mail software, Arnott performs her job just as well as if she were at her old office in Chicago. (Well, meeting her coworkers in the hallway to chat about the latest goings-on within Morningstar is a little more difficult.)

Although the idea of virtual employees seems to be catching on in the world of business, you, as a manager, need to consider some pros and cons when your thoughts turn to the idea of telecommuting.

Following are some advantages to telecommuting:

- ✔ Depending on the job, employees can set their own schedules.

- ✔ Employees can spend more time with customers.

- ✔ Employees can conduct more work because everything is there where they need it. (And, when they get bored on a Saturday afternoon, they just may do an hour or two of work.)

- ✔ You can save money by downsizing your facilities.

- ✔ Costs of electricity, water, and other overhead are reduced.

- ✔ Employee morale is enhanced.

And following are some of the disadvantages to telecommuting:

- ✔ Monitoring employee performance is more difficult.

- ✔ Scheduling meetings can be problematic.

- ✔ You may have to pay to set up your employees with the equipment that they need to telecommute.

- ✔ Employees can lose their feelings of being connected to the organization.

- ✔ Managers must be more organized in making assignments.

For many employees, the prospect of being able to work out of their own home is much more appealing than merging onto the freeway each morning. For example, Scott Bye still gets out of bed at about the same time as he did when he worked at a large corporate publisher, but now his commute is a few steps down the hall instead of an hour and 15 minutes of bumper-to-bumper, smog-filled, Los Angeles stop-and-go traffic. By 9:30 a.m. — 15 minutes before his old starting time — Bye has already made several calls to his East Coast clients, sent a fax or two to publishing contacts overseas, and created a sales presentation on his computer.

Top five virtual management Web sites

Wondering where to find the best information on the Web about the topics addressed in this chapter? Well, you've come to the right place! Here are our top five favorites:

- ✔ Virtual-Organization.net: www.virtual-organization.net

- ✔ @Brint: www.brint.com/EmergOrg.htm

- ✔ StartWright: www.startwright.com/virtual.htm

- ✔ Center for Coordination Science: http://ccs.mit.edu

- ✔ CoWorking: http://coworking.com

Chapter 13

Focusing on Ethics and Office Politics

*E*thics and office politics are very powerful forces in any organization. *Ethics* is the framework of values that employees use to guide their behavior. You've seen the devastation that poor ethical standards can lead to — witness the string of business failures attributed to less than sterling ethics in more than a few large, seemingly upstanding businesses. Today, more than ever, managers are expected to model ethical behavior and to ensure that their employees follow in their footsteps — and to purge the organization of employees who refuse to align their own standards with that of their employer.

At its best, *office politics* means the relationships that you develop with your coworkers — both up and down the chain of command — that allow you to get tasks done, to be informed about the latest goings-on in the business, and to form a personal network of business associates for support throughout your career. Office politics help to ensure that everyone works in the best interests of the organization and their coworkers. At its worst, office politics can degenerate into a competition, where employees concentrate their efforts on trying to increase their personal power at the expense of other employees — and their organizations. (For more on office politics, see *Office Politics For Dummies* by Marilyn Moats Kennedy and Linda Mitchell [Wiley].)

This chapter is about building an ethical organization, determining the nature and boundaries of your political environment, understanding the unspoken side of office communication, unearthing the unwritten rules of your organization, and, in the worst-case scenario, becoming adept at defending yourself against political attack.

Doing the Right Thing! Ethics and You

With an endless parade of business scandals — overstated revenues, mistaken earnings, and misplaced decimals — hitting the daily news, rocking the stock market, and shaking the foundations of the global economic system, you often wonder whether anyone in charge knows the difference between right and wrong. Or, if they do know the difference, whether they really care.

Of course, the reality is that many business leaders do know the difference between right and wrong, despite appearances to the contrary. Now more than ever, businesses and the leaders who run them are trying to do the right thing, not just because the right thing is politically correct, but also because it's good for the bottom line.

Ethics are in. And that's good for all of us.

Defining ethics

Do you know what ethics are? In case you're a bit rusty on the correct response, the long answer is that ethics are standards of beliefs and values that guide conduct, behavior, and activities — in other words, a way of thinking that provides boundaries for our actions. The short answer is that ethics are simply doing the right thing. And, not just talking about doing the right thing, but really doing it!

Although each of you comes to a job with your own sense of ethical values — based on your own upbringing and your own life experiences — organizations and leaders for which you work are responsible for setting clear ethical standards.

When you have high ethical standards on the job, you generally exhibit some or all of the following personal qualities and behaviors:

- Honesty
- Integrity
- Impartiality
- Fairness
- Loyalty
- Dedication
- Responsibility
- Accountability

A sample code of ethics

Because of the nature of the public trust that they are charged with (they're spending our tax dollars, after all!), government workers have long been held to a higher standard of ethical behavior than those in private industry. Here is the Code of Ethics for Government Service, adopted by the U.S. Congress on July 11, 1958 (and still just as valid today).

Any person in government service should:

1. Put loyalty to the highest moral principals and to country above loyalty to Government persons, party, or department.

2. Uphold the Constitution, laws, and legal regulations of the United States and of all governments therein and never be a party to their evasion.

3. Give a full day's labor for a full day's pay; giving to the performance of his duties his earnest effort and best thought.

4. Seek to find and employ more efficient and economical ways of getting tasks accomplished.

5. Never discriminate unfairly by the dispensing of special favors or privileges to anyone, whether for remuneration or not; and never accept for himself or his family, favors or benefits under circumstances which might be construed by reasonable persons as influencing the performance of his governmental duties.

6. Make no private promises of any kind binding upon the duties of office, since a Government employee has no private word, which can be binding on public duty.

7. Engage in no business with the Government, either directly or indirectly, which is inconsistent with the conscientious performance of his governmental duties.

8. Never use any information coming to him confidentially in the performance of governmental duties as a means for making private profit.

9. Expose corruption wherever discovered.

10. Uphold these principles, ever conscious that public office is a public trust.

Ethical behavior starts with you. As a manager, you're a leader in your organization, and you set an example — both for other managers, and for the many workers who are watching your every move. When others see you behaving unethically, you're sending the message loud and clear that ethics don't matter. The result? Ethics won't matter to them, either.

However, when you behave ethically, others follow your example and behave ethically, too. And, if you practice ethical conduct, it also reinforces and perhaps improves your own ethical standards. As managers, we have a responsibility to try to define, live up to, and improve our own set of personal ethics.

Creating a code of ethics

Although most people have a pretty good idea about what kinds of behavior are ethical and what kinds of behavior aren't, ethics are — to some degree — subjective, and a matter of interpretation to the individual employee. One worker may, for example, think that making unlimited personal phone calls from the office is okay, while another worker may consider that to be inappropriate.

So, what's the solution to ethics that vary from person to person in an organization? A code of ethics.

By creating and implementing a code of ethics, you spell out for all employees — from the very top, to the very bottom — your organization's ethical expectations, clearly and unambiguously. A code of ethics isn't a substitute for company policies and procedures; the code complements them. Instead of leaving your employees' definition of ethics on the job to chance — or someone's upbringing — you clearly spell out that stealing, sharing trade secrets, sexually harassing a coworker, and other unethical behavior is unacceptable and may be grounds for dismissal. And, when you require your employees to read and sign a copy acknowledging their acceptance of the code, then your employees can't very well claim that they didn't know what you expected of them.

Four key areas form the foundation of a good code of ethics:

- ✔ Compliance with internal policies and procedures
- ✔ Compliance with external laws and regulations
- ✔ Direction from organizational values
- ✔ Direction from individual values

Of course, a code of ethics isn't worth the paper it's printed on if it doesn't address some very specific issues, as well as the more generic ones listed previously. The following are some of the most common issues addressed by typical codes of ethics:

- ✔ Equal opportunity
- ✔ Sexual harassment
- ✔ Diversity
- ✔ Privacy and confidentiality
- ✔ Conflicts of interest
- ✔ Gifts and gratuities
- ✔ Employee health and safety

In addition to working within an organization, a well-crafted code of ethics can be a powerful tool for publicizing your company's standards and values to people outside your organization, including vendors, clients, customers, investors, potential job applicants, the media, and the public at large. Your code of ethics tells others that you value ethical behavior and that it guides the way you and your employees do business.

What's in a comprehensive code of ethics?

According to the Ethics Resource Center Web site (www.ethics.org), a comprehensive code of ethics has seven parts. These parts include:

1. **A memorable title.** Examples include Price Waterhouse's *The Way We Do Business* and the World Bank Group's *Living Our Values*.

2. **Leadership letter.** A cover letter that briefly outlines the content of the code of ethics and clearly demonstrates commitment from the very top of the organization to ethical principles of behavior.

3. **Table of contents.** The main parts within the code, listed by page number.

4. **Introduction-prologue.** Explains why the code is important, the scope of the code, and to whom it applies.

5. **Statement of core values.** The organization lists and describes its primary values in detail.

6. **Code provisions.** This part is the meat of the code, the organization's position on a wide variety of issues including such topics as sexual harassment, privacy, conflicts of interest, gratuities, and so forth.

7. **Information and resources.** Places that employees can go for further information or for specific advice or counsel.

Of course, simply having a code of ethics isn't enough. You and your employees must also live it. Even the world's best code of ethics does you no good if you file it away and never use it.

Living ethics

You may have a code of ethics, but if you never behave ethically in all your day-to-day business transactions and relationships, what's the purpose in having a code in the first place? Ethical challenges abound in business — some are spelled out in your company's code of ethics, or in its policies and procedures, and some aren't. What, for example, would you do if:

- ✔ One of your favorite employees gives you tickets to a baseball game?

- ✔ An employee asks you not to write her up for a moderate infraction of company policies?

- ✔ You sold a product to a client that you later found out to be faulty, but your boss wants you to forget about it?

- ✔ Your department's financial results are actually lower than what appears in your boss's presentation to the board of directors?

- ✔ You find out that your star employee actually didn't graduate from college as he claimed in his job application?

- ✔ You know that a product you sell doesn't actually do everything your company claims it does?

We all make ethical choices on the job every day — how do you make yours? According to Trainingscape (www.trainingscape.com), you have six keys to make better ethical choices:

- ✔ **E** — **Evaluate** circumstances through the appropriate filters (filters include culture, laws, policies, circumstances, relationships, politics, perception, emotions, values, bias, and religion).

- ✔ **T** — **Treat** people and issues fairly within the established boundaries. Fair doesn't always mean equal.

- ✔ **H** — **Hesitate** before making critical decisions.

- ✔ **I** — **Inform** those affected of the standard/decision that has been set/made.

- ✔ **C** — **Create** an environment of consistency for yourself and your working group.

- ✔ **S** — **Seek** counsel when you have any doubt (but from those who are honest and who you respect).

Evaluating Your Political Environment

How political is your office or workplace? As a manager, having your finger on the political pulse of the organization is particularly important. Otherwise, the next time you're in a management meeting, you may blurt out, "Why is it so difficult to get an employment requisition through human resources? You'd think it was their money!" only to find out that the owner's daughter-in-law heads the human resources department.

With just a little bit of advance information and forethought, you could've approached this issue much more tactfully than you did. Getting in touch with your political environment can help you be more effective, and it can help your department and your employees have a greater impact within the organization.

Assessing your organization's political environment

Asking insightful questions of your coworkers is one of the best ways to assess your organization's political environment. Such questions show you to be the polite, mature, and ambitious employee that you are, and the questions are a sure sign of your well-developed political instincts. Why don't you give these questions a try?

- ✔ "What's the best way to get a nonbudget item approved?"

- ✔ "How can I get a product from the warehouse that my client needs today when I don't have time to do the paperwork?"

- ✔ "Can I do anything else for you before I go home for the day?"

Although asking politically savvy questions gives you an initial indication of the political lay of the land in your organization, you can do more to assess the political environment. Watch out for the following signs while you're getting a sense for how your organization really works:

- ✔ **Find out how others who seem to be effective get tasks done.** How much time do they spend preparing before sending through a formal request for a budget increase? Which items do they delegate and to whose subordinates? When you find people who are particularly effective at getting tasks done in your organization's political environment, model their behavior.

- ✔ **Observe how others are rewarded for the jobs they do.** Does management swiftly and enthusiastically give warm and personal rewards in a sincere manner to make it clear what behavior is considered important? Is credit given to everyone who helped make a project successful, or does only the manager get his or her picture in the company newsletter? By observing your company's rewards, you can tell what behavior is expected of employees in your organization. Practice this behavior.

- ✔ **Observe how others are disciplined for the jobs they do.** Does your management come down hard on employees for relatively small mistakes? Are employees criticized in public or in front of coworkers? Is everyone held accountable for decisions, actions, and mistakes even if they had no prior involvement? Such behavior on the part of management indicates that they don't encourage risk taking. If your management doesn't encourage risk taking, make your political style outwardly reserved as you work behind the scenes.

- ✔ **Consider how formal the people in the organization are.** When you are in a staff meeting, for example, you definitely show poor form if you blurt out, "That's a dumb idea. Why would we even consider doing such a thing?" Instead, buffer and finesse your opinions like so: "That's an interesting possibility. Could we explore the pros and cons of implementing such a possibility?" The degree of formality you find in your company indicates how you need to act to conform to the expectations of others.

Identifying key players

So now that you've discovered that you work in a political environment (did you really have any doubt in your mind?), you need to determine who the key players are. Why? Because they are the individuals who can help make your department more effective and who can provide positive role models to you and your employees.

Key players are those politically astute individuals who make things happen in an organization. You can identify them by their tendency to make instant decisions without having to refer people "upstairs," their use of the latest corporate slang, such as *Six Sigma,* and their affinity for always speaking up in meetings if only to ask, "What's our objective here?"

Sometimes influential people don't hold influential positions. For example, Jack, as the department head's assistant, may initially appear to be nothing more than a gofer. However, you may later find out that Jack is responsible for scheduling all his boss's appointments, setting agendas for department meetings, and vetoing actions on his own authority. Jack is an informal leader in the organization and, because you can't get to your boss without going through Jack, you know that Jack has much more power in the organization than his title may indicate.

All the following factors are indicators that can help you identify the key players in your organization:

✔ Which employees are sought for advice in your organization?

✔ Which employees are considered by others to be indispensable?

✔ Whose office is located closest to those of the organization's top management and whose are located miles away? *(Have we arrived in Siberia yet?)*

✔ Who eats lunch with the president, the vice presidents, and other members of the upper management team?

As you figure out who the key players in your organization are, you start to notice that they have different office personalities. Use the following categories to help you figure out how to work with the different personality types of your organization's key players. Do you recognize any of these players in your organization?

✔ **Movers and shakers:** These individuals usually far exceed the boundaries of their office positions. For example, you may find a mover and shaker in charge of purchasing, helping to negotiate a merger. Someone in charge of the physical plant may have the power to designate a wing of the building to the group of his or her choosing. Nonpolitical individuals, on the other hand, tend to be bogged down by responsibilities — such as getting their own work done.

✔ **Corporate citizens:** These employees are diligent, hardworking, company-loving who seek slow but steady, long-term advancement through dedication and hard work. Corporate citizens are great resources for getting information and advice about the organization. You can count on them for help and support, especially if your ideas seem to be in the best interest of the organization.

- ✔ **The town gossip:** These employees always seem to know what's going on in the organization — usually before those individuals who are actually affected by the news know it. Assume that anything you say to these individuals will get back to the person about whom you say it. Therefore, always speak well of your bosses and coworkers when you are in the presence of town gossips.

- ✔ **Firefighters:** The individual who relishes stepping into a potential problem with great fanfare at the last conceivable moment to save a project, client, deadline, or whatever. Keep this person well informed of your activities so that you aren't the subject of the next "fire."

- ✔ **The vetoer:** This person in your organization has the authority to kill your best ideas and ambitions with a simple comment such as, "We tried that and it didn't work." In response to any new ideas that you may have, the favorite line of a vetoer is, "If your idea is so good, then why aren't we already doing it?" The best way to deal with vetoers is to keep them out of your decision loop. Try to find other individuals who can get your ideas approved or rework the idea until you hit upon an approach that satisfies the vetoer.

- ✔ **Techies:** Every organization has technically competent workers who legitimately have a high value of their own opinions. Experts can take charge of a situation without taking over. Get to know your experts well — you can trust their judgments and opinions.

- ✔ **Whiners:** A few employees are never satisfied with whatever is done for them. Associating with them inevitably leads to a pessimistic outlook, which is not easily turned around. Or worse, your boss may think that you're a whiner, too. In addition, pessimistic people tend to be promoted less often than optimists. Be an optimist: Your optimism makes a big difference in your career and in your life.

Redrawing your organization chart

Your company's organization chart may be useful for determining who's who in the formal organization, but it really has no bearing on who's who in the informal political organization. What you need is the real organization chart. Figure 13-1 illustrates a typical official organization chart.

Start by finding your organization's official organization chart — the one that looks like a big pyramid. Throw it away. Now, from your impressions and observations, start outlining the real relationships in your organization in your mind. (You don't want someone to find your handiwork lying around in your office or in the recycling bin!) Begin with the key players whom you've already identified. Indicate their relative power by level and relationships by approximation. Use the following questions as a guideline:

✔ **Whom do these influential people associate with?** Draw the associations on your chart and connect them with solid lines. Also connect friends and relatives.

✔ **Who makes up the office cliques?** Be sure that all members are connected, because talking to one is like talking to them all.

✔ **Who are the office gossips?** Use dotted lines to represent communication without influence and solid lines for communication with influence.

✔ **Who's your competition?** Circle those employees likely to be considered for your next promotion. Target them for special attention.

✔ **Who's left off the chart?** Don't forget about these individuals. The way that today's organizations seem to change every other day, someone who is off the chart on Friday may be on the chart on Monday. Always maintain positive relationships with all your coworkers and never burn bridges between you and others within and throughout the company. Otherwise, you may find yourself left off the chart some day.

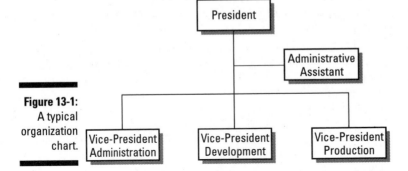

Figure 13-1:
A typical organization chart.

The result of this exercise is a chart of who really has political power in your organization and who doesn't. Figure 13-2 shows how the organization really works. Update your organization chart as you find out more information about people. Take note of any behavior that gives away a relationship — such as your boss cutting off a coworker in mid-sentence — and factor this observation into your overall political analysis. Of course, understand that you may be wrong. You can't possibly know the inner power relationships of every department. Sometimes, individuals who seem to have power may have far less of it than people who have discovered how to exhibit their power more quietly.

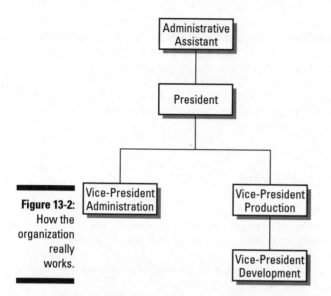

Figure 13-2:
How the organization really works.

Scrutinizing Communication: What's Real and What's Not?

One of the best ways to determine how well you fit into an organization is to see how well you communicate. But, deciphering the real meaning of communication in an organization takes some practice. So how do you determine the real meaning of words in your organization? You can best get to the underlying meanings by observing behavior, reading between the lines, and, when necessary, knowing how to obtain sensitive information.

Believing actions, not words

One way to decipher the real meaning of communication is to pay close attention to the corresponding behavior of the communicator. The values and priorities (that is, the ethics) of others tend to come through more clearly in what they do rather than in what they say.

So, for example, if your manager repeatedly says he is trying to get approval for a raise for you, look at what actions he has taken toward that end. Did he make a call to his boss or hold a meeting? Did he submit the necessary paperwork or establish a deadline to accomplish this goal? If the answers to these questions are no, or if he is continually waiting to hear, the action is probably going nowhere fast. To counter this situation, try to get higher up on your boss's list of priorities by suggesting actions that he can take to get you your raise. You may find that you need to do some or all of the footwork yourself. Alternatively, your manager's actions may indicate that your boss is not a power player in the organization. If that's the case, then make a point to attract the attention of the power players in your organization who can help you get the raise you deserve.

Reading between the lines

In business, don't take the written word at face value. Probe to find out the real reasons behind what is written. For example, here's a typical notice in a company newsletter announcing the reorganization of several departments:

> With the departure of J. R. McNeil, the Marketing Support and Customer Service department will now be a part of the Sales and Administration division under Elizabeth Olsen, acting vice president. The unit will eventually be moved under the direct supervision of the sales director, Tom Hutton.

Tools for success?

Every organization has someone who mistakenly believes that power comes from the accessories one carries, rather than from within himself. For people like this, no political image makeover is complete without the right accessories. If you believe that the items on this list create power, we have news for you: they don't. In fact, they may indicate a deep insecurity about not having any real power — the kind that comes from within an individual.

Wireless phone: Automatically rings anytime you have been in a meeting for more than five minutes. After you answer your phone, excuse yourself from the meeting, explaining that you have an important client on the line.

Antacid tablet container: Don't fake an ulcer when you can have a real one! Show your commitment to the team with a large bottle of these chalk tablets on your desk. Collects many times its weight in first impressions.

Rolex watch face: Exchange the face of your no-name watch for one that commands attention. Two-tone 18K gold and stainless steel wristband, add $1,000.

Mont Blanc pen: An expensive pen ensures that every word you write is concise, witty, and important. (Or so you think.)

Political scorecard: This handy reference card helps you to easily remember who is in favor and who is out. Use for scoring points for political moves and deciding when you have enough points to make a move yourself.

Such an announcement in the company newsletter may seem to be straight-forward on the surface, but if you read between the lines, you may be able to conclude:

> J. R. McNeil, who never did seem to get along with the director of sales, finally did something bad enough to justify getting fired. Tom Hutton apparently made a successful bid with the board of directors to add the area to his empire, probably because his sales were up 30 percent from last year. Elizabeth Olsen will be assigned as acting vice president for an interim period to do some of Tom's dirty work by clearing out some of the deadwood. Tom will thus start with a clean slate, 20 percent lower expenses, and an almost guaranteed increase in profits for his first year in the job. This all fits very nicely with Tom's personal strategy for advancement. (*P.S.: A nice congratulatory call to Tom may be in order.*)

Announcements like these have been reworked dozens of times by so many people that they appear to be logical and valid when you initially read them. By reading between the lines, however, you can often determine what is really going on. Of course, you have to be careful not to jump to the wrong conclusions. J.R. may have simply gone on to better opportunities and the company has taken advantage of that event to reorganize. Make sure to validate your conclusions with others in the company to get the real story.

Probing for information

In general, you can get ongoing information about your organization by being a trusted listener to as many people as possible. Show sincere interest in the affairs of others, and they'll talk about themselves openly. After they begin talking, you can shift the topic to work, work problems, and eventually more sensitive topics. Ask encouraging questions and volunteer information as necessary to keep the exchange equitable.

Even after you've developed such trusted relationships, you need to know how to probe to uncover the facts about rumors, decisions, and hidden agendas. Start by adhering to the following guidelines:

- ✔ Have at least three ways of obtaining the information.
- ✔ Check the information through two sources.
- ✔ Promise anonymity whenever possible.
- ✔ Generally know the answers to the questions you ask.
- ✔ Be casual and nonthreatening in your approach.
- ✔ Assume that the initial answer is superficial.
- ✔ Ask the same question different ways.
- ✔ Be receptive to whatever information you're given.

One more thing: If you find yourself in an organization rife with political intrigue, where you're always looking over your shoulder and are worried when the next rumor is going to be about you, seriously consider changing jobs! While every organization has its share of politics, spending too much time worrying about it is certainly counterproductive, and it can't be good for your well-being.

Uncovering the Unwritten Rules of Organizational Politics

Every organization has rules that are never written down and seldom discussed. Such unwritten rules pertaining to the expectations and behavior of employees in the organization can play a major role in your success or failure. Because unwritten rules aren't explicit, you have to piece them together by observation, insightful questioning, or simply through trial and error.

Interpreting the company policy manual

Even when written in black and white, an organization's policies are rarely what they appear to be. Most policies came about as a directive from the top to solve a particular problem. For example, if the company employed a single employee who preferred to wear gaudy jewelry, the individual could be confronted in a two- to three-minute discussion that would probably settle the matter. What is more often the case, however, is that management appoints a task force to develop a dress code and company plan for personal hygiene. Even after the policy is enacted, the targeted individual is likely to be oblivious to any perceived problem and may even wholeheartedly endorse the new code "for all those who need it" — that is, seemingly everyone except her.

A similar explanation can be made for most policies, and you should be alert to the following ways in which some employees try to skirt their responsibilities:

✔ Refer to the policy only when it clearly supports exactly what they want to do.

✔ Always assume that a policy that doesn't support what they want was intended for others.

✔ Claim an inability to equitably enforce policies they don't like by citing a rumored abuse or possible misinterpretation.

✔ When a conflict arises about policy implementation, argue that the policy is too specific (for general application) or too general (for specific circumstances).

✔ Argue that all policies should be considered flexible guidelines.

The point is that sometimes policies don't work. Your job is to recognize that some policies don't work and to try to change those policies. For example, if you want to give your employees the flexibility to set their own work schedules, but company policy prohibits that, do whatever you can to get management to buy off on a new policy that accomplishes your goal.

Never underestimate the power of the unwritten rules of organizational politics. In many companies, the unwritten rules carry just as much importance, if not more, than the written rules contained in the company's policy manuals.

Be friendly with all

The more individuals you have as friends in an organization, the better off you are. If you haven't already done so, start cultivating friends in your immediate work group and then extend your efforts to making contacts and developing friendships in other parts of the organization. The more favorably your coworkers view you, the greater your chances of becoming their manager in the future. Cultivate their support by seeking advice or by offering assistance.

You never know whom you'll be reporting to in the future. As the saying goes, "Be nice to people on the way up because you may meet them on the way down."

Build a network by routinely helping new employees who enter your organization. As they join, be the person who takes them aside to explain how the organization really works. As the new employees establish themselves and move on to other jobs in other parts of the organization, you have a well-entrenched network for obtaining information and assistance.

Knowing others throughout the organization can be invaluable for clarifying rumors, obtaining information, and indirectly feeding information back to others. An astute manager maintains a large number of diverse contacts throughout the organization, all on friendly terms. The following are excellent ways to enlarge your network:

- ✔ **Walk around:** Those managers who walk the halls tend to be better known than those managers who don't. Return telephone and e-mail messages in person whenever possible. Not only do you have the opportunity for one-on-one communication with the individual who left you the message, but also you can stop in to see everyone else you know along the way.

- ✔ **Play company sports or games:** You can meet employees from a wide range of functions and locations by joining a company sports league. Whether bowling, golf, or softball is your cup of tea, surely something catches your fancy. If you prefer, start or join a lunchtime bridge or chess group.

- ✔ **Join committees:** Whether the committee has been formed to address employee security or simply to determine who cleans out the refrigerator in the employee lounge, take part. You get to meet new people in an informal and relaxed setting.

Help others get what they want

A fundamental, unwritten rule of office politics is: Getting what you want is easier when you give others what they want. Win the assistance of others by showing them what they stand to gain by helping you. When a benefit isn't readily apparent, create or allude to one that may occur if they offer to help. Such benefits can include:

- ✔ **A favor returned in kind:** Surely, you can provide some kind of favor to your counterparts in exchange for their assistance. Lunch or the temporary loan of an employee is always a popular option.

- ✔ **Information:** Don't forget: Information is power. You may find that many of your coworkers crave the latest and greatest information in an organization. Perhaps you can be the one to give it to them.

- ✔ **Money:** Perhaps you have a little extra money in your equipment budget that you can allocate to someone's project in exchange for that person's help.

- ✔ **A recommendation:** The higher-ups trust your judgment. Your willingness to recommend a coworker for promotion to a higher position or for recognition for extraordinary performance is a valuable commodity. The right words to the right people can make all the difference to someone's success in an organization.

We're not suggesting that you do anything unethical or illegal. When you provide these kinds of benefits to others in your organization, make sure that you are within your company's rules and policies. And, as a side benefit, you may actually find satisfaction in giving. Don't violate your personal set of ethics or company policy to get ahead.

Don't party at company parties

Social affairs are a serious time for those employees seeking to advance within a company. Social events offer one of the few times when everyone in the company is supposed to be on equal footing. Don't believe it. Although social functions provide those managers at the top a chance to show that they're regular people and give those employees below a chance to ask questions and laugh at their bosses' jokes, they are also a time to be extremely cautious.

Beware of whom you talk to and, of course, what you say. Social functions, such as holiday parties and company picnics, are neither the time nor the place to sink your career by making some injudicious comment or by making a fool of yourself. Managing most social encounters involves art and skill, especially those encounters that involve coworkers. Proper poise begins with proper mingling techniques. Use these techniques at your next company party:

- ✔ Use the middle of the room to intercept individuals that you especially want to speak to. As an alternative strategy for getting their attention, watch the hors d'oeuvres table or the punch bowl. Go for refills when the person you are seeking does so.

- ✔ Keep discussion loose and light and avoid discussing work topics with anyone other than your boss. Try to move on before the person you're speaking to runs out of topics to discuss and is overcome with a blank expression. Don't fawn or brown-nose. These behaviors are more likely to lose respect for you than to gain it.

- ✔ Leave the social function only after the departure of the highest-ranking company official. If you're forced to leave before, let him or her know why.

Manage your manager

Successful managers know the importance of managing not just their employees, but their manager as well. The idea is to encourage your manager to do what most directly benefits you and your staff. The following tried-and-true techniques for manager management have evolved through the ages:

- ✔ **Keep your manager informed of your successes:** "That last sale puts me over quota for the month."

- ✔ **Support your manager in meetings:** "Gadsby is right on this. We really do have to consider the implications of this change on our customers."

- ✔ **Praise your manager publicly:** "Ms. Gadsby is probably the best manager I have ever worked for."

Although a well-controlled relationship with your manager is important, you need connections to those above your manager, too. A key relationship to develop is with your manager's manager — an individual who is likely to have a very big influence on your future career.

Volunteer for an assignment that happens to be a pet project of your manager's boss. If you do a good job, you'll more than likely be asked to do another project. If you don't have an opportunity like a pet project, try to find an area of common interest with your manager's boss. Bring up the topic in casual conversation and agree to meet later to discuss it in more detail. But be careful not to press your boss too hard. You don't want to appear overly anxious or like you're stalking your boss.

Move ahead with your mentors

Having a *mentor* is almost essential for ensuring any long-term success within an organization. A mentor is an individual — usually higher up in the organization — who provides advice and helps to guide your progress. (See our in-depth discussion about mentors in Chapter 20.) Mentors are necessary because they can offer you important career advice, as well as become your advocate in higher levels of the organization — the levels that you don't have direct access to.

Make sure the person whom you select as your mentor (or who selects you, as is more often the case) has organizational clout and is vocal about touting your merits. If possible, get the support of several powerful people throughout the organization. *Sponsorships* (your relationships with your mentors) develop informally over an extended period of time.

Seek out a mentor by finding an occasion to ask for advice. If you find the advice extremely helpful, frequently seek more advice from the same person. Initially, ask for advice related to your work, but as time goes on, you can ask for advice about business in general and your career advancement specifically. Proceed slowly, or your intentions may be suspect. Always display tact and discretion in your approach to your mentor:

- **The wrong approach:** "Mr. Fairmont, I've been thinking. In the marketing department, a lot of bad rumors have been going around about you and Suzy. I could try to squelch some of them if I see something in it for me. You know: You take care of me, and I take care of you. What do you say?"

- **The right approach:** "Here's that special report you asked for, Ms. Smith. Correlating customer color preferences with the size of orders in the Eastern region was fascinating. You seem to be one of the forward-looking people in this organization."

Be trustworthy

Similar to having a mentor is being a loyal follower of an exceptional performer within the organization. Finding good people to trust can be difficult, so if you're trustworthy, you're likely to become a valued associate of a bright peer. As that person rises quickly through the organization, he or she can bring you along. However, whenever possible, hitch your wagon to more than one star: You never know when a star may fall and leave you all alone in the stardust.

Protecting Yourself

Inevitably, you may find yourself on the receiving end of someone else's political aspirations. Astute managers take precautions to protect themselves — and their employees — against the political maneuverings of others. These precautions can also help if your own strategies go wrong. What can you do to protect yourself?

Document for protection

Document the progress of your department's projects and activities, especially when expected changes in plans or temporary setbacks affect your project. Documenting the changes or setbacks gives you an accurate record of your projects' history and ensures that individuals who don't have your best interest at heart don't forget (or inappropriately use them against you). The form of the documentation can vary, but the following are most common:

- ✔ Confirmation memos
- ✔ Activity reports
- ✔ Project folders
- ✔ Correspondence files
- ✔ Notes

Don't make promises you can't keep

Avoid making promises or firm commitments for your employees when you don't want to or you can't follow through. Don't offer a deadline, final price, or guarantee of action or quality unless you're sure you can meet it. When you make promises that you can't fulfill, you risk injuring your own reputation when deliveries are late, or costs are higher than expected. If you find yourself forced to make promises when you aren't certain you can meet them, consider taking one of the following actions:

- ✔ **Hedge:** If forced to make a firm commitment to an action that you're not sure you can meet, hedge your promise as much as possible by building in extra time, staff, money, or other qualifier.

- ✔ **Buffer time estimates:** If you're forced to make a time commitment that may be unrealistic, buffer the estimate (add extra time to what you think you really need) to give yourself room to maneuver. If your employees deliver early, they'll be heroes.

✔ **Extend deadlines:** As deadlines approach, bring any problems you or your staff encounter — even the most basic ones — to the attention of the person who requested that you do the project. Keeping people informed prevents them from being surprised if you need to extend your deadlines.

Be visible

To get the maximum credit for the efforts of you and your staff, be sure to publicize your department's successes. To ensure that credit is given where credit is due, do the following:

✔ **Advertise your department's successes.** Routinely send copies of successfully completed projects and letters of praise for every member of your staff to your manager and to your manager's boss.

✔ **Use surrogates.** Call on your friends in the organization to help publicize your achievements and those of your employees. Be generous in highlighting your employees' achievements. If you highlight your own achievements at the expense of your hard-working employees, you appear tactless and boastful.

✔ **Be visible.** Make a name for yourself in the organization. The best way to do that is to perform at a level that separates you from the rest of the pack. Work harder, work smarter, and respond better to the needs of the organization and your customers, and you'll be noticed!

Top five ethics and office politics Web sites

Wondering where to find the best information on the Web about the topics addressed in this chapter? Well, you've come to the right place! Here are our top five favorites:

✔ Business for Social Responsibility: www.bsr.org

✔ Ethics Resource Center: www.ethics.org

✔ Office Politics: www.officepolitics.co.uk/frame.html

✔ CareerLink: http://careerlink.devx.com/articles/hc1199/hc1199.asp

✔ Business.com: www.business.com/directory/human_resources/workforce_management/office_politics

---

Part V
Tough Times for Tough Managers

"This proposed Shackleton-like management plan seems to rely heavily on team building, crisis prevention, and an inordinate amount of raw seal meat."

In this part . . .

No one ever said that being a manager is easy. Rewarding? Yes. Easy? No. In this part, we present strategies for managing change in the workplace, disciplining employees easily and effectively, conducting employee terminations, and taking care of yourself.

Chapter 14

Managing Change on the Job

• •

In This Chapter

▶ Dealing with crisis

▶ Putting up roadblocks to change

▶ Helping others through change

▶ Inspiring initiative in others

▶ Moving on with your life

• •

*N*othing stays the same, in business or in life. Change is all around us — it always has been, and it always will be. But, while many people consider change something to be feared and avoided at any cost, the reality is that change brings with it excitement, new opportunities, and growth.

So what does change mean to you as a manager? The world of business is constantly changing, and the pressures on managers to perform are greater than they've ever been before. In addition, most organizations have gone from being bastions of stability and status quo in the stormy seas of change to being agile ships, navigating the fluid and ever-changing seas in which they float. "Heywood, we have decided to reorganize the division. Starting tomorrow, you're in charge of our new factory in Singapore. I hope you like Chinese food!"

The words *business* and *change* are quickly becoming synonymous. And the more things change, the more everyone in an organization is affected. This chapter is about managing and thriving on change and about helping your employees find ways to take advantage of it (instead of change taking advantage of them!).

What's the Rush?

What's your typical business day like? You get into the office, grab a cup of coffee, and scan your appointment calendar. Looks like a light day for meetings — two in the morning and only one in the afternoon. Maybe you can finally get a chance to work on the budget goal you've been meaning to complete for the past few months, plus have some extra time to go for a walk at lunch to unwind. Wouldn't that be nice! Next, you pick up your telephone to check your voice mail. Of the 25 messages that have stacked up since you last checked, 10 are urgent. When you check your e-mail, you find much the same ratio.

As you begin to think how you can respond to these urgent messages, an employee arrives with his own crisis that needs your immediate attention. He tells you that the computer network has broken down, and until someone fixes it, the entire corporate financial system is on the fritz. While you're talking to your employee, your boss calls to tell you to drop everything because you've been selected to write a report for the president that absolutely has to be done by the close of business today.

So much for working on your budget goal. And you can forget that relaxing walk at lunch. This day is turning out to be just another fun day in management!

Choosing between legitimate urgency and crisis management

Urgency has its place in an organization. The rate of change in the global business environment demands it. The revolutions in computer use, telecommunications systems, and information technology demand it. The need to be more responsive to customers than ever before demands it. In these urgent times, companies that provide the best solutions faster than anyone else are the winners. The losers are the companies that wonder what happened as they watch their competitors streak by.

However, an organization has a real problem when its managers fall into the behavior of managing by crisis and the trap of reacting to change instead of leading change. When every problem in an organization becomes a drop-everything-else-that-you-are-doing crisis, the organization isn't showing signs of responsiveness to its business environment. Instead, the business is showing signs of poor planning and lousy execution. Someone (perhaps a manager?) isn't doing his or her job.

Recognizing and dealing with crises

Sometimes outside forces beyond your control as a manager cause crises. For example, suppose that a vital customer requests that all project designs be submitted by this Friday instead of next Friday. Or perhaps the city sends you a notice that a maintenance crew plans to cut off the power to your plant for three days while the crew performs needed maintenance on switching equipment. Or a huge snowstorm in the Northeast cuts off all flights, in and out, for the rest of the week.

On the other hand, many crises occur because someone in your organization drops the ball, and now you (the manager) have to fix everything. The following are avoidable crisis situations:

- ✔ Hoping that the need will go away, a manager avoids making a necessary decision. Surprise! The need didn't go away, and now he or she has a crisis to deal with.

- ✔ An employee forgets to relay an important message from your customer, and you're about to lose the account as a result. Another crisis. (See Chapter 15 for details about disciplining an employee.)

- ✔ A coworker decides that informing you about a major change to a manufacturing process isn't important. Because of your experience, you would have quickly seen that the change would lead to quality problems in the finished product. When manufacturing grinds to a halt, you come in after the fact to clean up the mess. One more crisis to add to your list.

You have to be prepared to deal with externally generated crises. You have to be flexible, you have to work smart, and you have to work hard. But your organization can't afford to become a slave to internally generated crises. Managing by crisis forgoes one of the most important elements in business management. That element is *planning*.

You establish plans and goals for a reason — to make your company as successful as possible. However, if you continually set your plans and goals on a back burner because of today's crisis, why waste your time making the plans? And where does your organization go then? (See Chapter 7 for a discussion on the importance of having plans and goals.)

When you, as a manager, allow everything to become a crisis through your own inaction or failure to anticipate change, not only do you sap the energy of your employees, but also eventually, they lose the ability to recognize when a real crisis is upon them. Remember the old fable about the boy who cried "Wolf"? After the boy issued several false alarms in jest, the villagers didn't bother to respond to his cries when some wolves really appeared to attack his sheep. After responding to several manufactured crises, your employees begin to see the crises as routine, and they may not be there for you when you really need them.

Change Happens

Change happens, and you can't do anything about it. You can try to ignore it, but does that stop change? No, you only blind yourself to what is really happening in your organization. You can try to stop it, but does that keep change from happening? No, you're only fooling yourself if you think that you can stop change — even for a moment. You can try to insulate yourself and those employees around you from the effects of change, but can you really afford to ignore it? No, to ignore change is to sign a death warrant for your organization and, quite possibly, for your career.

Unfortunately, from our personal observations, most managers seem to spend their entire careers trying to fight change — to predict, control, and harness change and its effects on the organization. But why? Change is what allows organizations to progress, products to get better, and people to advance — both personally, and in their careers.

When Bill Taylor, owner of Lark In The Morning (a seller of musical instruments located in Ft. Bragg, California) discusses the topic of change with his employees, he likes to tell the following story about swinging on a trapeze — inspired by an essay published in *The Essene Book of the Days,* 1994, by Danaan Parry: You have a good grip. You get some confidence, and maybe even do a pike or hang by your ankles. It begins to feel really good and really comfortable. Then, off in the darkness, you see another trapeze bar swinging toward you, and you get that old familiar feeling in your stomach. You have to completely let go of this trapeze, fly through the air, and grab the next trapeze. You've done this before. You know you can do it again. But it always creates anxiety and uncertainty, maybe even a sense of dread. So you let go, and start flying through the air. And what you have to remember is that the very uncomfortable place in mid-air is the only place that personal growth takes place. Maybe you don't get comfortable with being in the air, but at least you recognize the value it adds to your life. When you grab the new trapeze, then personal growth is over.

Identifying the four stages of change

Change is not a picnic. Despite the excitement that change can bring to your working life — both good and bad — you've probably had just about all the change you can handle right about now, thank you. But as change continues, you go through four distinct phases in response to change:

1. **Deny change.** When change happens, the first response you have (if you're like most people) is one of immediate denial. "Whose dumb idea was that? That idea is never going to work here. Don't worry, they'll see their mistake and go back to the old way of doing things!" Operating with this attitude is like an ostrich sticking its head in the sand: If you can't see it, it'll go away. You wish!

2. **Resist change.** At some point, you realize that the change isn't just a clerical error; however, this realization doesn't mean that you have to accept the change lying down! "Nope, I'm sticking with the old way of doing that job. If that way was good enough then, why isn't it good enough now?" Resistance is a normal response to change — everyone

goes through it. The key isn't to let your resistance get you stuck. The quicker you get with the program, the better for your organization and the better for your career.

3. **Explore change.** By now, you know that further resistance is futile and the new way just may have some pluses. "Well, maybe that change actually does make sense. I'll see what opportunities can make the change work for me instead of against me." During this stage, you examine both the good and bad that come from the change, and you decide on a strategy for managing the change.

4. **Accept change.** The final stage of change is acceptance. At this point, you have successfully integrated the change into your routine. "Wow, this new system really works well. It beats the heck out of the old way of doing things!" Now, the change that you so vigorously denied and resisted is part of your everyday routine; the change is now the status quo.

At the end of your change responses, you come full circle, and you're ready to face your next change.

Are you fighting change?

You may be fighting change and not even know it. Besides watching the number of gray hairs on your head multiply, how can you tell? Look out for these seven deadly warning signs of resistance to change:

- **You're still using the old rules to play a new game.** Sorry to be the ones to bring you this bad news, but the old game is gone, kaput. The pressures of global competition have created a brand new game with a brand new set of rules. For example, if you're one of those increasingly rare managers who refuses to find out how to use a computer (don't laugh, they do exist!), you're playing by the old rules. Computer literacy and information proficiency is the new rule. If you're not playing with the new rules, not only is this a warning sign that you're resisting change, but you can bet on being left behind as the rest of your organization moves along the path to the future.

- **You're ducking new assignments.** Usually, two basic reasons cause you to avoid new assignments. First, you may be overwhelmed with your current job and can't imagine taking on any more duties. If you're in this situation, try to remember that new ways often make your work more efficient or even wipe out many old things that you do. Second, you may simply be uneasy with the unknown, and so you resist change.

Ducking new assignments to resist change is a definite no-no. Not only are you interfering with the progress of the organization, but also you're effectively putting your own career on hold.

✔ **You're trying to slow things down.** Trying to slow down is a normal reaction for most people. When something new comes along — a new way of doing business, a new assignment, or a new wrinkle in the marketplace — most people tend to want to slow down, to take the time to examine, analyze, and then decide how to react. The problem is that the newer something gets, the slower some people go.

As a manager, you want to remain competitive in the future. You don't have the luxury of slowing down every time something new comes along. From now on, the amount of new that you have to deal with is going to greatly outweigh the old. Instead of resisting the new by slowing down (and risking an uncompetitive and obsolete organization), you need to keep up your pace. How? When you're forced to do more with less, focus on less.

✔ **You're working hard to control the uncontrollable.** Have you ever tried to keep the sun from rising in the morning? Or tried to stop the dark clouds that drop rain, sleet, and snow on your house during a storm? Or tried to stay 29-years-old forever? Face it: You just can't control many things in life — you waste your time when you try.

Are you resisting change by trying to control the uncontrollable at work? Perhaps you want to try to head off a planned corporate reorganization or stop your foreign competitors from having access to your domestic markets or delay the acquisition of your firm by a much larger company. The world of business is changing all around you, and you can't do anything about it. You have a choice: You can continue to resist change by pretending that you're controlling it (believe us, you can't), or you can concentrate your efforts on figuring out how to most effectively respond to change to leverage it to your advantage.

✔ **You're playing the role of victim.** Oh, woe is me! This response is the ultimate cop-out. Instead of accepting change and finding out how to respond to it (and using it to the advantage of your organization and yourself), you choose to become a victim of it. Playing the role of victim and hoping that your coworkers feel sorry for you is easy to do. ("Poor Samantha, she's got a brand new crop of upstart competitors to handle. I wonder how she can even bring herself to come to work every morning!")

But today's successful businesses can't afford to waste their time or money employing victims. If you're not giving 110 percent each day that you go to work, your organization will find someone who can.

✔ **You're hoping someone else can make things better for you.** In the old-style hierarchical organization, top management almost always took responsibility for making the decisions that made things better (or worse) for workers. We have a news flash: The old-style organization is changing, and the new-style organization that is taking its place has empowered every employee to take responsibility for decision making.

The pressures of global competition and the coming of the Information Age require that decisions be made quicker than ever. In other words, the employees closest to the issues must make the decisions; a manager who is seven layers up from the front line and 3,000 miles away can't do it. You hold the keys to your future. You have the power to make things better for yourself. If you wait until someone else makes things better for you, then you're going to be waiting an awfully long time.

✔ **You're absolutely paralyzed, like a deer in the headlights.** This condition is the ultimate sign of resistance to change and is almost always terminal. Sometimes change seems so overwhelming that the only choice is to give up. When change paralyzes you, not only do you fail to respond to change, but also you can no longer perform your current duties. In today's organization, such resistance is certain death.

Instead of allowing change to paralyze you, become a leader of change. Here are some ideas how:

- Embrace the change. Become its friend and its biggest cheerleader.

- Be flexible and be responsive to the changes that swirl all around you and through your organization.

- Be a model to those employees around you who continue to resist change. Show them that they can make change work for them instead of against them.

- Focus on what you can do — not what you can't do.

- Recognize and reward employees who have accepted the change and who have succeeded as a result.

If you notice any of these seven warning signs of resistance to change — in yourself or in your coworkers — you can do something about it. As long as you're willing to embrace change instead of fight it, you hold incredible value for your organization, and you can take advantage of change rather than fall victim to it. Make responsiveness to change your personal mission: Be a leader of change, not a follower of resistance.

Change Affects Everyone

When your organization finds itself in the midst of change — whether because of fast-moving markets, changing technology, rapidly shifting customer needs, or some other reason — you need to remember that change affects everyone, not just you as a manager. And, although some of your employees can cope with these changes with nary a hiccup, others may have a very difficult time adjusting to their new environment and the expectations that come along with it. Be on the alert for employees who are resisting or having a hard time dealing with change, and then help them transition through the process.

The following tips can help your employees cope with change on the job:

- **Show that you care.** Managers are very busy people, but never be too busy to show your employees that you care — especially when they're having difficulties on the job. Take a personal interest in your employees and offer to help them in any way you can.

- **Widely communicate the potential for change.** Nothing is more disconcerting to employees than being surprised by changes that they didn't expect. As much as possible, give your employees a heads-up on potential changes in the business environment, and keep them up-to-date on the status of the changes as time goes on.

- **Seek feedback.** Let your employees know that you want their feedback and suggestions on how to deal with potential problems resulting from change, or how to capitalize on any opportunities that may result.

- **Be a good listener.** When your employees are in a stressful situation, they naturally are going to want to talk about it — this part of the process helps them cope with change. Set aside time to chat informally with employees, and encourage them to voice their concerns about the changes that they and the organization are going through.

- **Don't give false assurances.** Although you don't want to needlessly frighten your employees with tales of impending doom and gloom, also avoid sugarcoating the truth. Be frank and honest with your employees and treat them like the adults they are.

- **Involve employees.** Involve employees in planning for upcoming changes, and delegate the responsibility and authority for making decisions to them whenever practicable.

- **Look to the future.** Paint a vision for your employees that emphasizes the many ways that the organization will be a better place as everyone adapts to change and begins to use it to their benefit.

Change can be traumatic for those people who go through it. Stay alert to the impact of change on your employees, and help them work their way through it. Not only will your employees appreciate your support — showing their appreciation with loyalty to you and your organization — but also morale will improve and your employees will be more productive as a result.

Encouraging Employee Initiative

One of the most effective ways to help employees make it through the change process in one piece is to give them permission to take charge of their own work. You can encourage your employees to take the initiative to come up with ideas to improve the way they do their work, and then to implement those ideas.

The most successful organizations are the ones that actively encourage employees to take initiative, and the least successful ones are those organizations that stifle initiative.

Consider how these companies reward employee initiative:

- **Absolutely the best:** Federal Express, based in Memphis, Tennessee, awards the Golden Falcon to employees who go above and beyond to serve their customers. For example, one winner took the initiative to order new shipping forms for a regular customer after noticing that the customer had not thought to change his area code on a return address.

- **Above and beyond:** Employees who take the initiative to help others by going beyond what's expected at CIC Pharmaceuticals Group in Wilmington, Delaware, receive the Performance Excellence Award and $300. Peers, supervisors, or anyone else who knows of someone's special work can nominate an employee.

- **They add up:** At El Torito Restaurants, based in Irvine, California, employees receive a "Be a Star" award for going above and beyond their job description. Winners receive Star Bucks, which are entered for a monthly drawing for up to $1,000 worth of merchandise.

As a manager, you need to make your employees safe to take initiative in their jobs. Not only will your employees better weather the change that swirls all around them, but they also will create a more effective organization and provide better service to customers in the process. Ask your employees to take the following suggestions and put them to use:

- Look for ways to make improvements to the status quo, and follow through with an action plan.

- Focus suggestions on areas that have the greatest impact on the organization.

- Follow up suggestions with action. Volunteer to help implement your suggestions.

- Step outside of your box. Look for areas of improvement throughout the organization, not just within your department or business unit.

- Don't make frivolous suggestions. They degrade your credibility and distract you from more important areas of improvement.

When All Else Fails

If you've done everything you can to deal with change at work and take control of your business life, but you're still feeling lost, you may be facing a much deeper issue that's not readily apparent on the surface.

Top five change management Web sites

Wondering where to find the best information on the Web about the topics addressed in this chapter? Well, you've come to the right place! Here are our top five favorites:

✔ Change Management Resource Library: `www.change-management.org`

✔ ManagementFirst: Change Management: `www.managementfirst.com/experts/change.htm`

✔ Wharton Center for Leadership and Change Management: `http://leadership.wharton.upenn.edu`

✔ Change Management Learning Center: `www.change-management.com`

✔ HDI Managing Change Library: `www.hdinc.com/library.html`

When you read a book, do you ever wish that you had written it? When you go to a seminar, do you ever think that you could teach it? Have you ever wondered what owning your own business is like — to be your own boss and to be completely responsible for your company's profits or losses?

If you answered yes to any of these questions, you may not be truly happy until you pursue your dream. Maybe you want to start a new career or move to a new company. Or perhaps you have an opportunity with your current employer to make a job change that can take you to your dream. Maybe you want to go back to school to pursue an advanced degree. Or maybe you just want to take a vacation or short leave of absence. It may very well be that all the change you need to make is within yourself.

Chapter 15

Employee Discipline: Speaking Softly and Carrying a Big Stick

*W*ouldn't it be nice if all your employees always carried out their tasks perfectly? Wouldn't it be nice if they all loved the organization as much as you do? Winning the lottery would be nice, too, but you probably shouldn't quit your day job just yet.

The fact is that your employees will make mistakes, and some of them will exhibit attitudes that are, shall we say, poor. Every organization has employees (and managers) who exhibit varying degrees of these behaviors, but don't worry too much about it. However, when your employees make repeated, serious mistakes, when they fail to meet their performance goals and standards, or when it seems that they'd rather be working somewhere else (anywhere but where they are now!) (and they prove that by ignoring company policies), you have to take action to stop the offending behaviors — immediately and decisively. Why?

First, when employees aren't performing up to standard, or when they allow a poor attitude to overcome their ability to pull with the rest of the team, these employees cost your organization more than do the employees who are working at or above standard and pulling their share of the load. Poor performance and poor attitudes directly and negatively affect your work unit's efficiency and effectiveness.

Second, if other employees see that you're letting their coworkers get away with poor performance, they have little reason to maintain their own standards. "Hey! If Marty can get away with it, I can, too!" Not only do you create more management headaches, but also the morale and performance of your entire work unit decreases as a result.

In this chapter, you discover the importance of dealing with employee performance issues before they become major problems. You find out why you need to focus on performance and not personality. You also discover and implement a consistent system of discipline that can work for you, regardless of your line of business.

Understanding Employee Discipline

Employee discipline has lately gotten something of a black eye. Because of the abuses that more than a few overzealous supervisors and managers have committed, for many workers, the word *discipline* conjures up visions of crazed management tirades, embarrassing public scoldings, and worse.

What does discipline mean to you? What does discipline mean in your organization? Do your employees look forward to being disciplined? Do you?

The reality is that far too many employees confuse the terms *discipline* and *punishment*, considering them to be one and the same. This belief can't be farther from the truth — at least when discipline is done well. The word discipline comes from the Latin *disciplina*, meaning teaching or learning (no, not despicable). Punishment, on the other hand, is derived from the Latin root *punire*, which itself is derived from the Latin word *poena*, or penalty. Interestingly, the English word *pain* also found its beginnings in the Latin *poena*.

The whole point of this little digression is that employee discipline can be a positive experience. At least it should be when you do it the right way! Through discipline, you bring problems to your employees' attention so that they can take actions to correct them before they become major problems. Remember, however, to build a strong foundation of positives and trust that can be drawn upon when dealing with the negatives. The primary goal of discipline isn't to punish your employees; you want to help guide them back to a satisfactory job performance. Of course, sometimes this step isn't possible, and you have no choice but to terminate employees who can't perform satisfactorily.

Two main reasons to discipline your employees exist:

✔ **Performance problems:** All employees must meet goals as a part of their jobs. For a receptionist, a goal may be to always answer the telephone on the second ring or sooner. For a sales manager, a goal may be to increase annual sales by 15 percent. When employees fail to meet their performance goals, administering some form of discipline is required.

✔ **Misconduct:** Sometimes employees behave in ways that are unacceptable to you as a manager and to the organization. For example, if an employee abuses the company sick leave policy, you have a valid reason for disciplining that employee. Similarly, discipline employees who sexually harass or threaten other employees.

Discipline ranges from simple verbal counseling ("William, you turned in the report a day late. I expect future reports to be submitted on time.") to termination ("Sorry, Mary, I warned you that I wouldn't tolerate any further insubordination. You're fired."). A wide variety of options lies between these two extremes, the use of which depends on the nature of the problem, its severity, and the work history of the employee involved. For example, if the problem is an isolated incident, and the employee normally performs well, the discipline will be less severe than if the problem is repeated and persistent.

Always carry out discipline as soon after the incident as possible — you can deal with problems before they escalate. And, as with rewarding employees, your message is much stronger and relevant when it has the immediacy of a recent event. If too much time lapses between an incident and the discipline that you conduct afterward, your employee may forget the specifics of the incident. Not only that, but you also send the message that the problem isn't that serious because you don't bother doing anything about it for so long.

Managers practice effective discipline by noticing performance shortcomings or misconduct before these problems become serious. Effective managers help to guide their employees along the right path. Managers who don't discipline their employees have only themselves to blame when poor performance continues unabated or acts of misconduct escalate and get out of hand. Employees need the active support and guidance of their supervisors and managers to know what's expected of them. Without the guidance, employees sometimes find it difficult to keep from straying from the right path.

And don't forget: You get what you reward. Take a close look at the behavior you're rewarding in your employees. You may be surprised to find that you're inadvertently reinforcing negative behaviors and poor performance.

Don't put off discipline. Don't procrastinate. Don't look the other way and hope that your employees' bad behavior disappears. If you do look the other direction (or think you just don't have the time), you're doing a disservice to the employees who need your guidance, to the employees who are working at or above standard, and to your organization. Discipline your employees before you run out of time. Do it now.

Focusing on Performance, Not Personalities

You're a manager (or a manager-to-be). You're not a psychiatrist or psychologist — even if you feel that you sometimes do nothing but counsel your employees. Your job isn't to analyze your workers' personalities or to attempt to understand why your employees act the way they do — it's impossible to read minds about things like "attitude." Your job is to assess your employees' performance against the standards that you and your employees agree to and to be alert to employee violations of company policy. If your employees are performing above standard, reward them for their efforts. (See Chapter 5 for more information on rewarding and motivating your employees.) If, on the other hand, they're performing below standard, you need to find out why (possibly a process, motivation, or training problem is out of your employees' control) and, if necessary, discipline them.

We're not saying that you shouldn't be compassionate. Sometimes performance suffers because of family problems, financial difficulties, or other non-job–related pressures. Although you can give your employees the opportunity to get through their difficulties — you may suggest some time off or a temporary reassignment of duties — they eventually have to return to meeting their performance standards.

If an employee is overwhelmed by personal problems or other difficulties, encourage him or her to seek confidential help from professional sources — through your organization's employee assistance program (EAP), a therapist, or other professional counselor.

To be fair, and to be sure that discipline focuses on performance and not on personalities, ensure that all employees fully understand company policies and that you communicate performance standards clearly. When your organization hires new employees, do they get an orientation to key company policies? When your human resources representative drops off new employees at your door, do you or someone in your department take the time to discuss your department's philosophy and practices? Do you periodically sit down with your employees to review and update their performance standards? If you say no to any of these questions, you need to get to work!

When you apply discipline, use it consistently and fairly. Although you must always discipline your employees soon after a demonstrated shortfall in performance or act of misconduct, rushing to judgment before you have a chance to get all the facts is a mistake. Although proving that an employee submitted a report a week late is simple, uncovering the facts in a case of sexual harassment may not be so simple. When you discipline employees, know the facts and act impartially and without favoritism for certain employees. If one employee does something wrong, you can't ignore the same behavior in your other employees. To do so certainly risks the loss of employee respect for your management, and it definitely invites lawsuits and other such unpleasantness.

Remember, although your job is to point out your employees' shortcomings and to help guide your employees in their efforts to perform to standard, your employees are ultimately responsible for their performance and their behavior. You can't, and shouldn't, do their work for them, and don't cover for their mistakes and misdeeds. Sure, you can excuse an occasional mistake, but you must deal with an ongoing pattern of substandard performance or misconduct.

Identifying the Two Tracks of Discipline

As the beginning of this chapter explains, two key reasons for disciplining employees exist: performance problems and misconduct. The two-track system of discipline includes one set of discipline options for performance problems and another for misconduct. These tracks reflect the fact that misconduct, usually an employee's willful act, is considered a much more serious transgression than a shortfall in performance. Performance problems often aren't the employee's direct fault and can usually be corrected with proper training or motivation.

These two tracks reflect the concept of *progressive discipline*. Progressive discipline means that you always select the least severe step that results in the behavior that you want. For example, if your employee responds to a verbal warning and improves as a result, then you can move on to your next management challenge. However, if the employee doesn't respond to a verbal warning, you then progress to the next step — a written warning — and give that step a try. The hope is that your employee gets the hint and corrects his or her behavior before you get to heavy-handed steps, such as reductions in pay, demotions, or (*gulp!*) terminations.

As you prepare to discipline your employees, first decide whether you're trying to correct performance-related behaviors or misconduct. After you figure that out, decide the best way to get your message across. If the transgression is minor — a lack of attention to detail, for example — you may need only to conduct a verbal counseling. However, if you catch an employee sleeping on the job, you may decide to suspend your employee without pay for some period of time. The choice is yours.

In any case, make sure that the discipline takes place as soon as possible after the transgression occurs. You want to correct your employee's performance before the problem becomes significant. You definitely don't want to make discipline only an annual event by saving all your employee's problems for his or her periodic performance appraisal. *Ouch!*

Note: Your organization's system for disciplining employees may be somewhat different from the one that we outline in this chapter. If you're dealing with union-represented employees, you're likely required to work within the system proscribed by the contract between the union and your firm. You may, for example, be required to allow a union representative to sit in on any discipline sessions that you conduct with union-represented employees. Whatever the case, review your organization's policies and labor relations practices and procedures before you embark on the task of disciplining your employees.

Dealing with performance problems: The first track

If you've done your job right, each of your employees has a job description and a set of performance standards. The job description is simply an inventory of all the different duties that accompany a particular position. Performance standards, on the other hand, are the measurements that you and your employees agree to use in assessing your employees' performance. Performance standards form the basis of periodic performance appraisals and reviews. They also make great filler for your personnel files.

Although every organization seems to have its own unique way of conducting performance assessments, employees usually fall into one of three broad categories:

- ✔ Outstanding performance
- ✔ Acceptable performance
- ✔ Unacceptable performance

When it comes to employee discipline, you're primarily concerned with correcting unacceptable performance. You always want to help your good employees become even better employees, but your first concern has to be to identify employees who aren't working up to standard and to correct their performance shortcomings.

The following steps are listed in order of least to most severe. Don't forget: Use the least severe step that results in the behavior you want. If that step doesn't do the trick, move down the list to the next step:

- ✔ **Verbal counseling:** This form of discipline is certainly the most common, and most managers take this step first when they want to correct an employee's performance. A manager verbally counsels a variety of employees many times a day. Verbal counseling can range from a simple, spontaneous correction performed in the hallway ("Marge, you need to let me know when our clients call with a service problem.") to a more formal, sit-down meeting in your office ("Sam, I am concerned that you don't understand the importance of checking the correct address prior to shipping orders. Let's discuss what steps you're going to take to correct this problem and your plan to implement them."). *Note:* You usually don't document verbal counseling in your employees' files.

✔ **Written counseling:** When employees don't respond favorably to verbal counseling, or when the magnitude of performance problems warrants its use, consider written counseling. Written counseling formalizes the counseling process by documenting your employees' performance shortcomings in a written memo. Written counseling is presented to employees in one-on-one sessions in the supervisor's office. After the employees have an opportunity to read the document, verbal discussions regarding the employees' plans to improve their performance ensue. This documentation becomes a part of your employees' personnel files.

✔ **Negative performance evaluation:** If verbal and written counseling fail to improve your employees' performance, the situation warrants a negative performance evaluation. Of course, because performance evaluations are generally given only annually, if at all, they're not usually very useful for dealing with acute situations. However, if you give verbal and written counseling to no avail, negative performance evaluations are the way to go.

✔ **Demotion:** Repeated negative performance evaluations or particularly serious performance shortcomings may warrant demoting your employees to a lower rung on the organizational ladder. Often, but not always, the pay of demoted employees is also reduced at the same time. Face it: Some employees are hired or promoted into positions that they just can't handle. This situation isn't their fault, but you can't let your employees continue to fail if you have no hope of bringing performance up to an acceptable level with further training or guidance. Although demoralizing, demotions at least allow your employees to move into positions that they can handle. Before you resort to demotion, always first try to find a position at an equivalent level that the employee can handle. This step may help to improve your employee's motivation and self-confidence and result in a situation that is a "win" for both the employee and the organization.

✔ **Termination:** When all else fails, termination is the ultimate form of discipline for employees who are performing unsatisfactorily. As any manager who has fired an employee knows, terminating employees isn't fun. Consider it as an option only after you exhaust all other avenues. Perhaps needless to say, in these days of wrongful termination lawsuits and multimillion-dollar judgments, you must document employees' performance shortcomings very well and support them by the facts. For further information on the ins and outs of this important form of discipline, see Chapter 16.

Dealing with misconduct: The second track

Misconduct is a whole different animal from performance problems, so it has its own discipline track. Although both misconduct and performance problems can have negative effects on a company's bottom line, misconduct is usually considered a much more serious offense than performance shortcomings because it indicates a problem with your employees' attitudes or ethical beliefs. And modifying performance behaviors is a great first step in eventually modifying workers' attitudes or belief systems.

Even the terminology of the different steps in the second track indicates that something serious is going on. For example, although the first step on the first track is called verbal *counseling,* the first step on the second track is called verbal *warning.* You need to deal with misconduct more severely than you deal with performance problems.

The discipline that results from misconduct also has much more immediate consequences to your employees than does the discipline that results from performance problems. Although performance may take some time to bring up to standard — with preparing a plan, scheduling additional training, and so forth — misconduct has to stop right now! When you discipline your employees for misconduct, you put them on notice that you won't tolerate their behavior. Repeated misconduct can lead quickly to suspension and termination.

As in the first track, the following discipline steps are listed from least severe to most severe. Your choice depends on the severity of the misconduct and the employee's work record:

- ✓ **Verbal warning:** When employees' misconduct is minor or a first offense, the verbal warning provides the least severe option for putting your employees on notice that their behavior won't be tolerated. ("John, I understand that you have continued to pressure Susan into going to lunch with you — even though she has told you on numerous occasions that she is not interested. This isn't acceptable. I expect you to stop this harassing behavior immediately.") In many cases of misconduct, a verbal warning that demonstrates to your employees that you're aware of the misconduct is all the situation requires.

- ✓ **Written warning:** Unfortunately, not all your employees get the message when you give them a verbal warning. Also, the magnitude of the offense may require that you skip the verbal warning and proceed directly to the written warning. Written warnings signal to your employees that you're serious and that you're documenting their behavior for their personnel files. An employees' immediate supervisor gives the written warning.

- ✓ **Reprimand:** Repeated or serious misconduct results in a reprimand. A reprimand is generally constructed in the same format as a written warning. However, a manager higher up in the organization gives the reprimand instead of the employees' immediate supervisor. The reprimand is the employees' last chance to correct their behavior before suspension, demotion, or termination.

- ✓ **Suspension:** A *suspension,* or mandatory leave without pay, is used in cases of very serious misconduct or repeated misconduct that hasn't been corrected as a result of other, less severe attempts at employee discipline. You may have to remove employees from the workplace for a period of time to ensure the safety of your other employees or to repair your work unit's morale. Employees may also be given nondisciplinary suspensions while they're being investigated on charges of misconduct. During a nondisciplinary suspension, employees are usually paid while the manager, human resources representative, or other company official reviews the case.

✔ **Termination:** In particularly serious cases of misconduct, termination may be your first choice in disciplining a worker. This rule is particularly true for extreme violations of safety rules, theft, gross insubordination, and other serious misconduct. Termination may also be the result of repeated misconduct that less severe discipline steps don't correct. See Chapter 16 for more information about terminating employees.

Disciplining Employees: A Suite in Five Parts

A right way and many wrong ways to discipline employees exist. Forget the many wrong ways for now and focus on the right way.

Regardless of which kind of discipline you select for the particular situation, the approach that you take with your employees remains the same — whether you conduct verbal counseling or give a suspension or demotion (because of their finality, terminations are an exception here). Five steps must always form the basis of your discipline script. By following these steps, you can be sure that your employees understand what the problem is, why the problem exists, and what they need to do to correct the problem.

Describing the unacceptable behavior

Exactly what is your employee doing that is unacceptable? When describing unwanted behavior to an employee, make sure that you're excruciatingly specific. You don't have time for mushy, vague statements such as "You have a bad attitude," or "You make a lot of mistakes," or "I don't like your work habits." *Huh?*

Always relate unacceptable behaviors to specific performance standards that haven't been met or to specific policies that have been broken. Specify exactly what the employee did wrong and when the behavior occurred. And don't forget to focus on the behavior and not on the individual.

Following are some examples for you to consider:

✔ "Your performance last week was below the acceptable standard of 250 units per week."

✔ "You failed the drug test that you took on Monday."

✔ "The last three analyses that you submitted to me contained numerous computational errors."

✔ "You have been late to work three out of four days this week."

Expressing the impact to the work unit

When an employee engages in unacceptable behavior — whether his or her work doesn't meet standards or whether he or she engages in misconduct — the behavior typically affects a work unit negatively. When an employee is consistently late to work, for example, you may have to assign someone else to cover your employee's position until the offender arrives. Doing so takes your other employee away from the work that he or she should be doing, reducing the efficiency and effectiveness of the work unit. And if an employee engages in sexual harassment, the morale and effectiveness of the workers who are subjected to the harassment unnecessarily suffer.

Continuing with the examples that we use in the preceding section, following are the next steps in your discipline script:

✔ "Because of your below-standard performance, the work unit didn't meet its overall targets for the week."

✔ "This violation specifically breaks our drug-free workplace policy."

✔ "Because of these errors, I now have to take extra time to review your work much more thoroughly before I can forward it up the chain."

✔ "Because of your tardiness, I had to pull Marge from her position to cover yours."

Specifying the required changes

Telling your employee that he or she did something wrong does little good if you don't also tell that employee what he or she needs to do to correct the behavior. As a part of your discipline script, tell your employee the exact actions that you want him or her to adopt. Tell the employee that his or her behavior must be in accordance with an established performance standard or company policy.

Following are some examples of the third part of your discipline script:

✔ "You must bring your performance up to the standard of 250 units per week or better immediately."

✔ "You will be required to set an appointment with the company's employee assistance program for drug counseling."

- ✔ "I expect your work to be error free before you submit it to me for approval."

- ✔ "I expect you to be in your seat, ready to work, at 8:00 a.m. every morning."

Outlining the consequences

Of course, if the unacceptable behavior continues, you need to have a discussion about the consequences. Make sure that you get the message across clearly and unequivocally and that your employee understands it.

Here are some possibilities for the fourth part of your script:

- ✔ "If you can't meet the standard, you'll be reassigned to the training unit to improve your skills."

- ✔ "If you refuse to undergo drug counseling, you'll be suspended from work without pay for five days."

- ✔ "If the accuracy of your work doesn't improve immediately, I'll have to issue a written counseling to be placed in your employee file."

- ✔ "If you're late again, I will request that the general manager issue a formal reprimand in your case."

Providing emotional support

Give your employee an emotional boost by expressing your support for his or her efforts. Make this support sincere and heart-felt — you do want your employee to improve, right?

Finally, the icing on the pineapple upside-down cake that is employee discipline:

- ✔ "But let's try to avoid that — I know you can do better!"

- ✔ "I really want this to work out — let's find you the help you need."

- ✔ "Is there anything I can do to help you avoid that outcome?"

- ✔ "There's no reason we can't avoid that situation — I'm counting on you to turn this around!"

Molding it all together

After you develop the five parts of your discipline script, put them together into a unified statement that you deliver to your wayward employees. Although you'll undoubtedly discuss the surrounding issues in some detail, make the script be the heart of your discipline session.

The five parts of the script work together to produce the final product as follows:

- ✔ "Your performance last week was below our standard of 250 units per week. Because of your below-standard performance, the work unit didn't meet its overall targets for the week. You must bring your performance up to the standard of 250 units per week or better immediately. If you can't meet the standard, you'll be reassigned to the training unit to improve your skills. But let's try to avoid that — I know you can do better!"

- ✔ "You failed the drug test that you took on Monday. This violation specifically breaks our drug-free workplace policy. You'll be required to set an appointment with the company's employee assistance program for drug counseling. If you refuse to undergo drug counseling, you'll be suspended from work without pay for five days. I really want this to work out — let's find you the help you need."

- ✔ "The last three analyses that you have submitted to me contained numerous computational errors. Because of these errors, I now have to take extra time to review your work much more thoroughly before I can forward it up the chain. I expect your work to be error free before you submit it to me for approval. If the accuracy of your work doesn't improve immediately, I'll have to issue written counseling to be placed in your employee file. Is there anything I can do to help you avoid that outcome?"

- ✔ "You have been late to work three out of four days this week. Because of your tardiness, I had to pull Marge from her position to cover yours. I expect you to be in your seat, ready to work, at 8:00 a.m. every morning. If you're late again, I will request that the general manager issue a formal reprimand in your case. There's no reason we can't avoid that situation — I'm counting on you to turn this around!"

Making a Plan for Improvement

Managers love plans: plans for completing projects on time, plans for meeting the organization's financial goals in five years, and plans to develop more plans. In the case of employee discipline, one more plan exists. The *performance improvement plan* is a crucial part of the discipline process because it sets definite steps for the employee to undertake to improve performance within a fixed period of time.

If your employee's performance transgressions are minor, and you're giving only verbal counseling, working up a performance plan is probably overkill. Also, because most instances of misconduct must by nature be corrected right now or else, performance improvement plans generally aren't appropriate for correcting employee misconduct. However, if your employee's poor performance is habitual and you've selected counseling or more severe discipline, a performance plan is definitely what the doctor ordered. *Take two and call me in the morning!*

A performance improvement plan consists of the following three parts:

✓ **Goal statement:** The goal statement provides clear direction to your employees about what it takes to make satisfactory improvement. The goal statement, which is tied directly to your employee's performance standards, may be something along the lines of "Completes all his assignments on or before agreed deadlines," or "Is at her station ready to work at exactly 8:00 a.m. every day."

✓ **Schedule for attainment:** What good is a plan without a schedule? Not having a schedule is like eating an ice cream cone without the ice cream or like watching TV with the sound turned off. Every good plan needs a definite completion date with fixed milestones along the way if the plan for goal attainment is complex.

✓ **Required resources/training:** The performance improvement plan must also contain a summary of any additional resources or training that will be brought to bear to help your employee bring his or her performance up to snuff.

Here's a sample performance improvement plan for a worker who makes repeated errors in typed correspondence:

Performance Improvement Plan

Jack Smith

Goal statement:

✓ Complete all drafts of typed correspondence with two or fewer mistakes per document.

Schedule for attainment:

✓ Jack must meet the above goal within three months after the date of this plan.

Required resources/training:

✓ Jack will be enrolled in the company refresher course in typing and reviewing correspondence. This training must be successfully completed no later than two months after the date of this plan.

Implementing the Improvement Plan

After you put performance improvement plans in place, your job is to ensure that they don't just gather dust on your employees' shelves. Follow up with your employees to make sure that they're acting on their plans and making progress toward the goals that you both agreed to. Yes, following up on improvement plans takes time, but that time is well spent. Besides, if you can't find the time to check your employees' progress on their improvement plans, don't be surprised if they can't find the time to work on them.

Are your employees following through with the goal statements that you agreed to? Do they even have the goal statements that you agreed to? Are they keeping to their schedules, and are they receiving the training and other resources that you agreed to provide? If not, you need to emphasize the importance of the improvement plans with your employees and work with them to figure out why they haven't been implemented as agreed.

To assist your employees in implementing their improvement plans, schedule regular progress reporting meetings with them on a daily, weekly, or monthly basis. More extensive improvement plans necessitate more frequent follow-up. Progress meetings serve two functions.

- ✔ They provide you with the information that you need to know to assess your employees' progress toward meeting their plans.

- ✔ They demonstrate to your employees — clearly and unequivocally — that their progress is important to you. If you demonstrate that the plans are important to you, your employees can make the plans a priority in their busy schedules.

Set up performance improvement plans with your employees and stick with them. One of the most difficult challenges of management is dealing with a poor performer who improves under scrutiny, and then lapses again. Stick with your plan. If an employee can't maintain necessary performance standards, then you may want to consider whether he or she is really suited for continued employment.

Top five discipline Web sites

Wondering where to find the best information on the Web about the topics addressed in this chapter? Well, you've come to the right place! Here are our top five favorites:

- ✔ Fairfield and Woods: www.fwlaw.com/progressive.html

- ✔ CCH Business Owner's Toolkit: www.toolkit.cch.com/tools/coach_m.asp

- ✔ Employee Discipline: Building Blocks for Success: www.shrm.org/consultants/library/HRM0502.pdf

- ✔ HR Zone: www.hrzone.com/topics/firing.html

- ✔ Career Lab: www.careerlab.com/art_confrontation.htm

Chapter 16

Too Little, Too Late:
Terminating Employees

*B*eing a manager is a tough job. If people tell you that the job is easy, they're joking, lying, or totally confused. Challenging? Yes. Constantly changing? Yes. Satisfying? Yes. Easy? No. And of all the tough jobs that managers have to do routinely, firing employees has to be the absolute toughest. Take our word for it when we say that. No matter how many times you fire someone, terminating an employee is never a pleasant thing to do.

The mechanics of terminating employees — setting goals, gathering data, assessing performance, carrying out discipline, and completing the paperwork — aren't so tough. The tough part is all the emotional baggage that goes along with firing someone — especially someone who you've worked with for some time and have shared good and bad times. However, no matter how difficult, taking an employee aside and telling that employee that his or her services are no longer needed is sometimes your only option.

No matter how much you try to help someone succeed in your organization, sometimes that person's employment at your firm just isn't meant to be. This forces the questions: What's the best way for you to deal with the problem, and what's the best way for you to deal with the person?

You see, terminations aren't limited only to your discretion. Sometimes employees "fire" themselves. "I quit!" If you're lucky, they give you two weeks. If you're not so lucky, you get less. In any case, you're going to be awfully busy for a while as you work your way through the hiring process. (See Chapter 4 for more information about hiring good employees.)

This chapter deals with why employees are terminated, the different kinds of terminations, and exactly how you can carry them out. You discover the difference between a layoff and a firing as well as the importance of documentation to support your actions.

Terminations for Every Occasion

When you say the word *termination,* most people immediately think of the process of firing a worker who isn't doing his or her job. Although firing is the most dramatic and potentially volatile form of termination (just ask any manager who has had to deal with an employee who exploded during a termination), terminations come in many different flavors, depending on the situation.

Two major categories of employee termination exist: voluntary and involuntary. The key difference between the two is that an employee undertakes a voluntary termination of his or her own free will, while involuntary terminations are carried out against the will of the employee — often with the employee kicking and screaming. The following sections describe each category of termination.

Voluntary terminations

Employees have many reasons to terminate their own employment. Yeah, we know — that anyone would voluntarily choose to leave your particular brand of workers' paradise is hard to believe, but leave they do, and for all kinds of reasons. Sometimes employees find better promotional or pay opportunities with another firm. Sometimes employees find themselves in dead-end work situations or leave because of personality conflicts with their manager or other employees. Sometimes employees leave because of emotional stress, family needs, chemical dependency, or other personal reasons.

In some cases of voluntary termination, you don't want your employees to leave; in others, you actively encourage them to go. And every once in a while, an employee actually stays with your firm long enough to retire. Because so few people seem to stay anywhere long enough to retire anymore, this phenomenon is always a shock to employees.

So the following are the main reasons that employees voluntarily leave:

✔ **Resignation (not encouraged):** An unencouraged resignation occurs when an employee decides to quit his or her position with your firm with no prodding or suggestion to do so from you. Unfortunately, the best employees always seem to be the ones who resign. Although you can't force someone to stay with your organization forever (nor would you want to), you can make sure that people aren't leaving because your organization isn't adequately addressing problems. A certain department experiencing a lot of turnover, for example, is a warning sign that work conditions are too stressful or that a supervisor or manager may need an attitude adjustment. Conducting exit interviews of such employees as they are processing out of your organization can be a particularly useful tool for uncovering problems that need to be addressed. Don't let employees get away without first asking them why they decided to leave, and what the organization could do better.

✔ **Resignation (encouraged):** An encouraged resignation occurs when you suggest to an employee that he or she quit his or her job. Such resignations are often used as face-saving measures for employees who are about to be fired. Instead of firing your employees, you can offer them the opportunity to resign. This approach can help to dampen the hurt of being fired, plus it keeps a potentially damaging employment action off the employees' records.

✔ **Retirement:** Retirement happens when employees reach the end of their career and decide to terminate their employment finally and forever. Occasionally, organizations working to quickly cut costs offer certain employees early retirement — extending the benefits of regular retirement to those who are willing to retire from the company before they have reached the normal age of retirement. Retirement is generally a happy time for all involved, marked with celebrations and tokens of the organization's affection and gratitude (such as plaques, gold watches, and a very nice luncheon).

Involuntary terminations

Of course, not all terminations are as easy to deal with as the voluntary forms we mention in the preceding section. Involuntary terminations are seldom pleasant experiences — for either manager or employee — and you really have to be at the end of your rope before you invoke this ultimate sanction against an employee. Involuntary terminations come in two types:

✔ **Layoffs:** A layoff, also known as a reduction in force, occurs when an organization decides to terminate a certain number of employees for financial reasons. For example, your company loses several key contracts and the revenue that was projected to come with them. In order to stay afloat, your firm may have no choice but to reduce payroll costs through layoffs.

Every company has its own policy for determining the order of layoffs. In some organizations, the last employee hired is the first to go. In others, employee performance determines layoffs. Most organizations give hiring preference to laid-off employees if and when financial health is restored.

✔ **Firing:** Employees are fired when they have no hope of improving their performance, when job descriptions need to evolve and the people in the jobs aren't able to evolve along with them, or when they commit an act of misconduct that is so serious that termination is the only choice.

An 1884 Tennessee court decision (*Payne* v. *Western & A.R.P. Co.,* 81 Tenn. 507) established the termination-at-will rule within the United States. This rule said that employers have the right to terminate employees for any reason whatsoever — including no reason — unless a contract between employer and employee expressly prohibits such an action. However, more than 100 years of court decisions, union agreements, and state and federal laws have eroded the ability of employers to terminate employees at will. The federal government, in particular, has had the greatest effect on the termination-at-will rule, particularly in cases of discrimination against employees for a wide variety of reasons.

At-will does still exist on a state-by-state basis, and some companies require prospective employees to sign a statement confirming termination-at-will when they're hired. Be sure to check your local regulations.

Federal regulations, such as the Civil Rights Act of 1964, the Equal Employment Opportunity Act of 1991, the Age Discrimination in Employment Act, and others, prohibit terminating employees specifically because of their age, race, gender, color, religion, national origin, and other federally mandated exclusions. You need to double-check with any local and state regulations, too. To ignore these prohibitions is to invite a nasty and expensive lawsuit. Even the mere appearance of discrimination in the termination process (or anywhere else in your firm) can get you into trouble. In fact, most former employees — by some estimates, up to 90 percent — who bring wrongful termination cases to court today win their cases.

Good reasons for firing your employees

As long as you aren't discriminating against your employees when you terminate them, you still have quite a lot of discretion as a manager. Although you generally have the right to terminate employees at will, you may find yourself on thin legal ice depending on the specific grounds that you select for firing your employees.

People generally agree, however, on certain behaviors that merit firing. Some of these behaviors are considered *intolerable offenses* that merit immediate action — no verbal counseling, no written warning, and no reprimand or suspension. Immediate and unequivocal termination. Right now! They include:

✔ **Verbal abuse of others:** Verbal abuse includes cursing, repeated verbal harassment, malicious insults, and other similar behaviors. Your employees have the right to do their jobs in a workplace that is free of verbal abuse. And verbal abuse of customers and other business associates is just plain bad for business. If your employees continue to verbally abuse others after you give them fair warning, you can fire them without fear of legal repercussions. (And, keep in mind, if you don't take action by quickly firing a repeated offender, you put yourself and your company at risk of a lawsuit by those employees being harassed!)

✔ **Incompetence:** Despite your continued efforts to train them, some employees just aren't cut out for their jobs. If you have tried to help them and they still can't perform their duties at an acceptable level of competence, parting ways is clearly in the best interest of both the employee and the firm.

✔ **Repeated, unexcused tardiness:** You depend on your employees to get their jobs done as scheduled. Not only does tardiness jeopardize the ability of your employees to complete their tasks on time, but it also sets a very bad example for your employees who are punctual. If your employees continue to be late to work after you warn them that you won't tolerate this behavior, you have clear grounds for termination.

✔ **Insubordination:** *Insubordination* — the deliberate refusal to carry out one's duties — is grounds for immediate termination without warning. Although supervisors commonly encourage their employees to question why a decision is made, after the decision is made, the employees must carry it out. If they're unwilling to follow your direction, the basic employer-employee relationship breaks down, and you don't have to tolerate it.

✔ **Physical violence:** Most companies take employee-initiated physical violence and threats of violence very seriously. Employees have the right to do their jobs in a safe workplace; employers have the duty to provide a safe workplace. Physical violence jeopardizes your employees' safety and distracts them from doing their jobs. Never let an employee think that you don't take a physical threat seriously — the best way to communicate that is to call law enforcement immediately. The workplace is no place for violence or threats of violence. If the employee has a need to act tough, call security or law enforcement.

✔ **Theft:** Theft of company property and the property of coworkers or clients is another big no-no. Most companies that catch employees engaging in this nasty little practice terminate them immediately and without warning. If you decide to terminate an employee for theft, and you have concrete proof that the employee carried out the crime, you can do so knowing that you're on firm legal ground.

✔ **Intoxication on the job:** Although being drunk or under the influence of drugs on the job is sufficient grounds for immediate termination, many companies nowadays offer their employees the option of undergoing counseling with an employee assistance program or enrolling in a program such as Alcoholics Anonymous. In many cases, employees can rehabilitate themselves and return to regular service.

✔ **Falsification of records:** Falsifying records is another big no-no that can lead to immediate dismissal. This category includes providing fraudulent information during the hiring process (fake schools, degrees, previous jobs, and so on) and producing other fraudulent information during the course of employment (fake expense reports, falsified timecards, cheating on examinations, and so on).

Reasons that some managers avoid the inevitable

As you know, terminating an employee isn't a pleasant way to spend an afternoon. Most managers prefer doing most anything else. ("John, maybe we should go for a quick swim in the shark tank.") Although the reasons for terminating employees listed in the preceding section are clear cut and relatively easy for managers to use as leverage in a termination, having that leverage doesn't make the task any easier. But always keep in mind this old saying: Hire slow, fire quick. Few managers end up regretting firing a wayward employee too soon — far more regret not taking action more quickly when the writing is on the wall.

Some managers avoid carrying out a termination because of these reasons:

✔ **Fear of the unknown:** Terminating an employee can be a frightening prospect — especially if you're getting ready to do it for the first time. Is your employee going to cry? Have a heart attack or stroke? Get mad? Punch you out? Don't worry, every manager has to experience a first time. If you're in that particular boat, read up on the firing process before you do it. Reading about the firing process can help provide you with both logical and emotional support. Unfortunately, the last time never seems to come around until you retire.

✔ **Emotional involvement:** Considering that you likely spend from one-fourth to one-third of your waking hours at work, becoming friends with some of your employees is natural. Doing so is fine until you have to discipline or terminate one or more of your friends. Letting any employee go is tough enough, much less an employee with whom you have developed an emotional attachment.

✔ **Fear of a negative reflection upon yourself:** If you have to terminate one of your employees, what are you saying about yourself as a manager? In the case of a layoff, is it your fault that the organization didn't attain its goals? If you're firing an employee, did you make the wrong choice when you decided to hire that person? Many managers decide to put up with performance problems in their employees rather than draw attention to their own shortcomings — whether real or perceived.

✔ **Possibility of legal action:** The fear of legal action is often enough to stop a bull moose in his tracks at 50 paces. In these days of runaway, sue-at-the-drop-of-a-hat litigation, managers sometimes are afraid to terminate their employees.

✔ **Hope that the problem just goes away:** Yeah, right. Don't hold your breath.

Conducting a Layoff

Call it what you like: a reduction in force, a downsizing, a rightsizing, a re-engineering, or whatever. The causes and results are still the same. Your organization needs to reorganize its operations, or cut payroll and related personnel and facilities costs, and some of your employees need to go.

Although understandably traumatic for those employees involved, layoffs are different from firings because the employees who are terminated generally aren't at direct fault. They're usually good employees who follow the rules. They're productive and do their jobs. They're loyal and dedicated workers. They may even be your friends. The real culprits are usually external factors, such as changes in markets, mergers and acquisitions, and pressures of a more competitive global marketplace.

How to fire someone humanely

One of the hardest tasks any manager ever has to do is to fire an employee. Can you terminate an employee humanely? We'd like to think so. If you focus on being fair and keeping the person whole, you have a good chance of minimizing the negative impact while making the best of a situation that's not working. Here are some guidelines that can help you make this difficult transition a little easier.

✔ **Give them the benefit of the doubt.** You need to be sure that you're giving the employee a fair chance to succeed — not necessarily an endless number of chances — but a fair chance. This idea is especially important when the employee is new. You can say something like: "I don't know how you've been managed in the past, but I want to make it clear what is expected of you in this position so that we can agree on some mutual goals for your job." Summarize your expectations in writing and set up a time frame for reviewing progress on the employee's goals. Ask the employee to

come to you if he or she has questions or needs help in meeting the expectations and acknowledge when the employee has done good work. Don't expect your employees to know what you want without open, two-way communication.

✔ **Make it clear when expectations aren't being met.** You can have a much easier time dealing with problems when they're small than when they become huge. Bring up your concerns and the reasons why they are concerns. You can use a disclaimer, such as, "I know you're capable of improving in this area of your job," but you also at some point need to be clear that if improvement isn't forthcoming, the employee could lose the job. Document these discussions for clarity, reinforcement, and — if necessary — to provide evidence that you have made an honest attempt to manage the employee fairly.

(continued)

(continued)

✔ **Exhaust alternative approaches to dismissal.** Some managers find it useful to try one or more attempts to get through to an employee who isn't performing well. You can discuss other opportunities that may better match the employee's abilities, for example. Or you can offer the employee a "career day": "Tom, I'd like you to take a career day tomorrow. Take the day off and don't come to work. I'm still going to pay you, but I want you to go to the beach, a museum, your kid's school — or even watch TV all day — and simply focus on one question: 'Is this job really what you want to be doing with your life right now?' Come back and give me your answer, and if you do really want to stay in your position, we have to talk about what needs to change in order for you to keep your job."

Offer a zero-percent increase. "Jane, we have some mutually agreed upon goals, but I haven't seen where you have actually changed your behavior or achieved any of the results we have discussed. I don't like surprises, and I'm sure you don't either. So, I wanted to make it clear that your next performance review is in a few months and if you haven't shown any substantial improvement in your performance, you won't be getting any salary increase." Typically in this approach, the person quickly falls in line or ends up leaving of his or her accord and — either way — your problem is solved.

✔ **Act quickly to dismiss.** When all is said and done, if someone isn't working out well, the sooner that you deal with the situation the better off it will be — for the employee, yourself, and the workgroup. You have to move from hoping your employees improve to looking at the evidence as if they are, in fact, improving. Remember, sometimes the biggest motivator you can do for your workgroup is to get rid of the people who aren't performing, thereby sending a clear message to everyone else that the group can't afford to have anyone who isn't contributing per their level of responsibility and compensation. In reality, the reaction from other employees — who often know more about a coworker's performance than anyone else in the organization could ever hope to — is "What took you so long?" Even at dismissal, you can still be gracious: "I thought things would work out, but they haven't and we're going to let you go."

When it's time to conduct a layoff, use the following step-by-step guide to help you through the process:

1. **Determine the extent of the problem and figure out what departments will be affected.** How deep is the financial hole that your organization finds itself in? Does the possibility that fortunes will change anytime soon exist? If certain products or services aren't selling, what departments are affected?

2. **Freeze hiring.** Hiring employees during a layoff process doesn't make sense unless the position is absolutely critical. For example, if a receptionist quits, you still need someone to answer the phones and receive visitors. Not only do you risk laying off a new hire, but also

hiring at this time sends the wrong message to your employees that you don't care about your current employees. If you do have to hire, be sure to first consider previously laid off employees before you go outside the organization.

3. **Prepare tentative lists of employees to be laid off.** After you determine the extent of the problem and the affected departments, the next step is to determine which employees to lay off. Determine which employees have the most skill and experience in the areas that the organization needs, and which employees have the least. The first employees to go in a layoff are usually those employees whose skills and experience don't mesh with the organization's needs.

4. **Notify all employees of planned layoffs in advance.** When the need for a layoff seems certain, get the word out to all employees immediately and well in advance of the planned layoff. Fully disclose the financial and other problems that your organization faces and solicit employee suggestions for ways to cut costs or improve efficiency. Sometimes employee suggestions can save you enough money to avert the layoff or at least soften its blow on the organization. Err on the side of overcommunication.

5. **Prepare a final list of employees to be laid off.** After you turn the organization upside down to find potential savings, you need to prepare a list of employees to be laid off. Write the list in rank order in the event of a change that may allow you to remove employees from the list. Most companies have standard procedures for ranking employees for layoff — especially if a union represents workers. These procedures generally give preference to permanent employees over temporary ones and include seniority and/or performance in the formula for determining who stays and who goes. If you don't have a policy, you need to determine the basis for laying off employees. In this case, you want to consider your employees' experience and how long they've been with the organization. Be careful not to discriminate against protected workers — older employees, for example — who are good performers.

6. **Notify affected employees.** By now, many employees are probably paralyzed with the fear that they'll be let go. As soon as you finish developing the layoff list — updating it to account for employees who may have already found new jobs on their own — notify the affected employees. Private, one-on-one meetings are the best way to handle notification.

7. **Provide outplacement services to terminated employees.** If time and money permit, provide outplacement and counseling support to the employees being terminated. Your organization can provide training in subjects, such as resume writing, financial planning, interviewing, and networking, and allow the employees to use company-owned computers, fax machines, and telephones in their job searches. If you can help your employees by providing job leads or contacts, by all means do so.

8. **Terminate.** Conduct one-on-one termination meetings with employees to finalize arrangements and complete termination paperwork. Explain the severance package, continuation of benefits, and any other company-sponsored termination programs as appropriate. Collect keys, identification badges, and any company-owned equipment and property. Escort (you can do this personally, or have a security guard or human resources representative fill the role) your newly terminated, former employees out of the facility and wish them well.

9. **Rally the "survivors."** Rally your remaining employees together in an "all-hands" meeting to let them know that, now that the layoffs are completed, the firm is back on the road to good financial health. Tell the team that, to avoid future layoffs, you have to pull together to overcome this momentary downturn in the business cycle.

Heeding the Warning Before You Fire an Employee

Firing an employee is unpleasant enough without having to get dragged through the courts on a charge of wrongful termination. The problem is that, although most organizations have clear procedures for disciplining employees, some managers still ignore these procedures in the heat of the moment. Seemingly a manager's minor oversight can lead to major monetary damage awards in favor of former employees.

Before you fire an employee for cause, make sure that you can meet the following criteria and line your ducks up in a nice, neat row. Take our word for it: You'll be glad you did!

✔ **Documentation:** Remember the rule: Document, document, and then document some more. If you're firing an employee because of performance shortcomings, you had better have the performance data to back up your assertions. If you're firing an employee for stealing, you better have proof that this employee is the thief. You can never have too much documentation. This rule is always true when you take personnel actions, particularly when you terminate an employee.

✔ **Fair warning:** Were your employees' performance standards spelled out clearly to them in advance? Did you explain company policies and practices along with your expectations? Have you given your employees fair warning of the consequences of continued performance problems? Because of the American legal tradition of due process, terminating an employee without warning for performance-related behaviors is generally considered unfair. However, certain kinds of employee misconduct, including physical violence, theft, and fraud, are grounds for immediate termination without warning.

✔ **Response time:** Have you given your employees enough time to rectify their performance shortcomings? The amount of time considered reasonable to improve performance depends on the nature of the problem to be addressed. For example, if the problem were tardiness, you would expect the behavior to be corrected immediately. However, if the employee is to improve performance on a complex and lengthy project, demonstrating improvement may take weeks or months.

✔ **Reasonableness:** Are your company's policies and practices reasonable? Are the performance standards that you set with your employees achievable by the average worker? Does the penalty match the severity of the offense? Put yourself in your employee's shoes. If you were being terminated, would you consider the grounds for termination to be reasonable? Be honest!

✔ **Avenues for appeal:** Does your firm offer employees ways to appeal your decision to higher-level management? Again, due process requires that an avenue for terminated employees to present their cases to higher management exist. Sometimes a direct supervisor is too close to the problem or too emotionally involved, which can cause errors in judgment that someone, who is not personally involved in the situation, can see easily.

Firing an Employee in Three Steps

Don't forget: Although your job is to point out your employees' shortcomings and help your employees perform to standard, the employees are ultimately responsible for their performance and behavior. When you arrive at the last disciplinary step prior to firing your employees, letting them know that the responsibility and choice are theirs and theirs alone is important; you can't do this critical step for them. Your employees either improve their performance or leave. And if they decide to leave, have your employee express his or her choice in writing!

Assuming that the employee has made his or her choice, and that choice is to continue the misconduct or below-standard performance, the choice is then yours. And your choice is to terminate before the employee does any more damage to your organization.

Keep two key goals in mind when firing employees:

✔ **Provide a clear explanation for the firing.** According to legal experts, many employees file wrongful termination lawsuits simply in hopes of discovering the real reason why they were fired.

✔ **Seek to minimize resentment against your company and yourself by taking action to maintain your employee's dignity throughout the termination process.** The world is a dangerous enough place without incurring the wrath of potentially unstable former employees.

Fire an employee in a meeting in your office or other private location. Make the meeting concise and to the point; figure on setting aside approximately 5 to 10 minutes for the meeting. Termination meetings aren't intended to be discussions or debates. Your job is to inform your employee that he or she is being fired. This meeting isn't going to be fun, but keep in mind that you're taking the best course of action for all concerned. One more thing: Have a witness with you when you terminate an employee — especially when the person being terminated is of a different gender. Ideally, bring someone along from human resources who you can have step in with a discussion of the administrative details of the termination, such as turning in keys and equipment, continuing benefits, severance pay, and so forth.

Here, then, are the three steps for firing an employee:

- ✔ **Tell the employee that he or she is being terminated.** State simply and unequivocally that you've made the decision to fire. Be sure to note that you considered all relevant evidence, that you reviewed the decision and all levels of your organization's management agreed to it, and that the decision is final. If you did your homework and used a system of progressive discipline (see Chapter 15) in an attempt to correct your employee's behavior, the announcement should come as no surprise. Of course, no matter the circumstances, a firing shakes anyone to the core.

- ✔ **Explain exactly why the employee is being terminated.** If the firing is the result of misconduct, cite the policy that was broken and exactly what your employee did to break it. If the firing is due to a failure to meet performance standards, remind the employee of past attempts to correct his or her performance and the subsequent incidents that led to the decision to fire. Stick to the facts.

- ✔ **Announce the effective date of the termination and provide details on the termination process.** A firing is normally effective on the day that you conduct your termination meeting. Keeping a fired employee around is awkward for both you and your employee and should be avoided at all costs. If you're offering a severance package or other termination benefits, explain them to your employee as well as how he or she is to make arrangements for gathering personal effects from his or her office. Go through the termination paperwork with the employee and explain the handling of final wages due.

Termination can be quite traumatic for the employee on the receiving end of the news. Expect the unexpected. Although one employee may quickly become an emotional wreck, another may become belligerent and verbally abusive. To help defuse these situations, consider applying the following techniques:

- ✔ **Empathize with your employee.** Don't try to sugarcoat the news, but be understanding of your employee's situation. The news you have just delivered is among the worst news that anyone can get. If your employee becomes emotional or cries, don't try to stop it — hand the person a tissue and go on.

✔ **Be matter-of-fact and firm.** Even if your employee becomes unglued, you must maintain a calm, businesslike demeanor throughout the termination meeting. Don't lead your employee to believe that he or she is participating in a negotiating session or that he or she can do something to change your mind. Be firm in your insistence that the decision is final and not subject to change.

✔ **Keep the meeting on track.** Although letting your employee vent his or her feelings is appropriate, don't allow the employee to steer the meeting from the main goal of informing him or her about the termination. If the employee becomes abusive, inform the employee that you will end the meeting immediately if he or she can't maintain control.

You may find it helpful to prepare a *termination script* to read during the termination meeting. A script is beneficial because it helps to ensure that you don't forget to mention an important piece of information, and it provides instant documentation for your employee's personnel file (which you should retain for at least seven years after terminating the employee). Practice it before you go into the termination meeting.

Here is a sample termination script for an employee with ongoing performance problems:

> "Katie, we have decided that today is your last day of employment with the firm. The reason for this decision is that you can't maintain the performance standards that we agreed to when you were hired last year. As you know, we have discussed your failure to meet standards on many occasions over the past year. Specifically, the written counseling that I gave you on October 5th notified you that you had one month to bring your performance up to standard or you could be terminated. You didn't achieve this goal, and I therefore have no other choice but to terminate your employment, effective today. Jenny from personnel is here to discuss your final pay and benefits and to collect your office keys and voice-mail password."

Determining When Is the Best Time to Terminate

Any manager likely has his or her own idea of what day of the week and time of the day you should select to terminate your employees. Monday terminations are the way to go because of A, B, and C. Or Friday terminations are best because of X, Y, and Z. And is it better to carry out a termination the first task in the morning, or should you wait until the close of business?

Top five termination Web sites

Wondering where to find the best information on the Web about the topics addressed in this chapter? Well, you've come to the right place! Here are our top five favorites:

✔ HRZone: Firing and Disciplining Employees: `hrzone.com/topics/firing.html`

✔ CCH Business Owner's Toolkit: Firing and Termination: `toolkit.cch.com/text/P05_8101.asp`

✔ USLaw.com: Firing an Employee: `uslaw.com/problem.tcl?problem_id=118`

✔ Cheat Sheet: How to Fire or Be Fired: `business2.com/articles/mag/0,1640,9602,00.html`

✔ Inc. Magazine: Firing and Employee Resignations: `www.inc.com/articles/hr/manage_emp/fire_resign/`

We think that terminating an employee as soon as you decide it's necessary — regardless of what day of the week it may be — makes the most sense. Once you've decided an employee needs to go, every additional day is a drain on the organization — and on yourself.

So what time is the best to terminate? The best approach is when his or her coworkers aren't there to witness the termination, either prior to starting work, or when everyone's out to lunch. The idea is to minimize the embarrassment for the terminated employee.

If you terminate employees earlier in the day, they have to face their coworkers and explain why they are packing up their belongings and why the security guard is preparing to escort them off the premises. Your intent isn't to punish or embarrass your employees — you want to make the termination process as painless and humane as possible. Allow them to save face by scheduling the termination meeting at a time when you can avoid public display.

Chapter 17

Managing Me: Taking Care of No.1

*I*n all the hustle and bustle of a typical day at the office — proposals due yesterday, another rush order to get out, meetings stacked up one right after another, the latest crisis du jour — you can easily get caught up in work. Nothing is wrong with getting caught up in your work, but when work begins to intrude into your personal life — a bit too far and a bit too often — then you have a problem.

The problem is that work becomes your No.1 priority, and everything and everyone else — including yourself — is automatically required to take a back seat. And what results from this shift in priorities? You have poorer health because of all the junk food lunches caught on the run and infrequent exercise. You have increased stress because of your endless workdays and nights and because of your inability to take vacations or tear yourself away from your work. You also have a trail of ruined relationships as friends and family begin to tire of waiting for you to make room in your life for them.

No matter how high up in the organization you are, or how important your job is, or how much you're getting paid, you have to take care of yourself first. You have to be your No.1 priority. When you take care of yourself, you're in top form, and you're a more valuable asset to your organization, your customers, and your employees. And you also have a much better chance of surviving to retirement and having an opportunity to enjoy the fruits of all your hard work. Doesn't that sound nice?

Feeling the Work-Life Dilemma

Balancing your time on the job and your time away from the job can be a very difficult proposition. Everyone has to make money to pay for essentials like food, clothing, and shelter, and not-so-essential items like a cool new stereo or sports car.

You make money by working.

But, at the same time, everyone has a life outside of work. You have friends, you have families, and you have partners, lovers, and spouses. You have clubs, hobbies, groups, associations, avocations, and any number of other ways to keep busy. Sometimes just taking a few minutes to watch a sunset or walk on the beach can make all the difference in your perspective and frame of mind.

Workers in the United States put in more time on the job than workers in most other countries. Although American workers today toil on average 1,978 hours a year, Australian, Canadian, Japanese, and Mexican workers get by with about 100 hours — or 2.5 weeks — less each year, and British workers about 200 hours less. German workers work 500 fewer hours (or about 12 weeks) than their American counterparts. Only South Koreans (who put in 500 hours more a year) and Czechs (who put in 100 hours more a year) work more hours than workers in the United States.

Not surprisingly, most Americans feel tremendous pressure to spend more time on the job, to take work home, and even to work while on vacation, ill, or otherwise indisposed.

Reaping the benefits of a balanced work life and personal life

Finding the correct balance between your work life and your personal life is one of the most important steps you can take. Employees whose work and personal lives are in balance are happier, healthier, more productive, and a lot easier to live with. In addition, they provide better customer service. But, when employees allow their jobs to take over their lives, the results can be devastating.

Who benefits when your work life and personal life are balanced? You do, and your company, your partner, family, and loved ones do, as well. Here's how:

- Employees have improved self-esteem and health, are happier, and feel more valued by their employers.
- Employees have more control over their working lives.
- Employees are more motivated and more efficient and effective.
- Employees feel more loyalty and commitment to their jobs.
- Relationships between workers and managers improve.

✔ Absenteeism goes down.

✔ The number of worker's compensation and disability claims decreases.

✔ The organization transforms into an employer of choice.

✔ The organization enjoys increased employee retention rates.

Take a look at yourself. Are you in charge of your life, or is your job in charge? Are your relationships falling apart? Are you a stranger to your family and friends? Do you feel like you're constantly under stress? Does your work performance suffer because you're just too overwhelmed to take care of all the loose ends?

Now, how about your employees? Are they in the same boat as you? If so, you have to do something about these issues — and, the sooner the better.

Making the case for a more flexible workplace

You know that you and your employees need ways to move the balance of your lives more to the personal side and less to the work side. How exactly are you going to convince the powers that be that, first, this idea is good to implement and, second, that company policies should be modified to make it happen?

You have to develop a business case for creating a flexible workplace, clearly spelling out the benefits to your organization for making the changes. Suggest that the change first be made as an experiment or pilot program that can be permanently implemented if it is successful. As you move through the process, consider the impact of alternative work arrangements on your customers (in many cases, flexible work schedules can actually directly benefit your customers by extending the hours of service available to them), as well as on meetings and other ongoing company events.

Step 1: Identify core business needs

Does your organization truly need to adopt alternative work arrangements? Why or why not? Survey employees to find out what they think. Identify the core needs of your business, and then determine what kinds of alternative work arrangements may be appropriate. Consult with management (and with labor unions, if necessary) to determine what kinds of arrangements may be acceptable, and what kinds aren't. Quantify the benefits of making the desired change — and the costs — to the organization. Present your findings and your specific ideas to management for approval.

New ways to work

As a manager, not only do you have to watch out for yourself, but you also have to keep a close eye on your employees to ensure that they aren't showing the symptoms of overwork and burnout. Although managers have always had certain tools available to help their employees balance work and personal time — hiring them on a part-time basis or granting employees an unexpected day off with pay — a number of new tools are available in most managers' tool-boxes for accomplishing the same goal. What follows are some of the most popular tools.

- ✔ **Flextime:** Allowing employees to set their own work start and end times within a band of time approved by management

- ✔ **Compressed workweek:** Working a full-time, 40-hour-a-week schedule in fewer than five workdays each week (for example, four 10-hour days a week)

- ✔ **Shift swapping:** Allowing employees to trade shifts as desired among themselves

- ✔ **Self-rostering:** Allowing employees to sign up for their own work schedules each week or month

- ✔ **Job sharing:** Sharing a full-time job with another employee, with each person usually working 20 hours a week

- ✔ **Telecommuting:** Working from home or from a remote office, sometimes a day or two a week, sometimes on a full-time basis

Step 2: Develop policies and procedures

For alternative work arrangements to be successful — and to ensure that all employees are treated fairly — develop and implement clear and complete policies and procedures before any new program is rolled out. Don't reinvent the wheel. By doing a search on the Internet, you can find plenty of policies that you can model yours after. (See our "Top five work/life Web sites" sidebar at the end of the chapter for a start.)

Step 3: Have a trial period

When making a change that's as significant as this change will be to your employees, first run a pilot program before you finalize your alternative work arrangements. Communicate your new policies widely, and make sure that your employees understand them. Invite employees to participate, and then start your program. After a month or two, gather results and evaluate them. Are they positive or negative?

Step 4: Go final

Make changes to your program as determined in Step 3, and then create your final policies and procedures. Inaugurate your new program with much fanfare and celebration. You're on your way!

Avoiding Workaholics 'R Us

As the old saying goes, everything in moderation. Unfortunately, in regards to work, many people (both managers and workers alike!) don't find much moderation — you're in overdrive from the moment you arrive early in the morning until you go home, often late at night. You normally work long hours and accept them as a part of today's workplace. Work takes over your life, leaving precious little time to spend with friends, or family, or to pursue the kinds of physical or leisure activities that help you unwind after a hard day's work.

When overwork becomes more than an occasional event and you often push everything that isn't related to your job out of the picture, then you have a classic case of *workaholism*. And, workaholism isn't good. Not only can workaholism lead you to neglect your family and social life, but also it can actually make you less productive and less efficient. Although you may think you're getting more done with all the extra time you put into your job, chances are, you're actually getting less done.

So, how can you tell whether or not you're a workaholic? Here are the seven deadly warning signs of workaholism. How many do you have?

✔ When you go to parties, you talk mostly about work.

✔ You dream about work.

✔ You rarely miss a day of work or go on vacations.

✔ On the rare days that you do take a vacation, you take work with you and regularly call in to check your voice-mail messages.

✔ You work more than 45 hours a week.

✔ You eat lunch at your desk, or skip lunch altogether, because you don't have time for lunch.

✔ You're absolutely convinced that you're not a workaholic, even though you exhibit some or all of the preceding symptoms.

So, how did you do? When you look in the mirror, do you recognize any of the seven deadly warning signs of workaholism? Do others tell you that you're a workaholic? Are your relationships outside of work suffering, and do you have a hard time relaxing and having fun? If so, you can follow these steps to cure yourself of this obsessive addiction to work, including:

✔ Work fewer hours. Commit to a 40-hour-a-week schedule and stick to it.

✔ Clearly separate your work life from your personal life. Leave your work at the office when you go home every day.

✔ Spend more time with friends and family.

✔ Slow down!

- ✔ Take vacations (and don't bring your work with you or check in with the office before your vacation is over).
- ✔ Set up a regular exercise schedule and stick to it!
- ✔ Take time for lunch, and get outside the office as often as possible to eat it.

Make the time now to take positive steps to cure yourself of your work addiction. You can do it if you try. We guarantee that you'll be a changed person if you simply let go. Go ahead: What do you have to lose (besides an aggravated ulcer or two)?

Knowing the Symptoms of Stress

No matter how hard you try to prevent it, some amount of stress in the workplace is inevitable. Although you may be doing a great job leading change in your organization and creating flexible plans that allow for the unexpected, you may have to work with other employees who aren't doing such a great job. The presence of change and differences in individual working styles are bound to create stress for you and your organization.

And the stress that you experience on the job is multiplied by the stress that you bring with you from your everyday life. Is that house payment starting to weigh down your personal finances? Are you and your significant other embroiled in yet another conflict about how you squeeze your toothpaste out of the tube? Did you just get a call from the IRS about a little matter of auditing your tax records for the past three years?

So how do you know whether you're stressed out? The following list of stress indicators can help you identify the extent of stress in your business and personal lives. Because one affects the other, determining and dealing with the source of stress is important.

Table 17-1 shows a list of symptoms of stress with a place to check off the symptoms that you have. If you experience more than a couple of these symptoms, take a serious look at what creates the stress in your life. Quick! Do something about stress before it's too late!

Table 17-1	Symptoms of Stress
The Symptom	*Yes, I Have It!*
Aggression	❏
Hostility	❏
Headaches	❏

The Symptom	Yes, I Have It!
Indigestion	❏
Sleep disorders	❏
Defensiveness	❏
Poor judgment	❏
Nervousness	❏
High blood pressure	❏
Ulcers	❏
Fatigue	❏
Anxiety	❏
Depression	❏
Memory loss	❏
Inability to concentrate	❏
Mood swings	❏

Any one of these symptoms can indicate a stress problem, but the longer your list of symptoms, the greater the damage being done to your mind and body. Fortunately, you can figure out how to manage your stress. Although you can't always prevent stress from entering your life, you can take definite steps to reduce the negative effects. Discover how to take control of stress so that it doesn't take control of you.

Managing Your Stress

Have you ever wondered why so many organizations make such a big deal about stress management training? Organizations must deal with stress because, when employees allow stress to overcome them, they lose their effectiveness. And when employees lose their effectiveness, the organization loses its edge.

Most stress management training focuses on treating the symptoms of stress and not on curing the root causes within the organization. We see a problem with this approach. The training programs teach workers relaxation techniques to decrease their level of stress, but top management isn't forced to make better and faster decisions. The training shows employees how to use positive affirmations to reinforce their feelings of self-worth, but the lousy phone system that cuts customers off in mid-sentence isn't fixed. The program instructs the staff in better time management, but poor planning still leads to organizational crisis after organizational crisis.

These examples show that you can't wait for someone else to do something to reduce your stress. Find out how to manage stress yourself. Fortunately, managing stress isn't as hard as you may think. Effective stress management boils down to this: Change the things that you can change and accept the things that you can't change.

Changing the things that you can change

You can take several steps right now to change your work environment and decrease your stress. If these steps sound familiar, you've probably thought about doing them before, but you just couldn't seem to get around to it. Well, now is the time to get around to it! Don't delay and put it off until tomorrow. The life you save may be your own!

✔ **Get healthy:** You know that regular, vigorous exercise is one of the best steps that you can do for yourself. Not only do you make your mind and your body stronger, but you also work off tons of frustration and stress. And when you're under stress, your body quickly becomes depleted of certain vitamins and minerals. Eat right. Don't forget your fruit and veggies! Particularly use this advice when you're on the road. Don't forgo exercise and proper diet because you're making a business trip.

Avoid the temptation to stop at the Pizza Hut or Häagen-Dazs outlet in the airline terminal while you're waiting for your flight. When you're traveling, you have to make an extra effort to stick with your diet and exercise routine. And those espresso mochas you've grown so fond of on the way to work each day? They have at least 10,000 calories apiece (well, okay, we're exaggerating a bit). Watch it!

✔ **Have fun:** If you're not having fun, why bother? Look, you're going to spend roughly a fourth to a third of your adult life at work. Sure, you need the money, and you need the psychological satisfaction that doing a good job brings with it, but don't ever take work so seriously that you can't have fun with your job and your coworkers.

Someday, when you retire, do you want to be remembered as the manager who kept an eye on the company's cash flow, or do you want to be remembered as the manager who impacted your employees' lives and made their jobs more rewarding in the process?

✔ **Find out how to say no:** What's the old saying? "You can please some of the people some of the time, but you can't please all the people all the time." Recognize that you can't do everything. And when you try to do everything, the result is that nothing gets done well. When you already have a full plate of work to do and someone tries to give you more, say no.

✔ **Relax:** Relaxation is an extremely important part of any program of stress management. When you relax, you give your brain a break, and you provide yourself with the needed opportunity to recharge your batteries before going back into overdrive.

Every minute counts. Do you remember what breaks are? You may not have taken one for a while, so you may be a little rusty at it. When you take a break to relax, make a real break from your routine. Get up from your desk and go someplace where you can remove yourself from the day-to-day business at hand. If you stay at your desk, the chances are that someone will call and you'll feel compelled to answer the phone ("maybe the call is important!") or someone will barge into your office and need your immediate attention. ("Sorry, Bob, I hope I'm not interrupting anything, but you've got to help me out here!") Go for a walk outside your building. Smell some flowers. Listen to the birds. Relax!

✔ **Manage your schedule:** If you don't manage your own schedule, it will quickly find a way to manage you. Get a personal planner, desk calendar, or PDA, and take charge of the meetings you attend and the appointments you keep.

If someone invites you to a meeting, don't automatically agree to go. Find out the topic of the meeting and your expected role. If you don't think that the meeting is worth your time to attend, don't! When you're pursuing your goals and priorities, keeping the goals and priorities of others from intruding can be incredibly difficult. Steadfastly refuse to let someone else's crisis become yours!

✔ **Streamline:** Why make your job harder than it has to be? As a manager, you're in the perfect position to be on the lookout for ways to improve your organization's work processes and systems. Be brutal in reviewing everything that your department does and remove needless steps. Simplify, shorten, and condense. Fewer steps in a process translates into your workforce expending less effort, fewer problems going wrong, and, ultimately, less stress for you to endure. (Less stress is good.)

✔ **Look for silver linings:** Be an optimist. Look for the good in everything you do and everyone you meet. You'll be amazed by how much better you feel about your job, your coworkers, and yourself. And you'll be just as amazed by how much better your coworkers feel about you when they can depend on you to lift their spirits. Be an ambassador of optimism. You decrease your own stress and the stress of those employees around you, too.

Accepting the things that you can't change

You just can't change certain things, no matter how hard you try. Instead of changing the unchangeable, you only end up stressed, defeated, or ill. And such an outcome isn't good in anyone's book. When you can't change the unchangeable, you have one choice left: Change yourself.

✔ **Surrender:** Stop fighting change. To continue the fight simply causes your stress level to increase — along with your blood pressure and the number of bottles of antacid that it takes to quell the fire in your stomach. Surrender to change; become one with it. Instead of trying to row against the swift currents of change, let go and drift with them.

Understand that you can use change to your advantage. After you stop fighting change, you can concentrate on making change work for you and for your organization (see Chapter 14 for more on change).

✔ **Don't take change personally:** Change doesn't affect just you. Everyone has to deal with change and the effects of change on the working environment. But the question is not how everyone else responds to change; the question is how you respond to change. Do you retreat into your shell? Do you get frustrated and angry? Or do you take charge?

✔ **Adjust your attitude:** Losing perspective is sometimes easy to do. After you've worked at a job for a few years, you can begin to get visions of grandeur. "How would this place survive without me?" Before long, you become resentful when your opinion isn't given the widespread respect that you feel it deserves, and you begin to dislike performing the mundane tasks that are a part of your job.

As you get hot under the collar about your current status, remember that many people are only a couple of paychecks away from bankruptcy. How long could you survive if you lost your job? And don't be so sure that your organization will never have a layoff or reduction in force. Who do you think would be let go first: Employees who willingly do whatever they can to get the job done or employees who think that they're above all that? If you picked the former, you may be due for a major attitude adjustment. Adjust your own attitude before someone adjusts it for you!

✔ **Don't be a victim:** In this world, you can be a hammer, or you can be an anvil. If you're a victim of change, you've stopped fighting change (which is good), but you've also stopped responding at all to the changes going on around you (which is bad). Don't give up and unplug yourself from the organization. Refuse to be a victim of change and, instead, become its biggest fan. And, if you absolutely can't stand your organization any longer, then find another one.

✔ **Control your anger:** Getting mad when your job doesn't go your way may be expressive, but showing anger isn't a productive use of your time and energy. Being angry about something you can do nothing to change saps your energy and distracts you from accomplishing the tasks that you can do something about.

What do you do when you get stuck in rush-hour traffic? Do you stew and fume? Does your blood pressure go up as your face begins to take on the color of borscht? Does your anger help you go any faster or get you home any sooner? No! Instead of wasting time trying to change the unchangeable, catch up on some phone calls, relax to some new tunes, or listen to a book on tape. Exchange your anger for a productive activity, or the anger may eat you alive!

✔ **Don't sweat the small stuff:** Much of what happens during the course of a normal business day is small stuff — filling out forms, pulling messages off your voice-mail system, poking at a few buttons on your computer keyboard. The big stuff can be few and far between. We assume that something like 80 percent of your time is spent getting 20 percent of your results. The point is: Most of what you do is small stuff, so don't sweat the small stuff! If you're going to worry, at least save it for something that's really important!

Trying out some specific stress reduction exercises

While you're changing the things you can change and accepting the things you can't change, you can use specific exercises to reduce your stress. These exercises are great because you can do them anywhere: at the office, at home, or in your car on the way to work. In addition, the exercises are effective on any kind of stress, whatever the source. The next time you feel your stomach tying itself into knots and your blood pressure starting to rise, give these exercises a try:

✔ **Breath control:** In. Out. In. Out. That's it. Take a deep breath. Hold it; don't let go. Now, exhale slowly. Feel the stress leave your body as you let go of your breath. Controlled breathing can have a calming effect.

When you feel stressed, give this ancient yoga breathing exercise a try: Breathe in through one nostril for a count of one while placing a finger against the side of your nose to close your other nostril. Hold the breath for eight counts and then exhale through your other nostril for four counts. Then reverse the procedure starting with your other nostril and repeat the exercise for a total of four complete cycles. You should be as cool as a cucumber about now.

✔ **Positive affirmations:** Crowd the negatives out of your life with positive affirmations such as, "Gee, I really have this customer's needs figured out," or "I did a great job on that last assignment. I can't wait for another one so I can do a great job on that one, too." Get positive. The more positive your life, the less stress you experience. (Plus you're a lot more fun to be around than those naysayers you have to work with.)

✔ **Progressive relaxation:** Believe it or not, a guy who was bowling at the time discovered this highly beneficial exercise. Apparently, his arm had gotten quite tired from lugging his big bowling ball around the lanes. Somebody called his name and he dropped the ball. Hmmm. Nice trick.

Anyway, you can use progressive relaxation when you're away from the bowling lanes. Relax in your chair or, even better, lie down in a darkened room; starting with your feet, concentrate on tensing up your muscles for several counts, and then let the muscles in your feet relax. Next, move to your calves. Tense your calf muscles for several counts and then let them relax. Keep moving up the rest of your body until you get to the top of your head. Finally, tense all your muscles at once, and then relax. The result is a general release of tension and increased relaxation.

✔ **Mental vacation:** Imagination is a very powerful tool. No matter where you are, you can take a vacation anywhere you want, anytime you want. When the crowd at your door is five deep, your phone is ringing off the hook, everyone has a problem instead of a solution, and your blood pressure erupts like Krakatoa east of Java, a mental vacation is definitely in order.

Close your door, forward your phone to the operator or to voice mail, turn down your lights, kick your ergonomic chair back into its full relax mode, and let your mind float downstream. Picture yourself in a boat on a river with the sun shining and the birds chirping. Take yourself far away from the challenges of the day.

✔ **Laugh:** Don't take your job so seriously that you lose your sense of humor. Having fun with your job and with your coworkers is an important way to reduce stress on the job. Don't forget the saying, "All work and no play makes Johnny a very boring guy." Not only does a good laugh provide you with a great way to release stress, but it also reminds you that life is more than work. Right?

If you've done everything you can to reduce stress, have become a leader of change, and have taken control of your business life, but you're still stressed out, you may be facing a much deeper issue that's not readily apparent on the surface. Perhaps you need professional help — from a therapist, a member of the clergy, or someone who has the kind of experience that you need.

Top five work/life Web sites

Wondering where to find the best information on the Web about the topics addressed in this chapter? Well, you've come to the right place! Here are our top five favorites:

✔ **Work & Family Connection:** www.workfamily.com

✔ **Workoptions.com:** www.workoptions.com/articles.htm

✔ **Work-Life Balance in Canadian Workplaces:** http://labour-travail.hrdc-drhc.gc.ca/worklife

✔ **BlueSuitMom.com:** www.bluesuitmom.com

✔ **Families and Work Institute:** www.familiesandwork.org

Part VI
Tools and Techniques for Managing

The 5th Wave   By Rich Tennant

"Sorry, Cedric—the King cut my budget for additional fools. He said the project already had enough fools on it."

In this part . . .

Although you don't have to be a technical wizard to be a manager, you can benefit from staying familiar with some of the key tools and technologies that drive today's business. In this part, we consider the basics of accounting and budgeting and how to harness the power of technology. We also talk about how to develop employee skills and about some of the most recent management trends.

Chapter 18

Budgeting, Accounting, and Other Money Stuff

. . . .

In This Chapter

▶ Creating your budget

▶ Applying professional budget tricks

▶ Understanding accounting basics

▶ Interpreting financial statements

. . . .

*I*n any organization, money makes the world go around. No matter how great your department is, how exciting your products are, or what a swell bunch of workers you employ, you and your group are in big-time jeopardy if you don't have money. If profits are down and money is increasingly tight in your organization, you'd better take some actions to correct the situation (or revise your resume and warm up your personal network of business contacts).

As a manager, you need to understand the basics of budgeting and accounting. When your coworkers start throwing around terms, such as *labor budget, cash flow, income statement,* and *balance sheet,* don't you want to do more than simply nod your head and respond with a blank stare? Here's some good news: You don't need an MBA to grasp these basics.

If computers and computer networks are the central nervous system of a business, accounting and finance (and the money that they measure and manipulate) are the lifeblood — its veins, arteries, platelets, and corpuscles. So what does it mean when your business is feeling a little queasy and the room starts to spin? That's right — you need a cash infusion!

In this chapter, we cover the importance of budgeting in an organization, as well as putting together a budget by using some of the professional tricks of the budget trade. We then introduce the survival basics of accounting. We aren't going to make you an accountant (whew!), but this chapter can help you to remove that quizzical look that gets pasted to your face every time someone starts talking balance sheets or cash flow. And don't forget:

Although you may work for a governmental entity or nonprofit organization, and some of these concepts may not directly apply to you, you never know when you may find yourself in a new, private-sector job!

Exploring the Wonderful World of Budgets

A *budget* is an itemized forecast of an individual's or company's income and expenses expected for some period in the future. Budgets provide the baseline of expected performance against which managers measure actual performance. Accounting systems that generate reports to compare expected performance against actual performance provide financial information on an organization's actual performance. With this information, managers with budget responsibility act as physicians to assess the current financial health of their businesses.

When you receive the latest accounting report, it says that sales are too low compared to budget. What does that mean? As a responsible manager (this means you!), you need to figure out why. Are prices too high? Maybe your sales force is having problems getting the product delivered to your customers quickly. Or perhaps your competition developed a new thingamajig that is taking sales away from your product. Are labor costs exceeding your budget? Perhaps your employees are working too much overtime. Maybe a reduction in production quality has led to an increase in the amount of rework required. Or perhaps employee pay simply is too high.

Because change is highly prevalent in today's business, why should you bother having budgets? You go through all that work and then your budget is out-of-date the day after you finish it, right? Sure, planning becomes more difficult as the world changes all around you, but plan you must. Without a long-term plan and goals, your organization lacks focus and resources are wasted as employees wander aimlessly about. A budget isn't just an educated guess that reflects your long-term plans and allows you to act on them, it's a personal commitment about making a designated future happen. The best budgets are flexible, allowing for changes in different key assumptions, such as revenue results.

Experienced managers already know the importance of budgets. Budgets make plans happen. Through its interaction with lower-level managers during the budgeting process, upper management can have a tremendous impact on the direction that an organization and its employees take. Conversely, lower-level employees can also have a huge impact on the organization during the budgeting process by submitting budget requests to management for approval.

Budgets determine how many people you have on your staff and how much you pay them. Budgets determine the financial resources you have to improve your workplace or to buy necessary office equipment, such as computers and copiers. And budgets determine how much money you have available to support your efforts on projects. Furthermore, budgets allow you to use all that expensive spreadsheet software that the company bought last year.

But budgets also fulfill another important purpose: They provide a baseline against which you can measure your progress toward your goals. For example, if you're 50 percent of the way through your fiscal year but have actually spent 75 percent of your budgeted operating funds, then you have an immediate indication that a potential problem exists if you don't see any significant change in your expenditures. Either you've underbudgeted your expenses for the year, or you're overspending. Whenever budgeted performance and actual performance disagree, or are in *variance,* the job of the responsible manager is to ask why, and to then fix any problems that are found.

Budgets also can give you the opportunity to put together all kinds of snazzy graphs and charts to impress your employees and top management. Imagine yourself in the boardroom with the lights dimmed, the attention of every audience member riveted to your presentation. You alternately project full-color, multilevel spreadsheets, and then beautiful three-dimensional bar charts and graphs. You're in command as you click the remote control buttons. You captivate your audience when you present the numbers in an interesting way!

Depending on your organization's size, the budgeting process may be quite simple or, alternatively, very complex. Regardless of an organization's size, you can budget most anything in it. Following are some examples:

- ✔ **Sales budget:** The sales budget is an estimate of the total number of products or services that will be sold in a given period. Determine the total revenues by multiplying the number of units by the price per unit.

- ✔ **Labor budget:** Labor budgets consist of the number and name of all the various positions in a company along with the salary or wages budgeted for each position.

- ✔ **Production budget:** The production budget takes the sales budget and its estimate of quantities of units to be sold and translates those figures into the cost of labor, material, and other expenses required to produce them.

- ✔ **Expense budget:** Expense budgets contain all the different expenses that a department may incur during the normal course of operations. You budget travel, training, office supplies, and more as expenses.

- ✔ **Capital budget:** This budget is a manager's plan to acquire *fixed assets* (anything your organization owns that has a long useful life), such as furniture, computers, facilities, physical plant, and so forth to support the operations of a business.

Making a Budget

You have a right and a wrong way to do a budget. The wrong way is simply to make a photocopy of the last budget and submit it as your new budget. The right way is to gather information from as many sources as possible, review and check the information for accuracy, and then use your good judgment to guess what the future may bring. A budget is a *forecast* — a commitment to the future — and is only as good as the data that goes into it and the good judgment that you bring to the process.

So how do you actually put together a budget? Where does the information come from? With whom should you talk? The possibilities seem endless. However, experienced budgetmeisters know that when you understand your costs of doing business — and where they come from — the budgeting process is actually quite simple. Make a few phone calls. Have a couple of meetings. Look over some recent accounting reports. Crunch a few numbers. Bingo! Your budget is complete! Well, your budget may have a little more to it than that. Review the basic steps in putting together a budget:

✔ **Closely review your budgeting documents and instructions.** Take a close look at the budgeting documents that you're working with and read any instructions that your accounting staff provides with them. Although your organization may have done something the same way for years, you never know when that procedure may change.

Back when he used to work in a regular, 9-to-5 job (now he's a 24/7 kind of guy), Peter spent more hours than he would like to admit preparing an annual budget for his organization's liability and property insurance — something that he'd routinely done year after year. One year, he spent a lot of time preparing the budget as he always had, only realizing after he finished the job — and after reading the new budget instructions — that that responsibility for that particular task had moved to a different manager. *Oops!*

✔ **Meet with staff.** When you're starting the budget process, meet with your staff members to solicit their input. In some cases, you need the specific input of your employees to forecast accurately. For example, you may need to know how many trips your salespeople plan to make next year and where they plan to go. In other cases, you can simply ask for employee suggestions. One employee may ask you to include a pay increase in the next budget. Another may inform you that the current phone system is no longer adequate to meet the needs of employees and customers and that a new one should be budgeted. Whichever the case, your staff can provide you with very useful and important budget information.

✔ **Gather data.** Pull copies of previous budgets and accounting reports and then compare budgeted numbers to actual numbers. Were previous budgets overrun or underrun? By how much? If no historical data is available, find other sources of information that can help guide the development of figures for your budget. How much business do you plan to bring in during the next budget period, and what will it cost you to bring it in? Consider whether you need to hire more people, lease new facilities, or buy equipment or supplies. Furthermore, consider the possibility of large increases or decreases in sales or expenses and what effect they would have on your budget.

✔ **Apply your judgment.** Hard data and cold facts are very important in the budgeting process; they provide an unbiased, unemotional source of information on which to base your decisions. However, data and facts aren't everything — not by a long shot. Budgeting is part science and part art. Take the data and facts and then apply your own judgment to determine the most likely outcomes.

For example, Peter used to budget more for extraordinary maintenance of his office facility than he could ever justify on an item-by-item basis. He did this knowing that something would come up during the course of the year (and it always did), and he needed to have enough money available in his budget to accommodate it. So when the big boss decided to build an additional 20 offices or redo the entire building in pink wallpaper, the money was available.

When you're new to management, you have little experience on which to draw, so you have a natural tendency to rely more heavily on data. However, as you become more accomplished in management and budgeting, your personal experience and judgment come to the fore.

✔ **Run the numbers.** Depending on how your organization does business, either fill out your budget forms and send them to your budget folks for processing, or enter them in the budget model yourself. The result is a budget draft that you can review and modify before you finalize it. Don't worry if the draft is rough or is missing information. You'll have a chance to fill in the gaps soon enough.

✔ **Check results and run the budget again as necessary.** Check over your draft budget and see whether it still makes sense to you. Are you missing any anticipated sources of revenue or expenses? Are the numbers realistic? Do they make sense in a historical perspective? Are they too high or too low? Will you be able to support them when you present them to upper management? The fun part of budgeting is playing with your numbers and trying different scenarios and what-ifs. When you're satisfied with the results, sign off on your budget and turn it in. Congratulations! You did it!

The accuracy of your budget hinges on two main factors: the quality of the data that you use to develop your budget and the quality of the judgment that you apply to the data you're working with. Although judgment is something that comes with experience, the quality of the data you use depends on where you get it. You can use three basic approaches to develop the data for building a budget:

✔ **Build it from scratch.** In the absence of historical data, when you're starting up a new business unit, or when you just want a fresh view, you want to develop your budgets based strictly on current estimates. In this process, widely known as *zero-based budgeting,* you build your budget from scratch — determining the people, facilities, travel, advertising, and other resources that are required to support it. You then cost out each need, and the budget is complete. Perhaps not too surprisingly, the answer that comes out of building a budget from scratch is often quite different from one that results from using historical data. Funny how that works.

✔ **Use historical figures.** One of the easiest ways to develop data for your budget is to use the actual results from the preceding budget period. Although the past is not always an indication of the future — especially when an organization is undergoing significant change — using historical data can be very helpful in relatively stable organizations and it's interesting to see which numbers have gone up, and which have gone down.

✔ **Use the combination approach.** Many managers use a combination of both preceding methods for determining which data to include in their budgets. To use this approach, gather historical data and compare the figures to the best estimates of what you think performing a particular function will cost. You then adjust historical data up or down, depending on your view of reality.

Pulling Rabbits Out of Hats and Other Budget Tricks

In any organization, a certain amount of mystery and intrigue — some would call it "smoke and mirrors" — hovers around budgets and the budgeting process. Indeed, whether your organization is a one-person operation or the federal government, you can use many tricks of the budget trade to ensure that you get all the resources you need and desire. *Note:* In these days of big-business scandals and shenanigans, we definitely aren't suggesting that you do anything illegal, immoral, or unethical. The tricks we suggest in this section are quite legal, and they're time-honored techniques for budgeting used every day in all kinds of organizations around the world.

The budget game is a long-standing tradition in business and government. Managers who discover how to play the game prosper, as do the people who work for them. Managers who fail to find out how to play the game, and the employees who work for them, are doomed to always have to make do with insufficient resources, facilities, pay, and the other niceties of business life. If you're a manager, finding out how the game is played is definitely in your interest.

The top ten excuses for being over budget

In the long history of modern business, managers have used a million and one excuses for exceeding their budgets. Admittedly, trying to predict the future of a business that is going through dynamic change is not unlike trying to hit a gnat with a slingshot at 100 paces. Regardless, your boss expects you to stick to your budget, just as you expect your employees to stick to theirs. However, for those times when the future gets a little fuzzy, here are the top ten excuses for going over budget:

1. The accounting reports must be wrong.

2. Didn't you get my revised budget?

3. How was I supposed to know that it would rain (insert your own excuse here) this year?

4. You're not going to quibble over a measly couple of million dollars, are you?

5. What we lose in margin we'll make up for in volume!

6. My assistant worked up that budget — he must have messed it up.

7. It's an investment in our future.

8. Cathy's (insert name of another manager here) department didn't come through with the support that I was promised.

9. We're doing better than last year!

10. Well, two years out of three isn't bad, is it?

Generally, the goal of the budget game is to build in enough extra money to actually be able to get the job done. In the worst case, you'll have enough resources available to protect your employees and vital functions when the business goes south. In the best case, you'll have money left over after you pay all your necessary expenses. Either you can turn the money back into accounting with much fanfare and accept the accolades from the powers that be for your expert resource management skills, or you can apply the money to the purchase of some equipment or other department needs. Of course, if you work for the government, your goal is to spend every penny of your budgeted amount so that your budget won't be decreased in the following year.

You can play the budget game up front, when you develop the budget, or during the course of the budget period. The following sections tell you how to develop a solid budget.

Maneuvering up-front budgets

Following are some of the games that the pros play when they develop budgets.

Although these techniques are most appropriate for new or unstable departments or projects, you can use them when developing any budget. We may be exaggerating just a bit on some of these points, but most of them have a very clear ring of truth.

- **Do some selective padding.** Simple, but effective. The idea is to pad your anticipated expenses so that your budget targets are easy to achieve. You end up looking like a hero when you come in under your budget, plus you get some extra money to play with at the end of the year. This situation is known as win-win.

- **Tie your budget request to your organization's values.** This is the *Mom and apple pie* approach to budgeting. If you want to beef up your budget in a particular area, just pick one of your organization's values — for example, quality — and tie your request to it. When your boss asks you to justify why you have tripled your office furniture budget, just tell him that your employees can't do quality work without large, handcrafted walnut desks.

- **Create more requests than you need, and give them up as you have to.** You don't want to appear unreasonable in your budget demands — don't forget, you're a team player! When you draft your budget, build in items that are of relatively low priority to you overall. When your boss puts on the pressure to reduce your budget (and bosses always do), give up the stuff you didn't really care so much about anyway. Doing so ensures that you get to keep the items that you really do want.

- **Shift the time frame.** Insist that the budget items are an investment in the company's future. The secret is to tie these investments to a big payoff down the road. "If we double our labor budget, we'll be able to attract the talent that we need to expand our operations."

- **Be prepared.** The best defense is a good offense. Know your budget numbers cold and be ready to justify each budget item in intimate detail. Don't rely on someone else to prepare for you — it can be your finest hour as a manager. Be a star and go for it!

Staying on budget

After your new department or project starts up, you need to closely monitor your budget to make sure that you don't exceed it. If your actual expenditures start to exceed your budget, you need to take quick and decisive action. Following are some of the ways that experienced managers make sure that they stay on budget:

- **Freeze discretionary expenses.** Some expenses, such as labor, benefits, and electricity, are essential to an operation or project and can't be stopped without jeopardizing performance. Others, such as purchasing new carpeting, upgrading computer monitors, or traveling first-class, are discretionary and can be postponed without jeopardizing performance. Freezing discretionary expenses is the quickest and least painful way to get your actual expenditures back in line with your budgeted expenditures.

✔ **Freeze hiring.** Although you may have budgeted new hires, you can save money by freezing the hiring of new employees. Not only do you save on the cost of hourly pay or salaries, but you also save on the costs of fringe benefits, such as medical care and overhead expenses like water, electricity, and janitorial services. And because you aren't messing with your current employees' pay or benefits, most everyone will be happy with your decision. Of course, some critical positions in your organization may need to be filled, budget problem notwithstanding. You can determine which positions have to be filled if they become vacant, and which other employees can cover.

✔ **Postpone products and projects.** The development and production phases of new products and projects can burn up a lot of money. By postponing the start-up and rollout of these new products and projects, you can get your budget back on track. Sometimes it only takes a few weeks or months to make a difference.

✔ **Stretch payments to suppliers.** Instead of paying right on time, you can stretch out your payments over a longer period of time. If you're going to go this route, it's generally best to work this out with your suppliers in advance (that is, if you want them to continue to be your suppliers in the future).

✔ **Freeze wages and benefits contributions.** These kinds of savings directly affect your employees, and we can guarantee that they aren't going to like it one bit. Most employees are used to regular wage and benefits increases. Although increases aren't as generous as they were a decade ago, employees still consider them to be essential. However, if you have made cuts and still need to cut more, then you really don't have any choice but to freeze your employees' wages and benefits contributions (medical insurance, 401k matching, and so on) at their current levels.

✔ **Lay off employees and close facilities.** You are in business to make money, not to lose money. When sales aren't sufficient to support your expenses — even after enacting the cost-savings measures just mentioned — you must take drastic action. Action doesn't get much more drastic than laying off employees and closing facilities. However, if your budget is as far off as it must be if you reach this point, then cut you must. See Chapter 16 for more information on conducting employee layoffs.

Whether you're responsible for budgeting as a part of your managerial duties or not, you need to have a basic understanding of the process that your business goes through to account for the money it makes and the money it spends. In the section that follows, we present all the information that you need to know about accounting to achieve a basic level of comprehension.

Understanding the Basics of Accounting

The accounting system that takes up gigabytes of storage space on your company's network server is dependent on a few very basic assumptions. These assumptions determine how every dollar and cent that flows into and out of your organization is assigned, reported, and analyzed. (If you ever want to drive your accounting staff nuts, tell them that you noticed a two- or three-cent mistake in your accounting reports and want them to find the source.)

Some managers believe that they can skate by with little or no knowledge of accounting and finance. This attitude is a mistake. As a manager, you must be just as familiar with these accounting basics as are the employees who work in your accounting department. Not only does this knowledge help to ensure that you understand and control your organization's financial destiny, but also if you're in command of the financial side of your business as well as the technical side, then you're also much more likely to survive the next round of corporate layoffs.

No longer do you have to be dumbfounded when one of your fellow managers starts throwing around terms such as _ROI, accounts receivable,_ and _retained earnings._ After you read this section, you'll be in the driver's seat!

Figuring out the accounting equation

Daily events affect every business's financial position. A manager spends cash to buy a stapler and is reimbursed out of the petty cash fund. The company taps its bank line of credit to pay vendor invoices. Customers pay bills and those payments are deposited. Employees receive paychecks. Each of these _financial transactions_ and many more has its place in the accounting equation.

The accounting equation states that an organization's _assets_ are equal to its _liabilities_ plus its _owners' equity._ The accounting equation looks like this:

Assets = Liabilities + Owners' Equity

This simple equation drives the very complex system of accounting that is used to track every financial transaction in a business, provide reports to managers for decision making, and provide financial results to owners, shareholders, lenders, the IRS, and other stakeholders.

So what exactly does each part of the accounting equation represent? Take a look at each part and what it comprises.

Assets

Assets are generally considered to be anything of value — primarily financial and economic resources — that a company owns. The most common forms of assets in a business include the following:

- ✔ **Cash:** This asset encompasses money in all its forms, including cash, checking accounts, money market funds, and marketable securities, such as stocks and bonds. Every business likes to have lots of cash.

- ✔ **Accounts receivable:** This asset represents the money that customers who buy goods and services on credit owe to your company. For example, if your business sells a box of floppy disks to another business and then bills the other business for the sale instead of demanding immediate payment in cash, this obligation becomes an account receivable until your customer pays it. Accounts receivable are nice to have unless the companies or individuals that owe you money skip town or decide to delay their payments for six months.

- ✔ **Inventory:** Inventory is the value of merchandise held by your business for sale, the finished goods that you have manufactured but have not yet sold, as well as the raw materials and work in process that are part of the manufacture of finished goods. Inventory usually becomes cash or an account receivable when sold. Inventory that sits around on a shelf forever isn't the best way to tie up your company's assets. Keeping your inventory moving all the time is much better, because you are generating sales.

- ✔ **Prepaid expenses:** Prepaid expenses represent goods and services that your firm has already paid for but not yet used. For example, your company may pay its annual liability insurance premium at the beginning of the year, before the insurance policy actually goes into effect. If the policy is canceled during the course of the year, then part of the premium is refunded to your business.

- ✔ **Equipment:** Equipment is the property — machinery, desks, computers, phones, and similar items — that your organization buys to carry out its operations. For example, if your company sells computer supplies to individuals and other businesses, you need to purchase shelves on which to store your inventory of computer supplies, forklifts to move it around, and phone systems on which to take orders from your customers. As equipment ages, it loses value. You account for this loss through *depreciation,* which spreads the original cost of a piece of equipment across its entire useful lifetime. When in doubt, depreciate.

- ✔ **Real estate:** Real estate includes the land, buildings, and facilities that your organization owns or controls. Examples include office buildings, manufacturing plants, warehouses, sales offices, mills, farms, and other forms of real property.

Assets are divided into two major types: *current* assets and *fixed* assets.

- ✔ Current assets can be converted into cash within one year. Such assets are considered to be *liquid*. In the preceding list of assets, cash, accounts receivable, inventory, and prepaid expenses are considered current assets. Liquid assets are nice to have around when your business is in trouble and you need to raise cash quickly to make payroll or pay your vendors.

- ✔ Fixed assets require more than one year to convert to cash. In the preceding list of assets, equipment and real estate are classified as fixed assets. If your business gets into trouble and you need cash, fixed assets probably won't do you much good unless you can use them as collateral for a loan.

Liabilities

Liabilities are generally considered to be debts that you owe to others — individuals, other businesses, banks, and so on — outside the company. In essence, liabilities are the claims that outside individuals and organizations have against a business's assets.

The most common forms of business liabilities include the following:

- ✔ **Accounts payable:** Accounts payable are the obligations that your company owes to the individuals and organizations from which it purchases goods and services. For example, when you visit your local office supply store to buy a couple of pencils and bill the purchase to your company's account, this obligation becomes an account payable. You can conserve your company's cash in times of need by slowing down payments to your vendors and suppliers, although you have to be very careful not to jeopardize your credit in the process.

- ✔ **Notes payable:** Notes payable are the portion of loans made to your organization by individuals, financial institutions, or other organizations that are due to be paid back within one year. If, for example, your firm takes a 90-day loan to increase its inventory of floppy disks to satisfy a rapid increase in customer demand, the loan is considered a note payable.

- ✔ **Accrued expenses:** Accrued expenses are miscellaneous expenses that your company incurs but that aren't reimbursed. Examples include obligations for payroll, sick leave due to employees, taxes payable to the government, and interest due to lenders.

- ✔ **Bonds payable:** Some large companies issue bonds to raise money to finance expansion or achieve other goals. Bonds payable represent the money that a company owes to the individuals and organizations that purchase the bonds as an investment.

✔ **Mortgages payable:** When organizations purchase real estate, they often do so by incurring long-term loans known as *mortgages*. Mortgages differ from standard loans in that they're usually secured by the real estate that the mortgage finances. For example, if your company defaults in its payments on the mortgage used to purchase your office building, ownership of the office building reverts to the entity that originally issued the mortgage — usually a bank or investment group.

Like assets, liabilities are also divided into two major types: *current* liabilities and *long-term* liabilities.

✔ Current liabilities are repaid within one year. In the preceding list of liabilities, accounts payable, notes payable, and accrued expenses are considered current liabilities.

✔ Long-term liabilities are repaid in a period greater than one year. In the preceding list of liabilities, bonds payable and mortgages payable are both classified as long-term liabilities.

Owners' equity

All businesses have owners. In some cases, the owners are a few individuals who founded the company. In other cases, the owners are the many thousands of individuals who buy the company's stock through public offerings. Owners' equity is the owners' share of the assets of a business after all liabilities have been paid.

The most common forms of owners' equity include the following:

✔ **Paid-in capital:** Paid-in capital is the investment — usually paid in cash — that the owners make in a business. For example, if your firm sells common stock to investors through a public offering, the money that your firm obtains through the sale of the stock is considered paid-in capital.

✔ **Retained earnings:** These earnings are reinvested by a business and not paid out in dividends to shareholders. A certain amount of earnings are retained in hopes of increasing the firm's overall earnings and also to increase the dividends that are paid to owners.

Knowing double-entry bookkeeping

Double-entry bookkeeping is the standard method of recording financial transactions that forms the basis of modern business accounting. Invented in 1494 by Luca Pacioli, a bored Franciscan monk (he must have been really bored to invent accounting!), double-entry bookkeeping recognizes that every financial transaction results in a record of a *receipt* (also known as an asset) and a record of an *expense* (also known as a liability).

Consider this example: Your company buys $1,000 worth of computer floppy disks from a manufacturer to resell to your customers. Because your company has established an account with the floppy disk manufacturer, the manufacturer bills you for the $1,000 instead of demanding immediate cash payment. Do you remember the accounting equation that we discuss earlier in this chapter? Here's the double-entry version of the accounting equation illustrating the $1,000 purchase of floppy disks to stock in your inventory:

Assets	=	Liabilities	+	Owners' equity
$1,000	=	$1,000	+	$0
(Inventory)		(Accounts payable)		

In this example, assets (inventory) increase by $1,000 — the cost of purchasing the floppy disks to stock your shelves. At the same time, liabilities (accounts payable) also increase by $1,000. This increase represents the debt that you owe to your supplier of floppy disks. In this way, the accounting equation always stays balanced. Now, imagine the effect of the several hundreds or thousands of financial transactions that hit your accounting system on a daily, weekly, or monthly basis. Whew! And you wondered why your information systems manager is always complaining that the company's computer system isn't big enough or fast enough.

Identifying the Most Common Types of Financial Statements

An accounting system is nice to have, but the system is worthless unless it can produce data that is useful to managers, employees, lenders, vendors, owners, investors, and other individuals and firms that have a financial stake in your business. And believe us, a lot of people have a financial interest in your business.

The make-or-buy decision

One of the most common decisions made in business is whether to make — that is, build or perform with in-house staff — or buy goods and services that are necessary for the operation of a business. For example, say you decide that you need to assign a security guard to your reception area tc ensure the safety of your clients. Do you hire someone new as an employee, or does contracting with a company that specializes in providing security services make more sense?

When you consider such a make-or-buy decision, the first point to consider is the cost of each alternative to your firm. Say that in Case A, you hire your security guard as a full-time employee for $6.00 an hour. In Case B, a security services firm provides a guard for $8.00 an hour. On the surface, hiring a security guard as an employee seems to make the most sense. If the guard works 2,000 hours a year, then in Case A you spend $12,000 a year for your guard and in Case B you spend $16,000 a year. By employing the guard yourself, you stand to save $4,000 a year. Right?

Maybe not. See why.

Case A: Hire in-house security guard

Hourly pay rate
$6.00

Fringe benefits rate @ 35%
2.10

Overhead rate @ 50%
3.00

Total effective pay rate
$11.10

Hours per year
x 2,000

Total annual labor cost
$22,200

Annual liability insurance increase
4,000

Uniforms/cleaning
1,000

Miscellaneous equipment
500

Total annual cost
$27,700

Case B: Contract with security firm

Hourly pay rate
$8.00

Total effective pay rate
$8.00

Hours per year
x 2,000

Total annual cost
$16,000

Surprise, surprise. Instead of saving $4,000 per year by hiring an in-house security guard, you're actually going to spend almost $12,000 more each year because more costs are involved in hiring an in-house employee than just his or her hourly pay. You have to add all the fringe benefits, such as life insurance, medical and dental plans, and more, plus the employee's share of overhead — facilities, electricity, air conditioning, and so forth — to the basic wage rate to get a true picture of the cost of the employee to your organization. Furthermore, you need to purchase additional liability insurance, uniforms, uniform cleaning, and miscellaneous equipment such as a flashlight, Mace, and handcuffs.

On the other hand, when you contract with a security services firm, the firm bears the cost of fringe benefits, overhead, insurance, uniforms, and equipment. You simply pay the hourly fee and forget it. Furthermore, if the guard doesn't work out, you just make a phone call, and a replacement is sent immediately. No messy employee terminations or unemployment benefits to worry about.

Now, which deal do you think is the better one?

Does it surprise you to hear that almost everyone wants to know the financial health of your business? Well, they do. Managers want to know so that they can identify and fix problems. Employees want to know because they want to work for a company that's in good financial health and that provides good pay, benefits, and job stability. Lenders and vendors need to know your company's financial health to decide whether to extend credit. And owners and investors want to know because this knowledge helps them determine whether their investment dollars are being used wisely or are instead being frittered away.

Accountants invented *financial statements* to be able to measure the financial health and performance of a company.

Financial statements are nothing more than reports — intended for distribution to individuals outside the accounting department — that summarize the amounts of money contained within selected accounts or groups of accounts at a selected point or period of time. Each type of financial statement has a unique value to those people who use them, and different individuals may use some or all of an organization's financial statements during the normal course of business. The following sections review the financial statements that you're most likely to encounter during your career as a manager.

The balance sheet

The *balance sheet* is a report that illustrates the value of a company's assets, liabilities, and owners' equity — the company's financial position on a specific date. Think of it as a snapshot of the business. Although it can be prepared at any time, a balance sheet is usually prepared at the end of a definite accounting period — most often a year, quarter, or month.

Figure 18-1 shows a typical balance sheet.

As you can see, the balance sheet provides values for every major component of the three parts of the accounting equation. By reviewing each item's value in the balance sheet, managers can identify potential problems and then take action to solve them.

The income statement

Assets, liabilities, and owners' equity are all very nice, thank you, but many people really want to see the bottom line. Did the company make money or lose money? In other words, what was its profit or loss? This job belongs to the *income statement*.

Sample Balance Sheet

	January 31, 1997
ASSETS	
CURRENT ASSETS	
Cash and cash equivalents	$458,000
Accounts receivable	$11,759,000
Inventory	$154,000
Prepaid expenses and other current assets	$283,000
Refundable income taxes	$165,000
TOTAL CURRENT ASSETS	$12,819,000
EQUIPMENT AND FURNITURE	
Equipment	$4,746,000
Furniture, fixtures, and improvements	$583,000
	$5,329,000
Allowance for depreciation and amortization	($2,760,000)
	$2,569,000
COMPUTER SOFTWARE COSTS, NET	$3,199,000
NET DEPOSITS AND OTHER	$260,000
	$18,847,000
LIABILITIES AND SHAREHOLDERS' EQUITY	
CURRENT LIABILITIES	
Notes payable to bank	$1,155,000
Accounts payable	$2,701,000
Accrued compensation and benefits	$2,065,000
Income taxes payable	$0
Deferred income taxes	$990,000
Current portion of long-term debt	$665,000
TOTAL CURRENT LIABILITIES	$7,576,000
LONG-TERM DEBT, less current portion	$864,000
DEFERRED RENT EXPENSE	$504,000
DEFERRED INCOME TAXES	$932,000
STOCKHOLDERS' EQUITY	
Common stock	$76,000
Additional paid-in capital	$803,000
Retained earnings	$8,092,000
	$8,971,000
	$18,847,000

Figure 18-1:
A typical balance sheet.

An income statement adds all the sources of a company's revenues and then subtracts all the sources of its expenses to determine its net income or net loss for a particular period of time. Whereas a balance sheet is a snapshot of an organization's financial status, an income statement is more like a movie.

Figure 18-2 illustrates a simple income statement.

Revenues

Revenue is the value received by a company through the sale of goods, services, and other sources such as interest, rents, royalties, and so forth. To arrive at net sales, total sales of goods and services are offset by returns and allowances.

Expenses

Expenses are all the costs of doing business. For accounting purposes, expenses are divided into two major classifications:

- ✔ **Cost of goods sold:** For a firm that retails or wholesales merchandise to individuals or other companies, this figure represents the cost of purchasing merchandise or inventory. By subtracting the cost of goods sold from revenue, you end up with the company's *gross margin,* also known as *gross profit.*

- ✔ **Operating expenses:** Operating expenses are all the other costs of doing business not already part of the cost of goods sold. Operating expenses are usually further subdivided into *selling expenses,* which include marketing, advertising, product promotion, and the costs of operating stores, and *general and administrative expenses,* which are the actual administrative costs of running the business. General and administrative costs typically include salaries for accounting, data processing, and purchasing staff and the cost of corporate facilities including utilities, rent payments, and so on.

Net income or loss

The difference between revenues and expenses (after adjustment for interest income or expense and payment of income taxes) is a company's net income (profit) or net loss. Also commonly known as a company's *bottom line,* net income or loss is the cash you have on hand after you've paid all the bills, and it's the one number most often of interest to those people who want to assess the firm's financial health. Many corporate executives and managers have found themselves on the street when their companies' bottom lines dipped too far into the loss side of the equation.

The cash-flow statement

What's the old saying? "Happiness is a positive cash flow." Cash-flow statements show the movement of cash into and out of a business. It doesn't take an

Einstein to realize that when more cash is moving out of a business than is moving into the business for a prolonged period of time, the business may be in big trouble.

Sample Income Statement

Twelve months ended

January 31, 1997

REVENUES		
Gross sales	$58,248,000	
Less: Returns	$1,089,000	
Net Sales		$57,159,000
COST OF GOODS SOLD		
Beginning inventory		$4,874,000
Purchases	$38,453,000	
Less: Purchase discounts	$1,586,000	
Net purchases		$36,867,000
Cost of goods available for sale		$41,741,000
Less: Ending inventory		$6,887,000
Cost of Goods Sold		$34,854,000
GROSS PROFIT		$22,305,000
OPERATING EXPENSES		
Total selling expenses		$8,456,000
Total general expenses		$1,845,000
Total operating expenses		$10,301,000
Operating income		$12,004,000
Other income and expenses		
Interest expense (income)		$360,000
Total other income and expenses		$360,000
Income before taxes		$11,644,000
Less: Income taxes		$3,952,000
Net Income		$7,692,000
Average number of shares		3,500,000
Earnings per share		$2.20

Figure 18-2:
A simple income statement.

Cash is sort of like gasoline. Your car requires a plentiful supply of gasoline to run. If you run out of gas, your car is going to stop dead on the highway. One minute, you're going 65 miles an hour, and the next, you're going zero miles an hour. Similarly, if your company runs out of cash, the company is going to stop dead, too. Without cash to pay employees' salaries, vendors' invoices, lenders' loan payments, and so forth, operations quickly cease to exist.

✔ **Simple cash-flow statement:** The simple cash-flow statement arranges all items into one of two categories: cash inflows and cash outflows.

✔ **Operating cash-flow statement:** The operating cash-flow statement limits analysis of cash flows to only those items having to do with the operations of a business, and not its financing.

✔ **Priority cash-flow statement:** The priority cash-flow statement classifies cash inflows and outflows by specific groupings chosen by the manager or other individual who requests preparation of the statement.

Using financial ratios to analyze your business

If you don't know exactly what you're looking for, analyzing a company's financial records can be quite a daunting task. Fortunately, over a period of many years, expert business financial analysts have developed ways to assess the performance and financial health and well-being of an organization quickly by comparing the ratios of certain key financial indicators to established standards and to other firms in the same industries.

Current ratio: This ratio is the capability of a company to pay its current liabilities out of its current assets. A ratio of 2 or more is generally considered good. Consider this example:

Current ratio = Current assets ÷ Current liabilities

= $100 million ÷ $25 million

= 4.00

Quick ratio: The quick ratio (also known as the *acid-test* ratio) is the same as the current ratio with the exception that inventory is subtracted from current assets. This ratio provides a much more rigorous test of a firm's capability to pay its current liabilities quickly than does the current ratio, because inventory can't be liquidated as rapidly as other current assets. A ratio of 1 or better is acceptable.

Quick ratio = (Current assets - inventory) ÷ Current liabilities

= ($100 million - $10 million) ÷ $25 million

= $90 million ÷ $25 million

= 3.60

Receivables turnover ratio: This ratio indicates the average time that it takes for a firm to convert its receivables into cash. A higher ratio indicates that customers are paying their bills quickly, which is good. A lower ratio reflects slow collections and a possible problem that management needs to address, which is bad. Your boss isn't going to like it.

Receivables turnover ratio = Net sales ÷ Accounts receivable

= $50 million ÷ $5 million

= 10.00

You can gain one more interesting piece of information quickly from the receivables turnover ratio. By dividing 365 days by the receivables turnover ratio, you get the average number of days that it takes your firm to turn over its accounts receivable, which is commonly known as the *average collection period.* The shorter the average collection period, the better the organization's situation is, and the better your job security is.

Average collection period = 365 days ÷ Receivables = turnover ratio

= 365 days ÷ 10.00

= 36.5 days

Debt-to-equity ratio: This ratio measures the extent to which the organization depends on loans from outside creditors versus resources provided by shareholders and other owners. A ratio in excess of 1 is generally considered unfavorable because it indicates that the firm may have difficulty repaying its debts. And nobody — especially cranky bankers or vendors — wants to loan money to companies that have problems repaying their debts. A particularly low ratio indicates that management may be able to improve the company's profitability by increasing its debt.

Debt-to-equity ratio = Total liabilities ÷ Owners' equity

= $50 million ÷ $150 million

= 0.33 or 33 percent

Return on investment: Often known by its abbreviation, *ROI,* return on investment measures the capability of a company to earn profits for its owners. Don't forget: Profit is good and loss is bad. Because owners — shareholders and other investors — prefer to make money on their investments, they like an organization's ROI to be as high as possible.

Return on investment = Net income ÷ Owners' equity

= $50 million ÷ $150 million

= 0.33 or 33 percent

Top five accounting Web sites

Wondering where to find the best information on the Web about the topics addressed in this chapter? Well, you've come to the right place! Here are our top five favorites:

✔ *Business Finance* magazine: www. businessfinancemag.com

✔ CFO.com: www.cfo.com

✔ *Strategic Finance* magazine: www. strategicfinancemag.com/

✔ *AccountingWEB*: www.accountingweb. co.uk

✔ *SmartPros* Accounting: http:// finance.pro2net.com

Chapter 19

Harnessing the Power of Technology

*Y*ou gotta love technology. Unfortunately, like everything else in life, technology has its good and bad points. With computers, for example, managers and workers alike have more ways to waste time than ever before. Sure, computers make great typewriters and adding machines (and a year or two after you buy them, excellent boat anchors!), but do you really need to spend half an hour typing, editing, spell checking, and color printing a gorgeous, 64-shades-of-gray memo when a handwritten note or quick phone call works just as well? We automatically assume that our employees are more productive simply because they have computers at their fingertips, but are you (and your organization) really getting the most out of this innovative and expensive technology?

That is, of course, the million-dollar question. Or, considering how much companies spend on information technology each year, the question is more like the $29-million question — the amount that, according to Forrester Research, an average firm on the Global 3,500 list (a list of the top 3,500 firms worldwide) spends just on e-business technology in a year.

In this chapter, we explain how to harness information technology — technology used to create, store, exchange, and use information in its various forms. We examine the technology edge, and consider how technology can help or hinder an organization. We look at how technology can improve efficiency and productivity, and how to get the most out of it. Finally, we describe how to create a technology plan.

Using Technology to Your Advantage

Are we hallucinating, or does information technology seem to be taking over the world? Certainly, computers and telecommunications technology have taken over business. Even the most defiant CEOs are finally taking the plunge and are wireless telephoning and surfing the Web in ever-increasing numbers. Information technology can give you and your business tremendous advantages and, as a manager, you must capitalize on them — before your competition does.

The time to debate the advantages of information technology is over; the time to act is now. But, before you act, you must become technology savvy. The following are the four basic ways for doing just that.

Know your business

Before you can design and implement information technology in the most effective way, you first have to completely understand how your business works. What work is being done? Who's doing it? What do employees need to get their work done?

One way to know your business is to approach it as an outsider. Pretend you're a customer and see how your company's people and systems handle you. Do the same with your competitors to see how their people and systems handle you. What are the differences? What are the similarities? How can you improve your own organization using information technology as a result of what you've discovered?

Create a technology-competitive advantage

Few managers understand how technology can become a competitive advantage for their businesses. Although they may have vague notions of potential efficiency gains or increased productivity, they're clueless when dealing with specifics.

Information technology can create real and dramatic competitive advantages over other businesses in your markets, specifically by:

- ✔ Competing with large companies by marketing on a level playing field (the Internet)

✔ Helping to build ongoing, loyal relationships with customers

✔ Connecting with strategic partners to speed up vital processes, such as product development and manufacturing

✔ Linking everyone in the company, as well as with necessary sources of information both inside and outside the organization

✔ Providing real-time information on pricing, products, and so forth to vendors, customers, and OEMs (original equipment manufacturers)

Now is the time to create advantages over your competition. Keep in mind that the company that has the most data doesn't win today, but the company who manages that data best wins.

Develop a plan

If you're serious about using information technology as an edge, you must have a plan for its implementation. You can find details about creating a technology plan later in this chapter (see the section, "Having a Plan (And Sticking to It)"), but the following are several points to remember in the planning process:

✔ **Don't buy technology just because it's the latest and greatest thing.** You always enjoy shopping for the latest, whiz-bang gizmo. (Who doesn't?) Unfortunately, just because an item is new doesn't mean that it's right for your business. Be sure that whatever technology you include in your plan makes sense for your business.

✔ **Plan for the right period of time.** Different kinds of businesses require different planning horizons — the time periods covered by their plans. If you're in a highly volatile market — wireless communications, for example — then your planning horizon may be only six months or so out. If you're in a stable market — say, a grocery chain — your planning horizon may extend out three to five years into the future.

✔ **Make the planning process a team effort.** You're not the only one who's going to be impacted by all this new technology that you bring into your company. Make employees, customers, and vendors a part of your planning team.

✔ **Weigh the costs of upgrading your old system versus going to a new system.** Every system eventually comes to the end of its useful life. Rather than continuing to patch up a system that's becoming increasingly expensive to maintain, start fresh. Run the numbers and see what alternative makes the most sense for your organization before you finalize your plans.

Get some help

If you're a fan of technology and pretty knowledgeable in it, that's great — you have a head start on the process. But, if you're not, get help from people who are experts in information technology. Does your company have people who are knowledgeable? Can you hire a technician or technology consultant to fill in the gaps? Whatever you do, don't try it alone. Even if you're a full-fledged techno-geek, enlist others into your cause.

Weighing the Benefits and Drawbacks of Technology

Think for a moment about the incredible progress of information technology just in your lifetime. With so many tools at your fingertips, can you believe that a little more than two decades ago, the personal computer had yet to be introduced commercially? Whereas word processing used to mean a type-writer and a lot of correction fluid or sheets of messy carbon paper, computers have revolutionized the way in which business people can manipulate text, graphics, and other elements in their reports and other documents. Wireless telephones, fax machines, the Internet, and other business technology essentials are all fairly recent innovations.

So, how can technology help your business? Information technology can have a positive impact in two very important ways:

- **By automating processes:** Not too many years ago, business processes were manual. For example, your organization's accounting and payroll department may have calculated payroll entirely by hand with the assistance of only a ten-key adding machine. What used to take hours, days, or weeks can now be accomplished in minutes. Other processes that are commonly automated are inventory tracking, customer service, call analysis, purchasing, and more.

- **By automating personal management functions:** More managers than ever are taking their calendars and personal planners and moving them onto computers. Although paper-based planners won't die completely, many managers are finding out that computers are much more powerful management tools than their unautomated counterparts. Managers also use computers to schedule meetings, track projects, analyze numbers, manage business contact information, conduct employee performance evaluations, and more.

However, before you run off and automate everything, keep this piece of information in mind: If your manual system is inefficient or ineffective, simply automating the system won't necessarily make your system perform any better. In fact, automating it can make your system perform worse than the manual version. When you automate, review the process in detail. Cut out any unnecessary steps and make sure that your system is optimized for the new, automated environment. Believe us, the time you take now to improve your processes and functions will pay off when you automate.

But, just as information technology can help a business, it can also hinder it. Here are a few examples of the negative side of information technology:

- Widespread worker abuse of Internet access has reduced worker productivity by 10 to 15 percent. According to Forrester Research, 20 percent of employee time on the Internet at work doesn't involve their jobs.

- Hackers have sent periodic waves of computer viruses and malicious attacks through the business world, leaving billions of dollars of damage and lost productivity in their wake.

- E-mail messages can be unclear and confusing, forcing workers to waste time clarifying their intentions or covering themselves in case of problems.

- Employees are forced to wade through an ever-growing quantity of spam and junk e-mail messages.

- The slick, animated, and sound-laden computer-based full-color presentations so common today can take longer to prepare than the simple text and graphs that were prevalent a few years ago — especially if you're not technologically savvy.

So, you have to take the bad with the good. But don't take the bad lying down. You can maximize the positives of information technology while minimizing the negatives. You can do this by:

- **Staying current on the latest information innovations and news.** Although you don't need to become an expert on how to install a network server or configure your voice-mail system, you do need to become conversant in the technology behind your business systems.

- **Hiring experts.** Although you must have a general knowledge of information technology, plan to hire experts to advise you in the design and implementation of critical information technology-based systems.

- **Managing by walking around.** Make a habit of dropping in on employees — wherever they're located — and observe how they use your organization's information technology. Solicit their feedback and suggestions for improvement. Research and implement changes as soon as you discover the need.

One point is certain: You can't turn back the clock on technology. To keep up with the competition — and to beat it — you must keep pace with technology and adopt what can make your employees more productive, while improving products and services, customer service, and the bottom line. You really have no other choice.

Improving Efficiency and Productivity

The recent explosion of information technology accompanies the shift in American industry from old-line standards, such as steel mills and petroleum refineries to companies producing semiconductors, computers, and related products. The personal computer industry, which was still in its infancy two decades ago, has quickly grown into a market worth tens of billions of dollars in annual sales.

The idea that businesspeople who best manage information have a competitive advantage in the marketplace seems obvious enough. The sooner you receive information, the sooner you can act on it. The more effectively you handle information, the easier you can access that information when and where you need it. The more efficiently you deal with information, the fewer expenses you incur for managing and maintaining your information.

PC versus Apple

Only a few years ago, business managers took the question of whether to buy PC (IBM-compatible personal computer) or an Apple computer very seriously. Although Apple's products — with their intuitive, easy-to-learn operating interface, graphical icons, and computer mouse — were once vastly superior to their PC rivals, Microsoft Windows software changed all that. PCs using Microsoft Windows are virtually indistinguishable from their Apple equivalents in their ease of use, and they generally cost less to boot.

Although Apple almost crashed and burned some years ago, the return of Steve Jobs to the company has led to a resurgence both in Apple and in the popularity of its hardware. And, although the Macintosh is still the standard for specific applications such as video, graphics and design, and musical composition, the Mac is increasingly finding its way back into business — especially now that Apple prices its machines much more competitively than it did in past years.

Now that computer networks can accommodate both PCs and Apple computers, you have really no reason to limit yourself to one or the other. Your accounting employees can be blazing away on their multi-gigahertz PCs, while the graphics department happily designs and creates on their supercharged Apples.

Who says that we can't all coexist peacefully? PC or Apple — the choice is yours.

Management often cites the preceding reasons, and others like them, as justification for spending obscenely huge amounts of corporate resources to buy computers, install e-mail and voice-mail systems, and train employees to use these new tools of the Information Age. But, have all these expenditures made your workers more productive? Unfortunately, for years, researchers found no evidence to prove that office automation resulted in measurable productivity gains — leading many to label the phenomenon the "productivity paradox."

Author Eliyahu Goldratt defined information as "the answer to a question." Many of today's information systems are great at providing data, but not so hot at providing information (at least within this definition). A manager should first spend a lot of time identifying the "questions" that need an answer. Who needs the answer (customer, supplier, employee, management), how fast do they need the answer (real-time, one minute, one hour, one day), and how frequently do they need the answer (daily, weekly, monthly)? When this becomes clear, you have a rational basis to evaluate alternate technologies based on how well they meet the criteria needed for your "answers." Lots of technology seems to be designed to provide a real-time answer to a question that only needs to be asked once a month.

Information technology — planned and implemented wisely — can improve an organization's efficiency and productivity. More recent studies are beginning to show a relationship between the implementation of information technology and increased productivity. Examples like the following bear out this relationship:

- Implementation of a computerized inventory-management system at Warren, Michigan-based Duramet Corporation — a manufacturer of powdered metal — helped the company double sales over a three-year period without hiring a single new salesperson.

- By using information technology to provide employees with real-time information about orders and scheduling that cuts through the traditional walls within the organization, M.A. Hanna, a manufacturer of polymers, reduced its working capital needs by one-third to achieve the same measure of sales. Impressive as this reduction is, Martin D. Walker, CEO of M.A. Hanna, is convinced that his firm can further reduce its working capital by an equal amount simply by communicating with suppliers and customers through computer networks.

- At Weirton Steel Corporation — based in Weirton, West Virginia — the company uses only 12 people to run the hot mill that once required 150 people to operate, all because of the technology installed in the production line.

Although evidence is beginning to swing toward productivity gains, studies indicate that merely installing computers and other information technology doesn't automatically lead to gains in employee efficiency. As a manager, you must take the time to improve your work processes before you automate them. If you don't, office automation can actually lead to decreases in employee efficiency and productivity. Instead of the usual lousy results that you get from your manual, unautomated system, you end up with something new: garbage at the speed of light. Don't let your organization make the same mistake!

Getting the Most Out of Information Technology

The personal computer began revolutionizing business a decade ago, shifting the power of computing away from huge mainframes and onto the desks of individual users. Now, computer networks are bringing about a new revolution in business. Although the personal computer is a self-sufficient island of information, when you link these islands together in a network, individual computers have the added benefit of sharing with every computer on the network.

So does networking have any benefits? You bet it does! See what you think about these reasons:

✔ **Networks improve communication:** Computer networks allow anyone in an organization to communicate with anyone else quickly and easily. With the click of a button, you can send messages to individuals or groups of employees. You can send replies just as easily. Furthermore, employees on computer networks can access financial, marketing, and product information to do their jobs from throughout the organization.

✔ **Networks save time and money:** In business, time is money. The faster you can get something done, the more tasks you can complete during the course of your business day. Computer e-mail allows you to create messages, memos, and other internal communications, to attach work files, and then to transmit them instantaneously to as many coworkers as you want. And these coworkers can be located across the hall or around the world.

✔ **Networks improve market vision:** Information communicated via computer networks is, by nature, timely and direct. In the old world of business communication, many layers of employees filtered, modified, and slowed the information as it traveled from one part of the organization to another. With direct communication over networks, no one filters, modifies, or slows the original message. What you see is what you get. The sooner you get the information that you need and the higher its quality, the better your market vision.

Surfing the Intranet

If you think that the Internet is the greatest thing since sliced bread in business computing, guess again. Establishing a presence on the Internet is old news for most corporations. Now the real big addition in business is the *Intranet*. With few exceptions, America's largest corporations including Federal Express, AT&T, Levi Strauss, and Ford Motor Company, have built internal versions of the Internet *within* their organizations. For example, employees at DreamWorks SKG, the entertainment conglomerate created by Steven Spielberg, Jeffrey Katzenberg, and David Geffen, use their company's Intranet to produce films and to take care of production details such as tracking animation objects, coordinating scenes, and checking the daily status of projects.

Intranets take the basic tools of the Internet — Web servers, browsers, and Web pages — and bring them inside the organization. Intranets are designed to be accessible strictly by employees and aren't available to outside Internet users. For companies that have already made the investment in Web hardware and software, they're an inexpensive and powerful way to pull together an organization's computers — and its employees.

Not only are Intranets revolutionizing the development of computer networks within organizations, but they're also democratizing them. Where most company computer networks are the sole province of a small staff of computer systems administrators and programmers, Intranets allow novices and experts alike to create Web pages. At Federal Express, for example, employees created many of the company's Web pages.

Having a Plan (And Sticking to It)

When it comes to the fast-changing area of technology, having a *technology plan* — a plan for acquiring and deploying information technology — is a definite must. Why? Many businesses buy bits and pieces of computer hardware, software, and other technology without considering the technology that they already have in place, and without looking very far into the future. Then, when they try to hook everything together, they're surprised that their thrown-together system doesn't work.

Managers who take the time to develop and implement technology plans aren't faced with this problem, and they aren't forced to spend far more money and time fixing the problems with their systems.

What? You've never put together a technology plan before? No problem — here's how the process works:

1. **Create the plan.**

2. **Screen and select the vendors.**

3. **Implement the plan.**

4. **Monitor performance.**

Technology is no longer an optional expense; technology is a strategic investment that can help push your company ahead of the competition. And every strategic investment requires a plan. In their book, *eBusiness Technology Kit For Dummies,* (Wiley Publishing, Inc.), Kathleen Allen and Jon Weisner suggest that you take the following steps in developing your technology plan:

1. **Write down your organization's core values.**

2. **Picture where you see your business ten years from now. Don't limit yourself.**

3. **Set a major one-year goal for the company that is guided by your vision.**

4. **List some strategies for achieving the goal.**

5. **Brainstorm some tactics that can help you achieve your strategies.**

6. **Identify technologies that support your strategies and tactics.**

Gather your thoughts — and your employees' thoughts — together and write them down. Create a concise document — perhaps no more than five to ten pages — that describes your information technology strategies as simply and exactly as possible. After you create your plan, implement it.

Top five information technology Web sites

Wondering where to find the best information on the Web about the topics addressed in this chapter? Well, you've come to the right place! Here are our top five favorites:

- *Wired* magazine: www.wired.com

- *Computerworld*: www.computerworld. com

- *cNet*.com: www.cnet.com

- *PCWorld*.com: www.pcworld.com

- *Internet World*: www.internetworld. com

Chapter 20

Developing and Mentoring Employees

*T*ime for a quick pop quiz. What kind of manager are you? Do you hire new employees and then just let them go their merry way? ("Funny, I thought I recognized you from somewhere.") Or do you stay actively involved in the progress and development of your employees, helping to guide them along the way? If you're a manager-to-be, do you know what having a mentor is like — someone who takes a personal interest in your career development?

In every organization, you have a lot to figure out: internal and external office politics, formal and informal hierarchies, the right and wrong ways to get important tasks done, which people you should ignore, and which people you should pay close attention to. And this list doesn't even take into account the skills that you need to know to do your job: mastering a particular spreadsheet program or getting used to speaking in front of large groups of people, for example. Of course, every time you progress to a new level in the organization or take on a new task, your learning process starts anew.

Employee development doesn't just happen. Managers and employees must take a conscious, concerted effort. And beyond that, it takes time and commitment. When you do employee development right, you don't just talk about it once a year at your employees' annual performance reviews. The best employee development is ongoing and requires that you support and encourage your employees' initiative. Recognize, however, that all development is self-development; you can really only develop yourself. You can't force your employees to develop. They have to want to develop themselves. You can, however, help set an environment that makes it more likely that they will want to learn, grow, and succeed.

Why Help Develop Your Employees?

Many good reasons exist for helping your employees to develop and to improve themselves (not the least of which is that they'll perform more effectively in their current jobs). However, despite all the good reasons, development boils down to one important point: As a manager, you're in the best position to provide your employees with the support that they need to develop in your organization. Not only can you provide them with the time and money required for training, but also you can provide them with unique on-the-job learning opportunities and assignments, mentoring, team participation, and more. Besides, you'll need to have someone to take your job when you get promoted, right? Employee development involves a lot more than just going to a training class or two. In fact, approximately 90 percent of development occurs on the job.

The terms *training* and *development* can have two distinctly different meanings. *Training* usually refers to teaching workers the short-term skills that they need to know right now to do their jobs. *Development* usually refers to teaching employees the kinds of long-term skills that they'll need in the future as they progress in their careers. For this reason, employee development is often known as *career development*.

Now, in case you don't have any inkling whatsoever why developing your employees is a good idea, the following list provides just a few reasons. We're sure that many more exist, depending on your personal situation.

✔ **You may be taking your employees' knowledge for granted.** Have you ever wondered why your employees continue to mess up assignments that you know they can perform? Believe it or not, your employees may not know how to do those assignments. Have you ever actually seen your employee perform the assignments in question?

Say you give a pile of numbers to your assistant and tell him you want them organized and totaled within an hour. However, instead of presenting you with a nice, neat computer spreadsheet, your employee gives you a confusing mess. No, your employee isn't necessarily incompetent; your employee may not know how to put together a spreadsheet on his computer. Find out! The solution may be as simple as walking through your approach to completing the assignment with your employee and then having him give it a try.

✔ **Employees who work smarter are better employees.** Simply put, smarter employees are better employees. If you can help your employees to develop and begin to work smarter and more effectively — and doubtless you can — why wouldn't you? No one in your organization knows everything he or she needs to know. Find out what your employees don't know about their jobs and then make plans with them about how and when they can find out what they need to know. When your employees have achieved their development goals, they'll work smarter, your organization will reap the benefits in greater employee efficiency and effectiveness, and you'll sleep better at night.

✔ **Someone has to be prepared to step into your shoes.** Do you ever plan to take a vacation? Or get a promotion? How are you going to go anywhere or do anything outside of the office if you don't help to prepare your employees to take on the higher-level duties that are part of your job? We both know managers who are so worried about what's going on at the office when they're on vacation that they call the office for a status update several times a day. Whether they're in Niagara Falls, Walt Disney World, or at a beach in Hawaii, they spend more time worrying about the office than they do enjoying themselves.

The reason that many managers don't have to call their offices when they're on vacation is because they make it a point to help develop their employees to take over when they're gone. You can do the same thing, too; the future of your organization depends on it. Really.

✔ **Your employee wins, and so does your organization.** When you allocate funds to employee development, your employees win by learning higher-level skills and new ways of viewing the world — and your organization wins because of increased employee motivation and improved work skills. When you spend money for employee development, you actually double the effect of your investment because of this dual effect. Almost better than a trip to Las Vegas! And most important, you prepare your employees to fill the roles into which your organization will need them to move in the future.

✔ **Your employees are worth your time and money.** New employees cost a lot of money to recruit and train. And not only do you have to consider the investment in dollars, but also you and the rest of your staff have to make an investment in time.

Back when Peter used to work in a real job, his secretary accepted a promotion to another department. The result was a parade of three or four different temporary employees until Peter could recruit, interview, and hire a replacement. To say that this parade disrupted his organization is an understatement. After investing hours and hours of the staff's and his time in training the temp in the essentials of the job, a new one would suddenly appear in her place. Then it was time for another round of training, again and again. The morale of the story is this: When you have a trained employee, you should do everything to keep him or her. Constantly training replacements can be disruptive and very expensive.

When employees see that you have their best interests at heart, they're likely to want to work for you and learn from you. As a result, your organization will attract talented people. Invest in your employees now, or waste your time and money finding replacements later. The choice is yours.

Working in the coal mine: Not what it used to be

Many jobs that were formerly the province of relatively less educated blue-collar workers are becoming increasingly technical. For example, in coal mining, career development used to mean learning how to use a new type of pickax or pneumatic drill. Now, however, miners are using laptop computers to monitor water quality and equipment breakdowns. At the Twentymile Mine, located near Oak Creek, Colorado, employees of Cyprus Amax Mineral Company have many skills to master in addition to wielding a shovel or driving a tractor. According to an executive of the firm, Cyprus Amax Mineral is looking for employees with "high math skills, more technical background, more comfort with electronics." Indeed, workers at the Twentymile Mine have an average of two years of college under their belts.

(Source: *Business Week*)

✔ **The challenge stimulates your employees.** Face it: Not every employee is so fortunate as to have the kind of exciting, jet-setting, make-it-happen job that you have. Right? For this reason, some employees occasionally become bored, lackadaisical, and otherwise indisposed. Why? Employees constantly need new challenges and new goals to maintain interest in their jobs. And if you don't challenge your employees, you're guaranteed to end up with either an unmotivated, low-achievement workforce or employees who jump at offers from employers who will challenge them! Which option do you prefer?

Creating Career Development Plans

The career development plan is the heart and soul of your efforts to develop your employees. Unfortunately, many managers don't take the time to create development plans with their employees, instead trusting that, when the need arises, they can find training to accommodate the need. This kind of reactive thinking ensures that you're always playing catch-up to the challenges that your organization will face in the years to come.

Why wait for the future to arrive before you prepare to deal with it? Are you really so busy that you can't spend a little of your precious time planting the seeds that your organization will harvest years from now? No! Although you do have to take care of the seemingly endless crises that arise in the here and now, you also have to prepare yourself and your employees to meet the challenges of the future. To do otherwise is an incredibly shortsighted and ineffective way to run your organization.

All career development plans must contain at minimum the following key elements:

- ✔ **Specific learning goals:** When you meet with an employee to discuss his or her development plans, you identify specific *learning goals.* And don't forget: Each and every employee in your organization can benefit from having learning goals. Don't leave anyone out!

  For example, say that your employee's career path is going to start at the position of junior buyer and work up to manager of purchasing. The key learning goals for this employee may be to learn material requirements planning (MRP), computer spreadsheet analysis techniques, and supervision.

- ✔ **Resources required to achieve the designated learning goals:** After you identify your employee's learning objectives, you have to decide how he or she will reach them. Development resources include a wide variety of opportunities that support the development of your employees. Assignment to teams, job shadowing, *stretch assignments* (assignments that aren't too easy or too hard, and involve some learning and discomfort), formal training, and more may be required. Formal training may be conducted by outsiders, by internal trainers, or perhaps in a self-guided series of learning modules. If the training requires funding or other resources, identify those resources and make efforts to obtain them.

- ✔ **Employee responsibilities and resources:** Career development is a joint responsibility of an employee and his or her manager. A business can and does pay for things, but so can employees (as any employee who has paid out of his own pocket to get a college degree can attest). A good career development plan should include what the employee is doing on his or her own time.

- ✔ **Required date of completion for each learning goal:** Plans are no good without a way to schedule the milestones of goal accomplishment and progress. Each learning goal has to have a corresponding date of completion. Don't select dates that are so close that they're difficult or unduly burdensome to achieve, or so far into the future that they lose their immediacy and effect. The best schedules for learning goals allow employees the flexibility to get their daily tasks done while keeping ahead of the changes in the business environment that necessitate the employees' development in the first place.

- ✔ **Standards for measuring the accomplishment of learning goals:** For every goal, you must have a way to measure its completion. Normally, the manager assesses whether the employees actually use the new skills they've been taught. Whatever the individual case, make sure that the standards you use to measure the completion of a learning goal are clear and attainable and that both you and your employees are in full agreement with them.

The career development plan of a junior buyer may look like this:

Career Development Plan

Sarah Smith

Skill goal:

▮ ✔ Become proficient in material requirements planning (MRP).

Learning goal:

▮ ✔ Learn the basics of employee supervision.

Plan:

- ✔ Shadow supervisor in daily work for half days, starting immediately.
- ✔ Attend quarterly supervisor's update seminar on the first Wednesday of January, April, July, and October. (No cost: in-house.)
- ✔ Complete class "Basics of MRP" no later than the first quarter of fiscal year XX. ($550 plus travel costs.)
- ✔ Successfully complete class "Intermediate MRP" no later than the second quarter of fiscal year XX. ($750 plus travel costs.)
- ✔ Continue self-funded accounting certificate program at local community college.

As you can see, this career development plan contains each of the four necessary elements that we describe. A career development plan doesn't have to be complicated to be effective. In fact, when it comes to employee development plans, simpler is definitely better. Of course, the exact format that you decide on isn't so important. The most important point is that you do career development plans.

Helping Employees to Develop

Contrary to popular belief, employee development doesn't just happen all by itself. It takes the deliberate and ongoing efforts of employees with the support of their managers. If either employees or managers drop the ball, then employees won't develop, and the organization will suffer the consequences of not having the employees needed to meet the challenges that the future brings. This outcome definitely isn't good. As a manager, you want your organization to be ready for the future, not always trying to catch up to it.

The top 10 ways to develop employees

#1 Provide employees opportunities to learn and grow.

#2 Be a mentor to an employee.

#3 Let an employee fill in for you in staff meetings.

#4 Assign your employee to a team.

#5 Allow employees to pursue and develop any idea they have.

#6 Provide employees with a choice of assignments.

#7 Send your employee to a seminar on a new topic.

#8 Bring an employee along with you when you call on customers.

#9 Introduce your employee to top managers in your organization and arrange to have him or her perform special assignments for them.

#10 Allow an employee to shadow you during your workday.

The employees' role is to identify the areas where development can help to make the employees better and more productive workers and then to relay this information to their managers. After further development opportunities are identified, managers and employees work together to schedule and implement them.

As a manager, your role is to be alert to the development needs of your employees and to keep an eye out for potential development opportunities. Managers in smaller organizations may have the assignment of determining where the organization will be in the next few years. Armed with that information, you're responsible for finding ways to ensure that employees are available to meet the needs of the future organization. Your job is then to provide the resources and support required to develop employees so that they're able to fill the organization's needs.

To develop your employees to meet the coming challenges within your organization, follow these steps:

1. **Meet with your employees about their careers.** After you assess your employees, meet with them to discuss where you see them in the organization and also to find out where in the organization they want to go. This effort has to be a joint one! Having elaborate plans for an employee to rise up the company ladder in sales management isn't going to do you any good if your employee hates the idea of leaving sales to become a manager of other salespeople.

2. **Discuss your employees' strengths and weaknesses.** Assuming that, in the preceding step, you discover that you're on the same wavelength as your employee, the next step is to have a frank discussion regarding his or her strengths and weaknesses. Your main goal here is to identify areas the employee can leverage, that is, strengths that your employees can develop to allow their continued upward progress in the organization and to meet the future challenges that your business faces. Focus the majority of your development efforts and dollars on these opportunities.

Most importantly, you need to spend time developing your strengths than improving your weaknesses. You can be great at something that comes easy to you and this will have more value for you and your organization than forcing yourself to be merely adequate at things others excel in.

3. **Assess where your employees are now.** The next step in the employee development process is to determine the current state of your employees' skills and talents. Does Joe show potential for supervising other warehouse employees? Which employees have experience in doing customer demos? Is the pool of software quality assurance technicians adequate enough to accommodate a significant upturn in business? If not, can you develop internal candidates, or will you have to hire new employees from outside the organization? Assessing your employees provides you with an overall road map to guide your development efforts.

4. **Create career development plans.** Career development plans are agreements between you and your employees that spell out exactly what formal support (tuition, time off, travel expenses, and so on) they'll receive to develop their skills, and when they'll receive it. Career development plans contain milestones..

5. **Follow through on your agreements, and make sure that your employees follow through on theirs.** Don't break the development plan agreement! Make sure that you provide the support that you agreed to provide. Make sure that your employees uphold their end of the bargain, too! Check on their progress regularly. If they miss schedules because of other priorities, reassign their work as necessary to ensure that they have time to focus on their career development plans.

So when is the best time to sit down with your employees to discuss career planning and development? The sooner the better! Unfortunately, many organizations closely tie career discussions to annual employee performance appraisals. On the plus side, doing so ensures that a discussion about career development happens at least once a year; on the minus side, development discussions become more of an afterthought than the central focus of the meeting. Not only because of that limitation, but also with the current rapid changes in competitive markets and technology, once a year just isn't enough to keep up. Planning for career development only once a year is like watering a plant only once a year!

Conducting a career development discussion twice a year with each of your employees isn't too often, and quarterly is even better. Include a brief assessment in each discussion of the employee's development needs. Ask your employee what he or she can do to fulfill them. If those needs require additional support, determine what form of support the employee needs and when the support should be scheduled. Career development plans are adjusted and resources are redirected as necessary.

Finding a Mentor, Being a Mentor

When you're an inexperienced employee working your way up an organization's hierarchy, having someone with more experience to help guide you along the way is invaluable. Someone who's already seen what it takes to get to the top can advise you about the things that you must do and the things that you shouldn't do as you work your way up. This someone is called a *mentor*.

Isn't a manager supposed to be a mentor? No. A mentor is most typically an individual high up in the organization who isn't your boss. A manager's job is clearly to coach and help guide employees. Although managers certainly can act as mentors for their own employees, mentors most often act as confidential advisers and sounding boards to their chosen employees and therefore aren't typically in the employee's direct chain of command.

The day that a mentor finds you and takes you under his or her wing is a day for you to celebrate. Why? Celebrate because not everyone is lucky enough to find a mentor. And don't forget that someday you'll be in the position to be a mentor to someone else. When that day comes, don't be so caught up in your busy business life to neglect to reach out and help someone else find his or her way up the organization.

Mentors provide definite benefits to the employees they mentor, and they further benefit the organization by providing needed guidance to employees who may not otherwise get it. The following reasons are why mentors are a real benefit, both to your employees and to your organization:

✔ **Explain how the organization really works.** Mentors are a great way to find out what's really going on in an organization. You've probably noticed that a big difference exists between what's formally announced to employees and what really goes on in the organization — particularly within the ranks of upper management. Your mentor quite likely has intimate knowledge behind the formal pronouncements, and he or she can convey that knowledge to you (at least, the knowledge that isn't confidential) without your having to find it out the hard way.

✔ **Teach by example.** By watching how your mentor gets tasks done in the organization, you can discover a lot. Your mentor has likely already seen it all, and he or she can help you discover the most effective and efficient ways to get things done. Why reinvent the wheel or get beaten up by the powers that be when you don't have to?

✔ **Provide growth experiences.** A mentor can help guide you to activities above and beyond your formal career development plans that are helpful to your growth as an employee. For example, though your official development plan doesn't identify a specific activity, your mentor may strongly suggest that you join a group, such as Toastmasters, to improve your public-speaking skills. Your mentor makes this suggestion because he or she knows that public speaking skills are very important to your future career growth.

✔ **Provide career guidance and discussion.** Your mentor has probably seen more than a few employees and careers come and go over the years. He or she knows which career paths in your organization are dead ends and which offer the most rapid advancement. This knowledge can be incredibly important to your future as you make career choices within an organization. The advice your mentor gives you can be invaluable.

The mentoring process often happens when a more experienced employee takes a professional interest in a new or inexperienced employee. Employees can also initiate the mentoring process by engaging the interest of potential mentors while seeking advice or working on projects together. However, recognizing the potential benefits for the development of their employees, many organizations — including Merrill Lynch, Federal Express, and the Internal Revenue Service — have formalized the mentoring process and made it available to a wider range of employees than the old informal process ever could. If a formal mentoring program isn't already in place in your organization, why don't you recommend starting one?

Balancing Development and Downsizing

You've seen the numbers: x thousand employees laid off at IBM, y thousand employees laid off at AT&T, and z thousand employees laid off at General Motors. Most companies aren't immune when the economy turns south. Maybe your organization has felt the sharp knife of reengineering, downsizing, or reductions in force. If so, you may ask, "Isn't employee development too difficult to perform when everything is changing so fast around me? My employees may not even have careers next year, much less the need to plan for developing them."

Top five mentoring Web sites

Wondering where to find the best information on the Web about the topics addressed in this chapter? Well, you've come to the right place! Here are our top five favorites:

✔ Service Corps of Retired Executives: www.score.org

✔ Business Mentoring Scotland: www.businessmentoringscotland.org

✔ SBA Classroom: Business Mentoring Course: www.sba.gov/classroom/bizmentoring.html

✔ GreenBiz.com Mentor Center: www.greenbiz.com/reference/mentor.cfm

✔ SBA Office of Women's Business Ownership: www.sba.gov/womeninbusiness/wnet.html

Actually, nothing can be farther from the truth. Although businesses are going through rapid change, employee development is more important than ever. As departments are combined, dissolved, or reorganized, employees have to be ready to take on new roles — duties that they may never have performed before. In some cases, employees may have to compete internally for positions or sell themselves to other departments to ensure that they retain their employment with the firm. In this time of great uncertainty, many employees feel that they may have lost control of their careers and even their lives.

Career planning and development provide employees in organizations undergoing rapid change with the tools that they need to regain control of their careers. The following list tells what some of the largest American companies have done to help their employees get through massive corporate downsizings and reorganizations:

✔ As a result of dramatic organizational changes, General Electric provided targeted career training for its crucial engineering employees. The firm also scheduled informal follow-up meetings with graduates of this engineering career training.

✔ Raychem, a maker of industrial products located in Menlo Park, California, offers its employees the services of an in-house career center. At this center, employees can take courses in resume writing and interviewing techniques and search for transfer or promotional opportunities within their company.

✔ At AT&T, management offered special three-day career development seminars to its employees nationwide in response to dramatic staff reductions.

✔ IBM overhauled the career plans of thousands of employees who transitioned from staff positions to sales positions as a result of a massive corporate reorganization.

Despite the obvious negative effects of downsizing on employee morale and trust, these times of change provide managers with a unique opportunity to shape the future of their organizations. For many managers, this moment is the first time that they have such an opportunity to help remake the organization.

Employee development is more important than ever as employees are called upon to take on new and often more responsible roles in your organization. Your employees need your support now; make sure that you're there to provide it. This help just may be one of the most valuable gifts that you can give to your employees.

Chapter 21

Keeping Track of Recent Management Trends

A day doesn't pass without the unveiling of some new management trend — the latest-and-greatest system for harried managers that's guaranteed to improve employee morale, up the bottom line, or make even the dreariest workplace into a shining model of productivity and efficiency. Unfortunately, although some of these trends have a lasting impact on the organizations that employ them, others are little more than fads that are here today and gone tomorrow.

The graveyard of management innovation is littered with the wreckage of countless systems that were once hot, and now aren't. Zero defects, one-minute management, quality circles, knowledge management, and total quality management all had their time in the sun, and now all have been pushed onto the back shelf. Every management trend has its own unique lifecycle.

Most of these trends have value, but unfortunately, few organizations actually make the fundamental process and structural changes required to truly transform the organization. After the program's novelty wears off — often only a few short weeks or months after its introduction — the organization goes back to business as usual. But even the most fleeting management fad has the potential to leave some benefit and positive change within organizations. The secret is to look beyond the "fads" (some of them do have value) and see their place in the never-ending search for success.

In this chapter, we consider some of the latest management trends, including the return to basics, the learning organization, the flat organization, open-book management, and Six Sigma. Some of these may be around for years to come, and others may disappear soon after the ink on this page dries.

Going Back to Management 101

The new world of business has created all kinds of new opportunities in every industry. But, at the same time, the new world of business has created all kinds of new obstacles for managers and for their employees. How, for example, can managers best direct an employee when he or she may not even have physical contact with the manager for weeks or months at a time?

Answers to questions like this one have led many managers to step out of today's fast-paced, business-at-the-speed-of-light environment and return to the basics of managing others. These basics include:

- ✔ **Making time for people.** You have no substitute for face time when it comes to building trusting relationships. Managing is a people job, and you need to take time for people. (See Chapter 12 for ways to improve communication with your employees.)

- ✔ **Increasing communication as you increase distance.** The greater the distance from one's manager, the greater the effort both parties have to make to keep in touch. But, you can't depend on your employees to take the initiative to keep in touch; you have to keep the channels of communication flowing freely and often. (See Chapter 12 for ways to manage faraway employees.)

- ✔ **Using technology (and not letting it use you).** Technology is obviously great — and it's here to stay — but don't let technology use you. Instead, use technology as a way to leverage your communication with employees, not just as a way to distribute data. (See Chapter 19 for ways to use technology effectively.)

In the new world of business, managers have to work harder to be available to others. If you value strong working relationships and clear communication (we're assuming you do!), you need to return to basics — spending more and higher quality time with your employees rather than less.

Creating a Learning Organization

A *learning organization* is an organization skilled at creating, acquiring, and transferring knowledge and at modifying its original assumptions, purposes, and behaviors to reflect new knowledge and insights. Ever since Peter Senge's groundbreaking book *The Fifth Discipline* was published more than a decade ago, the question of how to create and lead organizations in which continuous learning occurs has been at the top of many managers' lists of management techniques to consider.

The problem with the old, command-and-control way of doing business is that your organization is built on the premise that the world is predictable. If you can just build a model that is large and complex enough, you can anticipate any eventuality, right? This particular view has a problem: The world isn't predictable. The global world of business is chaotic — what's true today surely is washed away tomorrow as the next wave of change hits. The only constant in today's organizations is change.

The learning organization is designed around the assumption that organizations are going through rapid change and that managers should expect the unexpected. Indeed, managers who work for learning organizations welcome unexpected events that occur within an organization, because they consider them to be opportunities, not problems. Instead of static organizations that are strictly hierarchical, learning organizations are flexible. This structure makes managers able to lead change instead of merely reacting to change.

So exactly how do you go about designing a learning organization? Several characteristics are particularly important as you consider turning your organization into a learning organization. The more of each characteristic that your organization exhibits, the closer it is to being a learning organization — one that thrives in times of rapid change.

✔ **Encourage objectivity.** Over the course of our careers, we've seen managers make many organizational decisions simply to please someone with power, influence, or an incredible ego. Managers made such subjective decisions, not through a reasoned consideration of the facts, but through emotion. As a manager, you must encourage objectivity in your employees and coworkers and practice objectivity in your own decision making.

✔ **Seek openness.** For an organization to grow, employees have to be willing to tell each other the truth. To make this openness possible, you must create safe environments for your employees to say what is on their minds and to tell you any bad news without fear of retribution. Drive fear out of the organization if you want to build a learning organization.

✔ **Facilitate teamwork.** Deploying employee teams is a very important part in the development of learning organizations. You'd be hard pressed to name any learning organization that hasn't implemented teams widely throughout the organization. When an organization relies on individuals to respond to changes, one or two individuals may pick up the torch and run with it; however, when an organization relies on teams to respond to change, many more employees are mobilized much more quickly. And this can mean the difference between life and death in the ever-changing global business environment.

✔ **Create useful tools.** Managers in learning organizations need the tools that enable employees to quickly and easily obtain the information that they need to do their jobs. Computer networks, for example, have to be set up with access for all employees, and they have to provide the kinds of financial and other data that decision makers need. The best tools are those that get the right information to the right people at the right time.

✔ **Consider the behavior you're rewarding.** Remember the phrase, "You get what you reward." What actions are you rewarding, and what behaviors are you getting in return? If you want to build a learning organization, reward the behaviors that help you create a learning organization. Stop rewarding behaviors that are inconsistent, such as subjectivity and individualism. The sooner you accomplish this mission, the better.

Making a Flat Organization

A growing trend exists today to flatten organizations by removing layers of management. When businesses flatten their organizations, they widen the span of control (the number of people directly supervised) of the remaining managers, and push authority farther down the chain of command.

Fewer layers of management, and increased decision making and participation by nonmanagement workers, typically results in:

✔ Less bureaucracy

✔ Faster decision making

✔ Organizations that are nimbler and better able to react to changing markets

✔ Increased reliance on self-managing teams

✔ More empowered and happier employees

✔ More satisfied and happier customers

✔ Reduced costs

✔ Increased profits

Instead of focusing on the structures and maintenance of hierarchy — departments, titles, and such — flat organizations

- ✔ Focus on their customers, both internal and external.

- ✔ Encourage all employees to become directly responsive to customer needs.

- ✔ Promote decision making by those employees closer to customers.

- ✔ Eliminate bottlenecks in the flow of information.

- ✔ Support open sharing of information.

As more and more organizations turn away from the restrictive culture that is a natural byproduct of hierarchy, the flat organization is becoming an obvious choice — and the best opportunity to capitalize on fast-changing markets.

Unlocking Open-Book Management

Until recently, the vast majority of companies treated accounting data — information on sales, revenues, expenses, profits, and more — as secrets that only managers and executives viewed and worked with. Managers used this approach as a way to solidify power at the top of organizations, and to prevent regular workers from providing their own input and suggesting improvements to vital financial processes.

This practice changed when — in a bid to make his company more competitive in a very tough market — Jack Stack, president and CEO of Springfield, Missouri-based engine rebuilder SRC Corporation, provided his employees with company financial reports, unit performance numbers, and production statistics. Thus, he empowered workers by teaching them how to understand and use the reports to help the company make more money — and inviting them to do just that.

The company did. SRC succeeded beyond all expectations, and the open-book management revolution was launched. Today, thousands of businesses are empowering their own employees — and reaping the benefits in the process — by providing them with financial data and then encouraging them to use the data to improve their jobs and their organizations.

According to Stack, three factors must be in place for open-book management to work:

- ✔ Everyone must know the rules and expectations.

- ✔ Everyone must have enough information to make the moves and keep score.

- ✔ Everyone must have a stake in the outcome.

Stack — and the business he created to teach the principles of open-book management, Great Game of Business (a subsidiary of SRC Holdings, Inc.) — has introduced countless businesspeople to the concept of open-book management through books, seminars, videos, and a Web site (www.greatgame. com). Throughout, the emphasis is on creating an environment where employees have major input:

✔ Creating the financials

✔ Setting up incentive programs that reward their progress

✔ Discovering how to forecast financial results

✔ Communicating progress to each other

✔ Sharing the rewards of good performance

Do the ends justify the means? Clearly they do. Davenport, Iowa-based staffing company Mid-States Technical saw its sales rise 79 percent in the two years after implementing an open-book management program, while profits tripled. Perhaps managers aren't the only ones who can understand and use company financial data to improve the bottom line after all.

Understanding Six Sigma

If any area of management is particularly subject to trends, it's the area of quality. One of the latest in a long line of such trends is Six Sigma, a quality-improvement system originated by electronics manufacturer Motorola some two decades ago, which has gained thousands of dedicated adherents over the past few years.

Top five management trend Web sites

Wondering where to find the best information on the Web about the topics addressed in this chapter? Well, you've come to the right place! Here are our top five favorites:

✔ *Fast Company* magazine: www.fast company.com

✔ *Inc.* magazine: www.inc.com

✔ *Business 2.0* magazine: www.business2. com

✔ *Bain & Company:* www.bain.com/ bainweb/expertise/tools/over view.asp

✔ *Wired* magazine: www.wired.com

So, what exactly is Six Sigma, and what's so special about it?

Six Sigma is a rigorous training program that gives managers highly specialized measurement and statistical analysis tools. They use the tools to reduce defects in products and processes, while cutting business costs (and improving customer satisfaction, to boot!). Key corporate fans include such business giants as General Electric (GE), Citicorp, Johnson & Johnson, and Allied Signal.

Six key concepts are at the heart of Six Sigma:

- **Critical to quality.** The attributes most important to the customer
- **Defect.** Failing to deliver what the customer wants
- **Process capability.** What your process can deliver
- **Variation.** What the customer sees and feels
- **Stable operations.** Ensuring consistent, predictable processes to improve what the customer sees and feels
- **Design for Six Sigma.** Designing to meet customer needs and process capability

According to Dr. Mikel Harry, originator of this management trend, application of Six Sigma principles can result in the following:

- Improved customer satisfaction
- Reduced cycle times
- Increased productivity
- Improved capacity and output
- Reduced total defects
- Increased product reliability
- Decreased work-in-progress (WIP)
- Improved process flow

And, the numbers seem to support Six Sigma. According to GE, the company saved $500 million in a recent year through the application of Six Sigma. In fact, GE is so excited about Six Sigma that it says in its corporate Six Sigma brochure, "Six Sigma has changed the DNA of GE — it is now the way we work — in everything we do and in every product we design."

Part VII
The Part of Tens

The 5th Wave — By Rich Tennant

Why can't I turn this guy around to my way of thinking?

STAY THE COURSE

LEAD DON'T FOLLOW

In this part . . .

These short chapters are packed with quick ideas that can help you become a better manager. Read them anytime you have an extra minute or two.

Chapter 22

Ten Common Management Mistakes

Managers make mistakes. Mistakes are nature's way of showing you that you're learning. Thomas Edison once said that it takes 10,000 mistakes to find an answer. As Peter's instructor once asked him at a frosty (32 degrees below zero at 9:00 a.m., no wind chill) ski school in Quebec, "Is that your nose lying there on the snow?" No, actually, Fritz's lesson was much more profound than that: "If you're not falling down, you're not learning." You get the idea.

This chapter lists ten traps that new and experienced managers alike can fall victim to.

Not Making the Transition from Worker to Manager

When you're a worker, you have a job and you do it. Although your job likely requires you to join a team or to work closely with other employees, you're ultimately responsible only for yourself. Did you attain your goals? Did you get to work on time? Was your work done correctly? When you become a manager, everything changes. Suddenly, you are responsible for the results of a group of people, not just for yourself. Did your employees attain their goals? Are your employees highly motivated? Did your employees do their work correctly?

Becoming a manager requires the development of a whole new set of business skills — people skills. Some of the most talented employees from a technical perspective become the worst managers because they fail to make the transition from worker to manager.

Not Setting Clear Goals and Expectations

Do the words *rudderless ship* mean anything to you? They should. Effective performance starts with clear goals. If you don't set goals with your employees, your organization often has no direction and your employees have few challenges. Therefore, your employees have little motivation to do anything but show up for work and collect their paychecks. Your employees' goals begin with a vision of where they want to be in the future. Meet with your employees to develop realistic, attainable goals that guide them in their efforts to achieve the organization's vision. Don't leave your employees in the dark. Help them to help you, and your organization, by setting goals and then by working with them to achieve those goals.

Failing to Delegate

Some surveys rank "inability to delegate" as the No.1 reason that managers fail. Despite the ongoing efforts of many managers to prove otherwise, you can't do everything by yourself. And even if you could, doing everything by yourself isn't the most effective use of your time or talent as a manager. You may very well be the best statistician in the world, but when you become the manager of a team of statisticians, your job changes. Your job is no longer to perform statistical analyses, but to manage and develop a group of employees.

When you delegate work to employees, you multiply the amount of work that you can do. A project that seems overwhelming on the surface is suddenly quite manageable when you divide it up among 12 different employees. Furthermore, when you delegate work to employees, you also create opportunities to develop their work and leadership skills. Whenever you take on a new assignment or work on an ongoing job, ask yourself whether one of your employees can do it instead (and if the answer is yes, then delegate it!).

Failing to Communicate

In many organizations, most employees don't have a clue about what's going on. Information is power, and some managers use information — in particular, the control of information — to ensure that they're the most knowledgeable and therefore the most valuable individuals in an organization. Some managers shy away from social situations and naturally avoid communicating with their employees — especially when the communication is negative in some way. Others are just too busy. They simply don't make efforts to communicate information to their employees on an ongoing basis, letting other, more pressing business take precedence by selectively "forgetting" to tell their employees.

The health of today's organizations — especially during times of change — depends on the widespread dissemination of information throughout an organization and the communication that enables this dissemination to happen. Employees must be empowered with information so that they can make the best decisions at the lowest possible level in the organization, quickly and without the approval of higher-ups.

Not Making Time for Employees

To some of your employees, you're a resource. To others, you're a trusted associate. Still others may consider you to be a teacher or mentor, while others see you as a coach or parent. However your employees view you, they have one thing in common: All your employees need your time and guidance during the course of their careers. Managing is a people job — you need to make time for people. Some workers may need your time more than others. You must assess your employees' individual needs and address them.

Although some of your employees may be highly experienced and require little supervision, others may need almost constant attention when they're new to a job or task. When an employee needs to talk, make sure that you're available. Put your work aside for a moment, ignore your phone, and give your employee your undivided attention. Not only do you show your employees that they are important, but when you focus on them, you also hear what they have to say.

Not Recognizing Employee Achievements

In these days of constant change, downsizing, and increased worker uncertainty, finding ways to recognize your employees for the good work that they do is more important than ever. The biggest misconception is that managers don't want to recognize employees. Most managers do agree that rewarding employees is important; they just aren't sure how to do so and don't take the time or effort to recognize their employees.

Although raises, bonuses, and promotions have decreased in many organizations as primary motivators, you can take many steps that take little time to accomplish, are easy to implement, and cost little or no money. In fact, the most effective reward — personal and written recognition from one's manager — doesn't cost anything. Don't be so busy that you can't take a minute or two to recognize your employees' achievements. Your employees' morale, performance, and loyalty will surely improve as a result.

Failing to Learn

Most managers are accustomed to success, and they initially learned a lot to make that success happen. Many were plucked from the ranks of workers and promoted into positions as managers for this very reason. Oftentimes, however, they catch a dreaded disease — *hardening of the attitudes* — after they become managers, and they only want things done their way.

Successful managers find the best ways to get tasks done and accomplish their goals, and then they develop processes and policies to institutionalize these effective approaches to doing business. This method is great as long as the organization's business environment doesn't change. However, when the business environment does change, if the manager doesn't adjust — that is, doesn't *learn* — the organization suffers as a result.

This situation can be particularly difficult for a manager who has found success by doing business a certain way. The model of manager as an unchanging rock that stands up to the storm is no longer valid. Today, managers have to be ready to change the way they do business as their environments change around them. They have to constantly learn, experiment, and try new methods. If a manager doesn't adapt, he or she is doomed to extinction — or at least irrelevance.

Resisting Change

If you think that you can stop change, you're fooling yourself. You may as well try standing in the path of a hurricane to make it change its course. Good luck! The sooner you realize that the world — your world included — will change whether you like it or not, the better. Then you can concentrate your efforts on taking actions that make a positive difference in your business life. You must discover how to adapt to change and use it to your advantage rather than fight it.

Instead of reacting to changes after the fact, proactively anticipate the changes that are coming your way and make plans to address them before they hit your organization. Ignoring the need to change doesn't make that need go away. The best managers are positive and forward looking.

Going for the Quick Fix over the Lasting Solution

Every manager loves to solve problems and fix the parts of his or her organization that are broken. The constant challenge of the new and unexpected (and that second-floor, corner office) attracts many people to management in the first place. Unfortunately, in their zeal to fix problems quickly, many managers neglect to take the time necessary to seek out long-term solutions to the problems of their organizations.

Instead of diagnosing cancer and performing major surgery, many managers perform merely what amounts to sticking on a Band-Aid. Although the job isn't as fun as being a firefighter, you have to look at the entire system and find the cause if you really want to solve a problem. After you find the cause of the problem, you can develop real solutions that have lasting effects. Anything less isn't really solving the problem; you're merely treating the symptoms.

Taking It All Too Seriously

Yes, business is serious business. If you don't think so, just see what happens if you blow your budget and your company's bottom line goes into the red as a result. You quickly learn just how serious business can be. Regardless — indeed, *because* — of the gravity of the responsibilities that managers carry on their shoulders, you must maintain a sense of humor and foster an environment that is fun, both for you and your employees. Invite your employees to a potluck at the office, an informal get-together at a local lunch spot, or a barbecue at your home. Surprise them with special awards, such as the strangest tie or the most creative workstation. Joke with your employees. Be playful.

When managers retire, they usually aren't remembered for the fantastic job that they did in creating department budgets or disciplining employees. Instead, people remember that someone who didn't take work so seriously and remembered how to have fun brightened their days or made their work more tolerable. Don't be a stick in the mud. Live every day as if it were your last.

Chapter 23

The Ten Best Ways to Recognize Employees

In This Chapter

▶ Providing no-cost praise

▶ Giving monetary recognition

Are you giving your employees the recognition they deserve? We certainly hope so! Why? Because recognizing your employees for doing a good job is one of the best ways to keep them motivated and engaged in their work. And furthermore, you don't have to break your budget to do it. You have countless ways to thank and appreciate employees for doing a good job, and many of them require little, if any, money. No, you don't need to send your employees to the Bahamas or give them $1,000 bonuses or gold-plated coffee warmers.

Bob Nelson's book, *1001 Ways to Reward Employees,* lists thousands of real-life positive rewards, most of which cost little or nothing. Following is a list of what Bob found out from thousands of employees across industries about what they consider most important in terms to recognition. The findings are categorized and prioritized in order of greatest importance from a list of 50 specific possibilities.

Support and Involvement

Your employees need information and support in order to do their jobs. Give them what they need when they need it, to do their best work. And if they make a mistake in the process, support them and help them to learn from that mistake. Mistakes are to be expected in any job, but how you handle mistakes when they occur can be critical to building ongoing trust, knowledge, and performance.

Every employee wants his or her manager's support after making a mistake. Furthermore, involve your employees when you're making key decisions — especially when those decisions affect your employees and their work. You can also involve employees by, when possible, asking them for their opinions and ideas. Doing so further shows that you respect and trust them — and that they actually have ideas worth sharing!

Personal Praise

Nearly 60 percent of employees report they never get a simple thank you from their manager for doing a good job — even though employees have reported this top motivator for many years.

Taking the time to thank employees personally shows them that no matter how busy you are and no matter what else you have to do, nothing is more important to you than them. By thanking them, you're saying that your employees are more important than everything else in your work life. Isn't that why employees are called "the organization's greatest asset"?

Remember to make your praise as timely, as sincere, and as specific as possible to have the greatest impact. Actively seek employees out when you have something to commend them for and don't be shy about acknowledging them in front of others — management, peers, or even customers.

Autonomy and Authority

Employees highly value being given the latitude to perform their work the way they see fit. No one likes a supervisor or manager who always hovers over their shoulders, micromanaging their every move, reminding them of the exact way everything should be done and making corrections every time they make a slight deviation. Guess what? Your employees actually may come up with a better way to do the task than your way if you give them a chance!

When you tell employees what you want done, provide them with the necessary training, and then give them the room to do the job. When you give them the training, you increase the likelihood that they will perform to — or even beyond — your expectations.

Flexible Working Hours

Another great, no-cost way to reward your employees is to give them flexibility in their working hours, which includes when they start work and when they finish, the ability to leave work early when needed, and time off. Because most of them are trying to balance multiple priorities on both the work and home fronts, time is very important. As such, flexibility and time off from work has become an increasingly valuable commodity.

People want to spend more time with their families and friends and less time in the office. Of course, with downsizing and reengineering, employees have more work to do, not less. Giving your employees flexible working hours can help them keep fresh and focused while on the job!

Learning and Development

Guaranteed employment may be gone for everybody, but guaranteed employability is still very much alive in today's job market. As a result, employees are increasingly interested in learning new skills where they work. They can enhance their abilities and the value they offer the organization. Remember, too, that most employee development happens on the job, not in the classroom. New work challenges and responsibilities and the chance to represent one's manager or group are ways to develop, grow, and master new skills.

Giving your employees new opportunities to perform is very motivating. You aren't going to motivate your employees by building a fire under them. Instead, find ways to build a fire within them to make work a place where they want and are able to do their best as they learn and grow. Talking with employees about their long-term hopes and career plans is also important. You develop an emotional bond and trust with each employee. If you know where someone wants to be in five years, you can think about aspects of their current job and circumstances that can help them prepare for the future.

Manager Availability and Time

Having access to one's manager is a big motivator. Access is different from being located physically near where your manager works. Access and accessibility today have less to do with physical proximity than with a manager's responsiveness in taking employees' questions and concerns seriously and in getting information, resources, or assistance back to employees in a timely manner.

In one executive position Bob held, he made a personal commitment that within 24 hours of any management or executive meeting he was a part of, he would communicate what was discussed and decided in those meetings with his immediate staff and get back to them if they had questions he couldn't answer. As a result, trust, respect, and teamwork flourished and his department attained higher levels of performance. Employees also report that they like their managers to take time to get to know them and spend time with them.

Written Praise

Employees also desire written praise as a form of recognition. Whether it comes in the form of letters of praise added to an employee's personnel file, a written note of thanks from one's manager or peers, or a simple thank-you card, written praise has a sense of permanence about it that can last for quite some time as the employee saves the communication.

Written praise also has a multiplier effect as employees refer to previous written thanks time and time again, perhaps posting a note at their work station or creating a "victory file" specifically for that purpose. They also may decide to share the written information with their families or friends.

Electronic Praise

Similar to written praise, electronic praise enables you to leverage positive communication as it occurs in your daily work. Use today's communication technologies not just to process information, but also to connect with others and to commend them when they've done good work.

In a recent Internet survey Bob conducted, some 28 percent of employees report it is "extremely important" to them to have positive e-mail messages forwarded to them and 65 percent say it's "extremely or very important" to be copied on positive e-mail messages.

Don't forget the use of voice mail as a way to leave a positive word of thanks — without rolling into another work assignment or project!

Public Praise

Most employees value being publicly praised. You have a nearly endless variety of ways to acknowledge employees publicly. Sharing positive letters from customers or posting them on a "Good News Bulletin Board" or even bringing some key customers in-house to acknowledge employees sends an important message to everybody in the organization that their work is important and valued.

Taking time at the beginning or end of department or company-wide meetings to thank performers or allowing employees to acknowledge one another at group meetings can also be very effective. Or using the company newsletter to post positive information, name top performers, or thank project teams are a few other possibilities that can work well to make people feel important and special when they've achieved.

Cash or Cash Substitutes

A manager can give an employee a nominal on-the-spot cash award when he or she "catches" an employee doing something right. The award can motivate and help remind employees what's truly important about their work. But cash has its drawbacks as well, having very little memory impact or "trophy value." Often when employees get extra money, they end up spending it on an immediate need or bill, quickly forgetting the reason for the award. *Cash substitutes,* however, such as gift certificates, vouchers, or entertainment tickets, provide variety, flexibility, and a chance to share a reward with a friend or family member, thus increasing the emotional impact and memory potential of the reward.

You don't have to spend a lot of time or money to show your employees how you feel about them and their work. Use the previous proven recognition strategies to create the most motivating work environment in which every employee feels valued, trusted, and respected!

Chapter 24

Ten Classic Business Books That You Need to Know About

. . . .

In This Chapter

▶ Finding traditional business tomes

▶ Locating useful managing books

. . . .

An incredible variety of business books is available for you to read and to buy. Becoming bewildered by all the choices is easy, and sorting out which books are of the greatest benefit to managers is difficult.

In the list that follows, we've already done the heavy lifting for you. Every manager should buy and read these ten classic business books (plus a bonus 11th) before reading any other business book (except this one, of course!).

Managing for Results

Peter F. Drucker (Harper & Row, 1964)

In this book — a real classic in the field of management — Drucker takes the development of his management theories a step further by showing readers what they must do to create an organization that will prosper and grow. Drucker encourages readers to focus on opportunities in their organizations rather than on problems. The book also suggests that managers take a hard look at an organization's strengths and weaknesses to develop effective plans and strategies.

The Human Side of Enterprise

Douglas McGregor (McGraw-Hill, 1960)

The first wake-up call for managers everywhere, this book proclaims that (big surprise) people play a major role in the success of any business. This book produced the birth of Theory X and its negative assumptions of human behavior ("People are lazy") and Theory Y, which focuses on the positive assumptions of human behavior ("People want to do a good job"). McGregor argues that relying on authority as the primary means of control in industry leads to "resistance, restriction of output, indifference to organizational objectives, the refusal to accept responsibility, and results in inadequate motivation for human growth and development." Still relevant reading for managers today who just don't get why employees are so important.

The Peter Principle

Dr. Laurence Peter and Raymond Hull (Morrow, 1969)

The Peter Principle says that in a hierarchy, every employee tends to rise to his or her level of incompetence. This book is an amusing look at how hierarchies work in organizations and what managers can do to ensure that employees aren't assigned to tasks beyond their capabilities. A must!

Up the Organization

Robert Townsend (Knopf, 1970)

This book, written by the former CEO of Avis, offers up some pithy advice for business people everywhere. Townsend discusses the strategies that helped drive Avis' success in a fun, readable format. The book includes such gems as: "Don't hire Harvard MBAs" (they just want to be CEOs anyway, so they focus on that as their main goal) and "Fire the human resources department" (Townsend believes that this function should be the job of every manager).

The One Minute Manager

Kenneth Blanchard and Spencer Johnson (Morrow, 1982)

Written in a unique parable format, this book became an instant business classic. Even today, it is a perennial resident on most business best-seller lists. *The One Minute Manager* teaches readers three very simple but important management skills (One Minute Goal Setting, One Minute Praisings, and One Minute Reprimands), and it does so in an entertaining but informative way. A true classic.

The Goal

Eliyahu Goldratt and Jeff Cox (North River Press, Second Edition, 1992)

This well-paced novel — a business parable — features Alex Rogo, a UniCo plant manager in fictional Bearington, U.S.A. Alex has big problems: He's been given three months to turn his plant around or face shutdown. Suddenly, Alex encounters his kindly old physics professor, Jonah, who sets him on an almost mystical quest for "the goal." Along the way, he learns that the real lesson is to avoid orthodoxies of all kinds and accept the need for constant reexamination of every process. Woven into this narrative is much valid information about various weighty concepts — among them, just-in-time manufacturing, total quality management, and computer-integrated factories.

Leadership Is an Art

Max Du Pree (Doubleday, 1989)

When Max Du Pree wrote this book, he was chairman of the board of furniture manufacturer Herman Miller — a firm well known for being a management innovator. Du Pree's main premise is that leadership isn't a science or a discipline; it's an art. For this reason, leadership has to be experienced, created, and felt. This perspective is quite different from the old-style model of management that depends on strict rules and policies and the measurement of results.

The Fifth Discipline: The Art and Practice of the Learning Organization

Peter Senge (Doubleday/Currency, 1990)

This book started the learning/systems fad in business, which is still going strong. It encourages organizations to apply systems thinking — seeing inter-relationships instead of just isolated events, incidents, and problems. Senge argues that organizations should make learning a continuous process rather than treat it as a series of distinct, unrelated events. He claims that everyone in an organization has a responsibility to help create a learning organization, with top managers playing a crucial role in the process. He also encourages organizations to realize the importance of reflection, as opposed to action, in business. ("Yeah, but who's going to help the customer?")

The Wisdom of Teams

Jon R. Katzenbach and Douglas K. Smith (Harvard Business School Press, 1993)

Katzenbach and Smith define a team as "a small number of people with com-plementary skills who are committed to a common purpose, performance goals, and [an] approach for which they hold themselves mutually account-able." The authors analyze teams broadly, dividing them by function into those that do things, those that recommend things, and those that run things. This analysis helps people understand why the meetings of an opera-tional team, an advisory board, and a quality team are often so different in purpose and format. ("But who's in charge of bringing the donuts?")

This book argues that team learning is the most important kind, and that "the same team dynamics that promote performance also support learning and behavioral change, and do so more effectively than larger organizational units or individuals left to their own devices."

Built to Last: Successful Habits of Visionary Companies

James C. Collins and Jerry I. Porras (HarperBusiness, 1994)

Built to Last identifies 18 "visionary" companies — including companies such as Disney, Wal-Mart, and Merck — and sets out to determine exactly what makes them so special. The result, based on meticulous research, shatters many of the hallowed myths of successful organizations, such as "It takes a great idea to start a great company," and "Visionary companies require great and charismatic visionary leaders." Truly a classic in its own time, and a must read for any manager.

First, Break All the Rules: What the World's Greatest Managers Do Differently

Marcus Buckingham and Curt Coffman (Simon & Schuster, 1999)

Buckingham and Coffman — consultants for the Gallup Organization — expose the fallacies of standard management thinking, debunking some cherished management myths in the process. Applying data gathered from more than 80,000 Gallup interviews with real, live managers, the authors discovered that cherished notions, including "treat people as you like to be treated," "people are capable of almost anything," and "great managers are revolutionaries," have no basis in fact. Instead, Buckingham and Coffman found that there are four keys to becoming a great manager:

- ✔ Finding the right fit for employees
- ✔ Focusing on strengths of employees
- ✔ Defining the right results
- ✔ Selecting staff for talent — not just knowledge and skills

Index

• D •

• E •

• Z •

FOR DUMMIES®

The easy way to get more done and have more fun

PERSONAL FINANCE & BUSINESS

0-7645-2431-3

0-7645-5331-3

0-7645-5307-0

Also available:

Accounting For Dummies
(0-7645-5314-3)

Business Plans Kit For Dummies
(0-7645-5365-8)

Managing For Dummies
(1-5688-4858-7)

Mutual Funds For Dummies
(0-7645-5329-1)

QuickBooks All-in-One Desk Reference For Dummies
(0-7645-1963-8)

Resumes For Dummies
(0-7645-5471-9)

Small Business Kit For Dummies
(0-7645-5093-4)

Starting an eBay Business For Dummies
(0-7645-1547-0)

Taxes For Dummies 2003
(0-7645-5475-1)

HOME, GARDEN, FOOD & WINE

0-7645-5295-3

0-7645-5130-2

0-7645-5250-3

Also available:

Bartending For Dummies
(0-7645-5051-9)

Christmas Cooking For Dummies
(0-7645-5407-7)

Cookies For Dummies
(0-7645-5390-9)

Diabetes Cookbook For Dummies
(0-7645-5230-9)

Grilling For Dummies
(0-7645-5076-4)

Home Maintenance For Dummies
(0-7645-5215-5)

Slow Cookers For Dummies
(0-7645-5240-6)

Wine For Dummies
(0-7645-5114-0)

FITNESS, SPORTS, HOBBIES & PETS

0-7645-5167-1

0-7645-5146-9

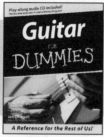

0-7645-5106-X

Also available:

Cats For Dummies
(0-7645-5275-9)

Chess For Dummies
(0-7645-5003-9)

Dog Training For Dummies
(0-7645-5286-4)

Labrador Retrievers For Dummies
(0-7645-5281-3)

Martial Arts For Dummies
(0-7645-5358-5)

Piano For Dummies
(0-7645-5105-1)

Pilates For Dummies
(0-7645-5397-6)

Power Yoga For Dummies
(0-7645-5342-9)

Puppies For Dummies
(0-7645-5255-4)

Quilting For Dummies
(0-7645-5118-3)

Rock Guitar For Dummies
(0-7645-5356-9)

Weight Training For Dummies
(0-7645-5168-X)

Available wherever books are sold.
Go to www.dummies.com or call 1-877-762-2974 to order direct

 **WILEY**

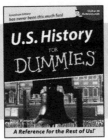

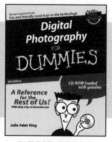

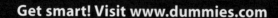

FOR DUMMIES

Helping you expand your horizons and realize your potential

GRAPHICS & WEB SITE DEVELOPMENT

0-7645-1651-5

0-7645-1643-4

0-7645-0895-4

Also available:

Adobe Acrobat 5 PDF
For Dummies
(0-7645-1652-3)

ASP.NET For Dummies
(0-7645-0866-0)

ColdFusion MX for Dummies
(0-7645-1672-8)

Dreamweaver MX For
Dummies
(0-7645-1630-2)

FrontPage 2002 For Dummies
(0-7645-0821-0)

HTML 4 For Dummies
(0-7645-0723-0)

Illustrator 10 For Dummies
(0-7645-3636-2)

PowerPoint 2002 For
Dummies
(0-7645-0817-2)

Web Design For Dummies
(0-7645-0823-7)

PROGRAMMING & DATABASES

0-7645-0746-X

0-7645-1626-4

0-7645-1657-4

Also available:

Access 2002 For Dummies
(0-7645-0818-0)

Beginning Programming
For Dummies
(0-7645-0835-0)

Crystal Reports 9 For
Dummies
(0-7645-1641-8)

Java & XML For Dummies
(0-7645-1658-2)

Java 2 For Dummies
(0-7645-0765-6)

JavaScript For Dummies
(0-7645-0633-1)

Oracle9i For Dummies
(0-7645-0880-6)

Perl For Dummies
(0-7645-0776-1)

PHP and MySQL For
Dummies
(0-7645-1650-7)

SQL For Dummies
(0-7645-0737-0)

Visual Basic .NET For
Dummies
(0-7645-0867-9)

LINUX, NETWORKING & CERTIFICATION

0-7645-1545-4

0-7645-1760-0

0-7645-0772-9

Also available:

A+ Certification For Dummies
(0-7645-0812-1)

CCNP All-in-One Certification
For Dummies
(0-7645-1648-5)

Cisco Networking For
Dummies
(0-7645-1668-X)

CISSP For Dummies
(0-7645-1670-1)

CIW Foundations For
Dummies
(0-7645-1635-3)

Firewalls For Dummies
(0-7645-0884-9)

Home Networking For
Dummies
(0-7645-0857-1)

Red Hat Linux All-in-One
Desk Reference For Dummies
(0-7645-2442-9)

UNIX For Dummies
(0-7645-0419-3)

Available wherever books are sold.
Go to www.dummies.com or call 1-877-762-2974 to order direct